*Gardening
with the
Native Plants
of Tennessee*

*Happy Birthday
to Angie, 2006*

Gardening with the Native Plants of Tennessee

THE SPIRIT OF PLACE

Margie Hunter

THE UNIVERSITY OF TENNESSEE PRESS / Knoxville

Copyright © 2002 by Margie Hunter.
All Rights Reserved. Manufactured in Hong Kong.
First Edition.

This book is printed on acid-free paper.

Unless otherwise noted, the illustrations were
provided by the author.

Library of Congress Cataloging-in-Publication Data

Hunter, Margie, 1955–
Gardening with the native plants of Tennessee:
the spirit of place/Margie Hunter.—1st ed.
        p. cm.
Includes bibliographical references (p.   ).
ISBN 1-57233-155-0 (pbk.: alk. paper)
1. Native plant gardening—Tennessee.
2. Native plants for cultivation—Tennessee.
I. Title.

SB439.24.T2 H86 2002
635.9'51768—dc21   2001003530

Contents

Acknowledgments

Y January 1996, my search for an easy source of information on Tennessee and its native plants was proving fruitless. It was becoming clear that many sources, some highly specialized, would have to be sought out and scattered information pieced together. At that point the idea for this book was born. Thus began the research and the invaluable assistance of numerous people.

Jenny Andrews, former education coordinator and wildflower horticulturist at Cheekwood Botanical Garden, Dr. Edward W. Chester, professor of botany at Austin Peay State University, and Dr. Edward E. C. Clebsch, professor emeritus at the University of Tennessee in Knoxville, reviewed the text in depth and played a significant role in shaping this book. Andrea Shea, Brian Bowen, Carl Nordman, and David Withers of the Tennessee Department of Environment and Conservation's Division of Natural Heritage and Jim Moore and Tom Hart of the Division of Geology, Bob Hatcher of the Tennessee Wildlife Resources Agency, Paul Moore of Moore and Moore Garden Center, Dr. Elsie Quarterman, professor emeritus at Vanderbilt University, Michael Wenzel formerly of Cheekwood, Nashville garden designer B. C. Hudson, and the wonderful staff at the Warner Park Nature Center also contributed greatly. I would also like to thank Jennifer Siler and the staff at UT Press as well as fellow authors Rob Simbeck, Mila Truan, Michael Sims, Jim Summerville, and Andy Wasowski for their advice and assistance throughout the exciting yet nerve-wracking experience of publishing my first book.

People often buy gardening books for the great color photographs, not the scintillating prose. To that end I am deeply indebted to Paul Moore, George Hornal, Bill Hall, Kurt Emmanuele, Scott Woodbury of Shaw Arboretum, Susan Felts, Nancy Fleisher, Dr. Edward Chester of Austin Peay State University, Clayton Oslund of Plant Pics, Jim Snyder, Carl Nordman of the state Natural Heritage Program, and the talented staff of Chromatics PhotoImaging in Nashville.

Finally, to my family—Nick, Kate, and Sam—thanks for being there.

I am a gardener, not a botanist, geologist, scientist, or horticulturist. While I have experience growing some of the plants discussed in this book, the majority of the information relies on the accumulated wisdom of others. The sources used in each chapter are listed at the end of that chapter. My task has been to gather and present the information in (I hope) an accessible way. I take full responsibility for any errors that may have resulted.

Introduction

R. AUGUSTIN GATTINGER, WHO IMMIGRATED FROM GERMANY IN 1849, PURsued his general love of science beyond his chosen field of medicine into the realms of geology and botany. In frequent travels across the state, he meticulously identified and collected samples of plants, including several species that he was the first to discover. In 1890 he donated this vast collection to the University of Tennessee in Knoxville, forming the backbone of its herbarium. (Sadly, the entire collection was destroyed by fire in the 1930s.) By 1901 he had persuaded the state legislature to underwrite his *Flora*, the first and only published record of Tennessee's botanical heritage.

Our state is unique. Running horizontally across the upper southeastern face of the United States, it encompasses a broad spectrum of geographically distinct areas, ranging from the 6,000-foot peaks in the Unaka Mountains to the swampy floodplain of the Mississippi River. Our approximately 2,850 plant species represent the crossroads of a mountain to prairie landscape transitioning from a northern to a southern climate. This mix forms the basis for an uncommonly rich and diverse flora. Given such central positioning and rich native opportunities, it's hard to imagine anyone being content to use the same old nursery lineup of cultivated plants—many if not most of which are non-native.

The reasons to consider native plants go well beyond mere variety of choice. In *Natural Landscaping: Designing with Native Plant Communities* John Diekelmann and Robert Schuster point to the evolutionary development of native species. In stable environments over time, plants become adept at tapping into the resources and surviving the dangers within their respective landscapes. This adaptation applies to the climatic progression of the seasons as well, providing a revolving smorgasbord of species. Diekelmann and Schuster credit this "diversity and intimate relationship with the land" for allowing native plants a measure of self-sufficiency; they do not require active maintenance to survive or reproduce. The impact of this evolutionary advantage extends to pests and diseases (native plants have developed strategies to cope with these predations) and wildlife. Native plants attract and support favorable native insects and animals in the fertilization of flowers, distribution of seed, and pest control.

In a day and age when most developments (whether rural or urban, north or south, east or west) are virtually identical in appearance, it is refreshing to see a landscape, human-made or natural, that truly fits and reflects the essential spirit and history of the place. For gardeners, the choice is between a garden that could be found anywhere and one that displays the essence of Tennessee's natural beauty, rooted in all that makes this state unique. It is the choice between an autumn olive or a winterberry, a Bradford pear or a sourwood, chrysanthemums or goldenrods and asters.

Interest in native plants has gone through periodic upswings in the past, and as we embark upon the new millennium native plants are once more a hot topic. They are beginning to make it into the mainstream nursery trade, and ecologically astute gardeners, savvy to the depredations of collecting in the wild, are insisting on nursery-propagated stock. The Perennial Plant Association selects a Perennial Plant of the Year, and of the eleven winners through 2000, five are native plants or their cultivars. Twenty plants native to Tennessee were selected among the most impressive perennials observed in the University of Tennessee Trial Gardens from 1996 through 1999. We are simply rediscovering what has been under our noses for over two hundred years.

In the mid-1770s, as the British colonists pondered their future in this bountiful land, William Bartram, a Philadelphia botanist, traveled throughout the southeastern portions of the North American continent in search of new and useful plants. Traversing areas of Florida, Georgia, South and North Carolina over four years, he wrote effusively about "the marvellous scenes of primitive nature, as yet unmodified by the hand of man." Who would not envy his immersion in a pure and unsullied landscape, the "fruitful fragrant groves," "limpid waters . . . transparent as the ether," "harmonious and soothing . . . native sylvan music," "air [filled] with the richest perfume." Yet he began to tire of his lonely voyage through the depths of this natural world and longed to finish his work and return to civilization. He even cast a lascivious eye on the bounty surrounding him and envisioned its transformation as a result of "the arts of agriculture and commerce, [by which] almost every desirable thing in life might be produced and made plentiful here, and thereby establish a rich, populous, and delightful region."

What would Bartram think if he could see the areas of his travel today, two hundred and thirty years later? Perhaps he would be a bit more circumspect regarding "the arts of agriculture and commerce." Perhaps he would register alarm at the populous and commonly *un*-delightful character of the region. He would most certainly mourn the widespread, often irreparable, damage sustained by primitive nature.

We cannot undo our past, but we can control our present and future. Who better to begin natural reparations than those in love with the soil, those drawn to the beauty of flowers, those happiest under the canopy of trees and sky, those enchanted by the lives of humanity's fellow earthly inhabitants. Discovering the interdependent relationships that shape Tennessee's landscape provides valuable insight. From our geologic past to the different plant communities inhabiting our countryside, from the wildlife feeding and nesting in our backyards to the exotic pest plants threatening our native diversity, this book seeks to inform and aid the understanding of our state and lists the garden-worthy native plants whose collective spirit infuses this place we call home. It is to Tennessee gardeners that this book is directed. Armed with knowledge about the treasures that surround us, we cannot fail "to appreciate and to preserve such great ornaments of [our] native land."

For those living outside Tennessee's borders, rest assured that native plants recognize no such boundaries. Most of our "great ornaments" are yours, too. Areas of the Mid-South adjacent to Tennessee share an overwhelming number of the plants listed here. The key is matching the natural conditions of your garden with the native plants adapted to those conditions. Use the information and resources in this book to guide you to the spirit of your place.

PART I

The Spirit
of Place

1

The Geography, Geology, and Soil of Tennessee

*Continued more than a mile through
this elevated plain to the pitch of the
mountain, from whence presented to
view an expansive prospect, exhibiting
scenes of mountainous landscape,
westward, vast and varied, perhaps
not to be exceeded any where.*

—William Bartram
Travels, 1791

View from Clingman's Dome,
Great Smoky Mountains National Park.

George W. Hornal.

Geography: The Lay of the Land

FROM THE MOUNTAINS ON THE EASTERN BORDER TO THE MISSISSIPPI RIVER FLOODPLAIN ON THE WESTERN BORDER, THE LANDSCAPE OF Tennessee exhibits amazing variety. In the science of geography, variations in the earth's surface are referred to as topography. The topography of Tennessee is among the most diverse in the United States. It is divided into three major physiographic provinces, each of which is subdivided into a total of seven physiographic regions.

The Appalachian Highlands Province—East Tennessee

East Tennessee is the Appalachian Highlands Province and consists of three regions: the Unaka Mountains (also known as the Blue Ridge Mountains), the Valley and Ridge (also called the Great Valley), and the Cumberland Plateau. The Unaka Mountains feature the peaks of Great Smoky Mountains National Park and Cherokee National Forest, including Chilhowee, English, Bean, Starr, Roan, and Meadow Creek Mountains. Many are higher than 6,000 feet, and Clingman's Dome is the highest point in Tennessee at 6,642 feet. The terrain is rugged, composed of steep, deeply forested slopes and swift streams with waterfalls. Low, flat coves, such as Cades, Wear, Millers, Tuckaleechee, and Bumpass, are tucked among the peaks. Valley floors range from 1,000 feet in elevation in the southern portions to 1,500 feet in the northern areas.

West of the Unaka Mountains is the Valley and Ridge Region, consisting of a series of long ridges alternating with valleys running northeast to southwest. The highest ridges to the north rise 3,097 feet above sea level; in the south they rise to 1,495 feet. Southern valleys are as low as 750 feet. A continuous, unbroken escarpment along the western edge of the Valley and Ridge announces the beginning of the Cumberland Plateau Region, characterized mainly by flat to rolling terrain 1,800 feet in elevation. There are some ridges cresting at 3,000 feet in the Cumberland Mountains in the plateau's northeastern corner and two valleys—Elk to the north and Sequatchie to the south. Sequatchie Valley runs northeast/southwest for over 60 miles, is about 4 to 5 miles wide, and sits 1,000 feet lower than the enveloping plateau. There are numerous waterfalls, including Fall Creek Falls, which is the highest falls east of the Rocky Mountains. The Cumberland Plateau's western edge is deeply dissected with gorges and valleys that mark the beginning of the Eastern Highland Rim.

The Interior Low Plateau Province—Middle Tennessee

Middle Tennessee, as part of the Interior Low Plateau Province, is composed of the Nashville or Central Basin Region and the Highland Rim Region. The Highland Rim is the largest physiographic region in Tennessee. It encircles the Central Basin and is bounded on the east by the irregular cliff face of the Cumberland Plateau and on the west by the valley of the Tennessee River and Kentucky Lake. It is mostly hilly uplands, especially the western half, which average 900 feet in elevation. The

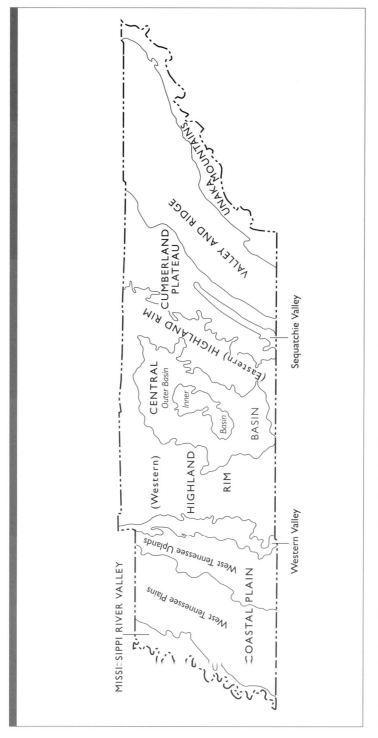

Physiographic Regions of Tennessee. Adapted from *The Geologic History of Tennessee*, Bulletin 74, Tennessee Divison of Geology.

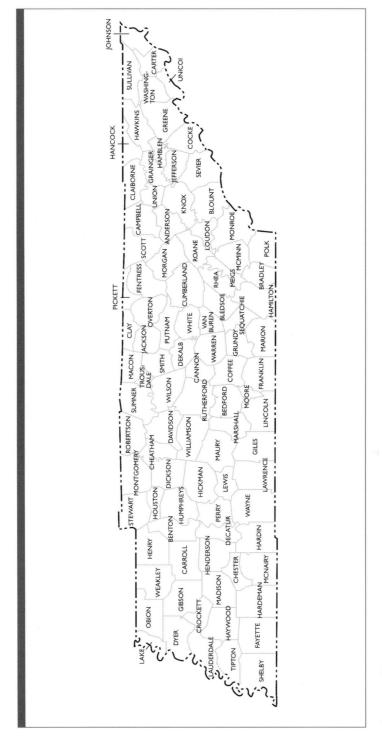

Counties of Tennessee.

Rutledge Falls in Coffee County.

eastern half of the Highland Rim is narrow and features areas of nearly flat land called barrens in Coffee, Cannon, and Warren Counties. Other areas are steep, averaging 1,000 feet, with deeply divided, narrow valleys and waterfalls.

The Central Basin is an elliptically shaped area with level or gently rolling to hilly terrain. It runs north to south about 120 miles, is 50 to 60 miles wide, and is divided into inner and outer parts. The inner basin has many nearly level areas, especially in Rutherford County, with an average elevation of 600 feet. The outer basin's terrain is hilly, rising as high as 1,300 feet, but averaging just 750.

The Coastal Plain Province—West Tennessee

West Tennessee is the Coastal Plain Province, which includes the Coastal Plain Region and the Mississippi River Valley Region. West Tennessee begins with the western valley of the Tennessee River, considered by some to be a separate physiographic region itself. The Coastal Plain Region encompasses most of the western one-third of the state and is divided into two parts—the West Tennessee Uplands and the West Tennessee Plain. The uplands area features hilly to rolling terrain with an elevation of 500 feet and includes the divide separating land draining east to the Tennessee River from land draining west to the Mississippi. The plain is flat to rolling land and slopes gently toward the low, 100-foot bluffs overlooking the Mississippi River. This great river's floodplain comprises the Mississippi River Valley Region with lakes, such as Reelfoot, and swamps.

Geology: The Genesis of Our Backyards

To best understand the essence of this land requires a journey through 600 million years of geologic time, a large part of which Tennessee spent as the ocean floor. Throughout the Paleozoic era Tennessee experienced nearly 300 million years of advancing and receding seas depositing layer upon layer of sedimentary limestone, shale, sandstone, siltstone, dolomite, chert, and claystone on top of a base of igneous and metamorphic rock. The waters over the area were often shallow and increasingly teeming with life. The Paleozoic periods progressed (Cambrian, Ordovician, Silurian, Devonian, Mississippian, Pennsylvanian), each depositing its own identifiable layer of sediment. The Pennsylvanian period, the Age of Forests, was the last to leave a record of areas of water over the central and eastern portions of Tennessee. Often the waters were so shallow as to be more swamp than sea. A continual mosaic of land emerged and lush plant life shifted with the water's depth, leaving in its wake lots of dead vegetation that would compress into coal along with the sandstones and shales.

By the start of the Mesozoic era, two significant events had taken place that would determine much of Tennessee's current topography. First, perhaps as early as the Ordovician period, came the uplift of the Nashville Dome centered roughly over present-day Murfreesboro. This uplift paradoxically set the stage for the current depression, the Nashville or Central Basin. Secondly, as the Paleozoic era waned, faulting associated with the collision of North Africa and North America caused a great fracturing, folding, and buckling. This event, called the Allegheny orogeny, resulted in the birth of the current southern Appalachian Mountain chain from Pennsylvania to Alabama. Violent movements brought Precambrian igneous and metamorphic rock to the surface. This tremendous restructuring of the land not only created the Unaka Mountains on the Tennessee–North Carolina border but also set the foundation for the development of the series of northeast to southwest ridges and valleys occupying a large part of East Tennessee. The effects of this restructuring reached as far west as the Cumberland Plateau where fault thrusts created ridges that have slowly eroded into the Sequatchie and Elk Valleys.

Time Units of the Geological Time Scale					Tennessee Events
			Duration		
Era	Period	Epoch	millions of years	millions of years	
Cenozoic	Quaternary	Holocene	Last 10,000 years		Loess deposits
Cenozoic		Pleistocene	1.7	1.7	
Cenozoic	Tertiary	Pliocene	3	5	
Cenozoic	Tertiary	Miocene	19	24	Central Basin deepens
Cenozoic	Tertiary	Oligocene	10	34	Central Basin deepens
Cenozoic	Tertiary	Ecocene	21	55	Seas leave West Tennessee
Cenozoic	Tertiary	Paleocene	10	65	Seas leave West Tennessee
Mesozoic	Cretaceous		80		Mississippi Embayment
Mesozoic				145	
Mesozoic	Jurassic		61		
Mesozoic				206	Erosion of Nashville Dome Highland Rim Valley and Ridge Sequatchie Valley
Mesozoic	Triassic		39		Erosion of Nashville Dome Highland Rim Valley and Ridge Sequatchie Valley
Mesozoic				245	
Paleozoic	Permian		45		Allengheny Orogeny
Paleozoic				290	
Paleozoic	Pennsylvanian		33		West Tennessee Uplift
Paleozoic				323	
Paleozoic	Mississippian		40		
Paleozoic				363	
Paleozoic	Devonian		46		
Paleozoic				409	
Paleozoic	Silurian		30		
Paleozoic				439	
Paleozoic					Nashville Dome Uplift
Paleozoic	Ordovician		71		
Paleozoic				510	
Paleozoic	Cambrian		60		
Paleozoic				570	
Paleozoic	Precambrian		4,000		

Source: Tennessee's Prehistoric Vertebrates, Bull. 84, Tenn. Div. of Geology.

This mountain-building episode drained the sea from the eastern half of Tennessee, bringing an end to the great deposition of materials, and the wind and rain began to take away what the sea had left behind. The uplift of the Nashville Dome became a liability. Standing above the surrounding landscape, the elements acted on its cracked surface with greater effect, chipping away at the tough Pennsylvanian sandstone deposits and readily undermining the softer limestones below. In the east, the soon-to-be Valley and Ridge Region got its start as the rearranged layers of sediment began to erode unevenly. Some exposed layers (the ridges) were more resistant; others (the valleys) did not hold up as well and wore away.

Once the Nashville Dome lost its protective cap of tough Pennsylvanian deposits, erosion sped up as the less resistant Mississippian layers of limestone succumbed to the slow but persistent onslaught of ground and surface water. This pattern of erosion slowly spread in all directions. The Pennsylvanian sandstones were worn eastward into an ever retreating escarpment that today announces the beginning of the Cumberland Plateau. Short Mountain (2,074 feet), 20 miles west of the plateau in Cannon County on the Eastern Highland Rim, is topped with the only remaining remnant of Pennsylvanian sandstone in Middle Tennessee.

The final barrier to the development of the Central Basin during the Cenozoic period was a tough layer of chert, a hard, dense sediment of crystalline silica named the Fort Payne formation. The breach of this lower Mississippian layer signaled more rapid erosion as the underlying limestones more readily dissolved. The dissolution of these sediments has produced a special type of terrain called karst, which denotes the presence of underground streams, caves, caverns, and sinkholes in the limestone bedrock. As the Mississippian layers continued to erode, the outlying Highland Rim continued to retreat, and the Central Basin continued to grow. The Central Basin has now eroded down to the Ordovician layer of deposits, which were put in place between 400 and 500 million years ago.

Forces responsible for the Nashville Dome periodically applied renewed pressure, generating more uplift here and on its western counterpart, the Ozark Dome. Between these domes the western half of Tennessee was lifted above the surface of the sea sometime during the Pennsylvanian period, permitting many of the fresh marine deposits to weather away over the next 250 million years. A north to south depression in the earth's crust formed from western Kentucky and eastern Missouri down through Louisiana, which gradually lowered West Tennessee and allowed the sea to return as the Mississippi Embayment near the end of the Mesozoic era. Waters spilled onto the Western Highland Rim as well. For 30 million years marine sediment and eroded material from the surrounding land left a soft bed to which early rivers and streams added their alluvium after the sea departed. As a final touch West Tennessee benefited from the four major glacial advances (the Ice Age) during the last 2½ million years. Movement of the ice sheets to the north ground rock into a fine powder called loess, which was carried southward into the Mississippi Valley by huge torrents of melting ice. As floodwaters receded, deposits dried and clouds of dust blew across Tennessee. Loess deposits accumulated to depths of 70 feet or more near the Mississippi Bluffs and thinned progressively eastward to the Highland Rim.

Billion-year-old Precambrian igneous and metamorphic rocks of the Unaka Mountains mark one end of the state, while 10,000-year-old glacial loess above the Mississippi River defines the other. Through hundreds of millions of years, Tennessee has been built up, eroded, lifted, folded, buckled, and dropped into the topography that so distinctly characterizes each region today.

The Soil and Climate of Tennessee

Soil Formation

Soil formation is the very slow but ongoing process of physical and chemical destruction followed by synthesis. Many soils in Tennessee develop on site from the weathering of underlying rock. As bedrock begins to break up from the action of temperature and erosion or the chemical action of water and oxygen, this fragmented residue becomes parent material for future soil. Further weathering of this parent material continues the process, which may be aided by deposits left by wind (loess) or water (alluvium). Plants and animals play a role through the action of roots and digging. The uppermost layer of soil is the most organic with the highest concentration of decayed or decaying vegetable and animal matter.

Soil plays a crucial role in plant growth by

- providing mechanical support for roots
- retaining heat
- containing tiny pockets of air
- holding water

- providing essential macronutrients (relatively large quantities of nitrogen, phosphorus, potassium, calcium, and sulfur) and micronutrients (relatively small quantities of iron, copper, magnesium, manganese, zinc, boron, and molybdenum).

Soil fertility is based on the supply of nutrients and the availability rate of nutrients to the plant, a complex process in which the plant itself takes an active role. Other fertility factors are the proportion of these nutrients and the influence of soil pH, relative acidity or alkalinity. Soil pH can affect the amount of nutrients, too much or too little, that a plant can access.

The texture of soil is a reflection of particle size, from gravel and sand on the large side to silt and clay on the small side. Too much of the large makes a loose, dry soil. Too much of the small results in a heavy, sticky soil that stays too wet and keeps out air. To avoid these problems a balanced combination of particle sizes, loam, is best. Larger particles allow spaces for air and drainage; smaller particles bind it together and hold water for plant use. Organic material, or humus, holds a great deal of water and returns essential nutrients to the soil to be used again. Millions of organisms reside in this layer, from highly visible rodents, insects, and worms to microscopic organisms and other forms of life, e.g., fungi, bacteria, algae, etc. All these living things work to break down organic matter, exhibiting nature's ability to recycle and reuse.

The primary factors contributing to soil formation are climate (particularly temperature and precipitation), native vegetation, area topography, the nature of the parent material, and time. Topographical influences include the accumulation of gravitational wash down slopes (called colluvium) and the erosion and deposition of material from the flow of water in bottomlands. The direction in which a slope faces (north, south, east, or west) can affect the resulting soil due to variations in prevailing winds, precipitation, sun exposure, and soil temperature. The type of vegetation growing exerts an influence, as do the animals and insects, via mixing the soil, recycling nutrients, building a humus layer, etc.

Tennessee's Climate

The prominent role of climate in soil formation and in establishing the range of native vegetation necessitates a brief look at the state's climate statistics. It will come as no surprise to read that Tennessee's climate is "characterized by erratic weather changes" (*Tennessee's Natural Resources,* vol. 2). The state's location in the middle latitudes means our weather systems arrive on westerly winds or arise from conflicting air masses. It also gives us our greatest asset: the appearance of four distinct seasons nearly equal in length. Winters are wet and humid; summers are warm and humid with thunderstorms bringing most of our rain. Autumns are mild, dry, and less humid; springs are mild with cool spells and, often, lower precipitation as the weather systems make the transition from winter to summer. Temperatures range from double-digit subzero to over 100 degrees in extremes. Average annual humidity is 70 percent. Annual winter snowfall averages 4 to 6 inches in most areas with higher amounts on the Cumberland Plateau and Unaka Mountains. Winds are strongest in the spring and lightest in autumn. The greatest amounts of precipitation usually fall in late winter and early spring.

Warmer temperatures and higher precipitation increase the rate of soil formation. The state requires 30 inches of rainfall per year to replace moisture lost through evaporation and the transpiration of plants. Normal yearly precipitation throughout much of Tennessee exceeds this by about 20 inches. Excess rainfall runs off or moves down through the soil, which leaches out nutrients and helps dissolve parent material in the

Climate Statistics for Tennessee					
	West Tennessee	Middle Tennessee	East Tennessee		
			C.P.	V/R	Unakas
Temperature (in degrees F)					
Average	60–62	58–60	56	58–60	44–56
Extremes	Memphis -13/108	Nashville -17/107		Knoxville -24/104	
Freeze Dates					
Last	Mar. 26–Apr. 10	Apr. 5–15	Apr. 15–30	Apr. 5–20	Apr.20–May 5
First	Oct. 20–Nov. 4	Oct. 20–30	Oct. 10–20	Oct. 20–Nov. 4	Oct. 10–20
Growing Season (length in days)	193–223 Ave. 208	188–208 Ave. 198	163–188 Ave. 175	183–203 Ave. 193	158–183 Ave. 170
Precipitation (in inches)	48–52	48–52	52–56	40–44 (north) 48–52 (south)	44–56(north) 56–76 (south)

Sources: *Soils of Tennessee,* Bulletin 596, University of Tennessee Agricultural Experiment Station and U.S. Dept. of Agriculture Soil Conservation Service, and National Oceanic and Atmospheric Administration.

never-ending production of new soil. In the hot, dry dog days of summer the importance of seasonal balance in rainfall becomes apparent. Good loamy soils with an organic layer can hold water longer and make it more readily available for use by plants during periodic dry spells.

The Soil of East Tennessee

The rearranged layers of bedrock in East Tennessee have produced a variety of soils. In the Unaka Mountains, metamorphic and igneous rocks are the primary parent material with contributions from other rocks and colluvium. The soils are loamy, high in organic matter, thicker on the lower slopes, and shallower at the top. Soils have a variable degree of stoniness and support thick, lush forests. Valleys and coves have deep, well-drained soils, derived from limestone, that are loamy and productive. Most of this land is used for agriculture and human habitation. Valley and Ridge soils are derived from limestones, sandstones, and shales. They are well drained, clayey, and loamy and, due to leaching, are often low in fertility and strongly acid. Stream bottoms are more fertile and less acid. The ridges are wooded, and the gentler slopes and valleys are used for pasture. The Cumberland Plateau is mostly forest with loamy, acid soil two to four feet deep from sandstone and shale. Soils down the steep escarpment sides have limestone, too, and are deeper and stony at the base. Rock outcrops are common.

The Soil of Middle Tennessee

In Middle Tennessee most of the soils are derived from the underlying limestones with minor contributions from sandstones, siltstones, and shales. There are also deposits interpreted as loess, particularly in the barrens of the Eastern Highland Rim and other flat or gently rolling areas. The soils of the steeper hills of the Highland Rim are well drained and somewhat droughty over tough, cherty limestone with outcrops. The leaching of alkalis raises the acidity of these soils that support forests and wildlife. Flatter areas that drain well are usually agricultural. Low areas with hard fragipans (impervious clay layers below the surface) do not drain well and are swampy forests or wet meadows. Descending to the hills of the outer basin, often called the Highland Rim outliers, the soils are high in phosphorus due to the limestone. These upland soils are mostly well drained and productive. In the flatter inner basin, the soils have lost a good part of the phosphorus and vary from a depth of several feet near rivers to a few inches in the endemic cedar glades, where large slabs of limestone bedrock are often exposed. In these areas, soil pH can vary from slightly acid to slightly alkaline.

The Soil of West Tennessee

Loess and its derivatives are characteristic of most West Tennessee soils. The hilly West Tennessee Uplands has a thin layer of loess over sandy or clay soils that are well drained, highly leached, and strongly acid. Forests and pastures are most common, with crops grown in the more fertile river bottoms. Thick deposits of loess form a silty, fertile soil on the West Tennessee Plain. Cropland predominates, with some forests on the steeper hills prone to erosion. Fragipan layers one to three feet down are quite common, but affect drainage only in flat areas. Soil pH varies from strongly acid to slightly alkaline. The Mississippi River Valley has very fertile, productive soil, which is loamy and silty, with a neutral to slightly alkaline pH. There are poorly drained areas of swampy forests with more acid, clayey soils.

The value of good soil cannot be overstated. Since soil formation goes well beyond the scale of human time, it makes sense to protect and preserve good soil and to work to improve soil that has been abused, exhausted, or eroded. Native plants can play an important role in this preservation through their adaptation to local soil and their subtle influence in its composition.

Sources for Further Reading

(Full citation information can be found in the bibliography.)

The Nature and Properties of Soil, Harry O. Buckman and Nyle C. Brady

The Soul of Soil: A Soil-Building Guide for Master Gardeners and Farmers, Grace Gershuny and Joe Smillie

Our Restless Earth: The Geologic Regions of Tennessee, Edward T. Luther

The Geologic History of Tennessee, Robert A. Miller

Soils of Tennessee, M. E. Springer and J. A. Elder

Tennessee's Natural Resources, Tennessee Dept. of Finance and Administration

Each county in Tennessee has a published Soil Survey available from that county's Natural Resources Conservation Service or the Soil Conservation District office. These surveys detail the location and makeup of different soil types throughout the county and give valuable information on the soils' suitability for various uses.

2

Plant Communities in Tennessee

Plant communities . . . are a dynamic and orderly element of landscapes. In reflecting the geology, climate, and history of the land, they give each region its own natural character.

—John Diekelmann
and Robert Schuster,
*Natural Landscaping:
Designing with Native Plant
Communities*, 1982

Mesic forest community: The Nature Conservancy of Tennessee's Taylor Hollow Preserve in Sumner County is home to an amazing variety of plants. *Diplazium pycnocarpon* (narrow-leaved spleenwort), *Collinsia verna* (blue-eyed Mary), *Phacelia bipinnatifida* (purple phacelia), *Stylophorum diphyllum* (wood poppy), *Cystopteris protrusa* (lowland bladderfern), *Pachysandra procumbens* (Allegheny spurge), *Valerian pauciflora* (valerian), *Asarum canadense* (wild ginger), *Jeffersonia diphylla* (twinleaf), and *Trillium* spp. are all visible here.

STOP A MOMENT AND CONSIDER YOUR IMMEDIATE HUMAN ENVIRONMENT. WE OFTEN USE THE TERM COMMUNITY TO DESCRIBE THE NEIGHborhood, town, or city in which we live. Its implications include the people, their occupations and entertainments, their buildings and infrastructure, their natural surroundings, and the interaction of all these parts. The natural world is an integral part of our community, and we often exert tremendous influence on nature's communities. The workings of nature's communities differ little philosophically from ours.

Communities in Nature

A community in nature is a group of interacting plant and animal populations within a similar environment. The combinations of individual species of plants and animals are unique to each community, imparting a distinct personality and appearance. There are five main factors that can alter an environment sufficiently to affect the make up of a community's inhabitants:

- climate
- geologic history
- topography
- hydrology (ground and flood water)
- soil type

It is hard to separate these factors, as each can play a determinative or reactive role with one or more of the others. The uniformity of these factors dictates the distribution of species. At some point one or more factors will change enough (through physical distance, elevation, or geologic time) to signal the growing limitations of certain species. Such species drop out and are replaced by others better suited to the prevailing conditions.

For example, much of the eastern half of the United States is forested with various deciduous trees. Moving north into Canada, these trees decrease in number and are replaced by evergreen conifers. In this region the growing season is just too short for a deciduous tree to manufacture the food it needs. Likewise, a move into the Deep South will find deciduous species being replaced by needle-leaved and broadleaf evergreens. In this case deciduous trees do not get the necessary dormancy due to the long—or even continual—growing season. In each instance, tree species better suited thrive where others cannot, and they put their unique stamp on the community.

Communities can be large and widespread or small and isolated. Middle Tennessee has a large concentration of cedar glade communities, yet they make up only a small part of the total area, scattered over a handful of counties. Some plants thrive on the warm, sunny, drier southern slope of a hillside. Others much prefer the cooler, shadier, and moister aspect facing north, which is less troubled by sun-sponsored temperature fluctuations. Some plants love having wet roots in a low, swampy area where others would promptly rot. Whether it is hard-baked clay on a roadside or humusy loam in the forest, the acid soil of a ridge-top or an alkaline crevice in limestone, the boreal forest of Clingman's Dome or the flooded alluvial plain of Reelfoot Lake, there is an adapted community of plants and animals that call that place home.

Within a larger community, smaller areas (called microhabitats) can differ sufficiently in various factors to support species not readily found outside this localized environment. When the determining factors in a community recur, so do many of the associated plants and animals. Gardeners can take advantage of microhabitats existing on their property—a drainage ditch or a rock outcrop—to increase the variety of plants in their landscape.

Plant Layers—Stratification

To define the community types in Tennessee, it is important to understand vegetative (plant) layers or stratification. Beginning on the ground these layers are:

- litter—dead and decaying organic matter
- herbaceous—grasses, ferns, and wildflowers
- shrub—woody stems from a few inches to 15 feet
- understory—small trees or large shrubs 15 to 50 feet
- canopy—largest trees 50 to 100 feet or more

Communities are usually characterized by one or two specific plants called indicator species or dominants, those that by their abundance, unique presence, or particular combination give a community a distinct identity. These dominants are usually in the canopy layer. Plant species in the lower layers can also be a strong indicator of certain communities, but their presence is often a result, at least in part, of the canopy's effect. In East Tennessee forests with a number of *Tsuga canadensis* (eastern hemlock) in the canopy will also likely feature *Rhododendron maximum* (rosebay rhododendron) in the understory and herbaceous plants such as *Mitchella repens* (partridgeberry) and *Medeola virginiana* (Indian cucumber-root). These plants thrive in the cool shade and strongly acid soil produced by the hemlocks.

Aside from the specialized plant communities associated with the barrens, cedar glades, and high mountain peaks, most forest communities in Tennessee can be broadly categorized as mixed mesophytic (consisting

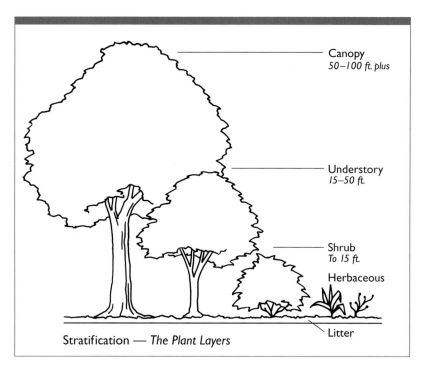

Canopy
50–100 ft. plus

Understory
15–50 ft.

Shrub
To 15 ft.

Herbaceous

Litter

Stratification — *The Plant Layers*

of moist soil with great plant diversity), mesic (moist soil), xeric (dry soil), or hydric (wet soil). The presence or absence of certain plant species within one of these broad categories often helps to denote a specific geographical area within the state. An examination of species in the *Atlas of Tennessee Vascular Plants* reveals interesting examples. *Taxodium distichum* (bald cypress) is a water-loving (hydric) species found throughout West Tennessee, yet aside from Stewart County, it has not been documented in hydric communities east of the Tennessee River's western valley.

Middle and West Tennessee comprise an area of transition between the moist forests of East Tennessee and the drier woods of the Ozarks. *Aesculus flava* (yellow buckeye) and *Tilia heterophylla* (white basswood) are considered indicator species for the rich and diverse mixed mesophytic forests, which are most common in the eastern one-third of Tennessee. Pockets of this forest type, signaled by the presence of white basswood and restricted to protected sites that are cool and moist, can be found as far west as the bluff ravines of Memphis. The yellow buckeye, though, appears to travel no farther west than Nashville.

When one species drops out another will often fill in the gap. *Trillium grandiflorum* (large-flowered trillium) stops its westward travel at the Eastern Highland Rim. *Trillium flexipes* (drooping white trillium) takes over on the Western Highland Rim. *Quercus montana* (chestnut oak), a common upland species in East and Middle Tennessee, all but disappears in West Tennessee. However, two coastal plain species, *Quercus nigra* (water oak) and *Quercus pagoda* (cherrybark oak), are very common in West Tennessee and infrequent to the east. Other plants with strong regional associations are noted in the plant descriptions in chapter 6.

Succession

When Europeans first arrived in this country the vast majority of the eastern half of the land was covered in dense, ancient forests. The intervening four hundred years have seen most of that original forest cut, resulting in a current patchwork quilt of forests in various stages of secondary growth. Does bare earth immediately regenerate itself with the same plant species that were lost? No, it truly develops in stages, each stage with its own identifiable species adapted to the current conditions. The flow of these stages is called succession, the progressive replacement of one plant community by another through natural development.

A forest may have been logged, cleared for agriculture, or damaged by a storm or fire. Regardless of the cause, the resulting changes to soil (erosion), light (shade to sun), temperature (cooler to warmer), and water (greater runoff) leave the environment unsuitable for most of the original plants and their associated wildlife. Pioneer plants, however, thrive in these disturbed areas. From weeds and grasses to sun-loving shrubs and trees, in a few years they've stabilized the raw site and begun their own set of changes: checking erosion, adding organic nutrients to the soil, providing shade, moderating the temperature, and improving soil- and air-moisture levels. These improvements allow the next level of successional plants to establish themselves in a more congenial setting.

Over the years these later plants grow in number and size and begin to make life more difficult for the sun-loving pioneers, which are often rather short-lived anyway. The pioneers eventually give way, and the process continues until an unchanging, sustainable set of conditions (shade, temperature, and moisture) occurs in which the dominant species can not only grow but also reproduce. The association of plants in the final stage is the stable community. Different areas support different stable communities, as demonstrated in the plant community lists below. Succession is not rapid. It can take up to a few hundred years to complete the process that nature has developed so patiently through the millennia. This process continues today as native plant and animal communities adapt to environmental changes both natural and human influenced.

Few people live within a stable community. Most developed property will be part of some early to mid-successional stage, which will be artificially managed and maintained through mowing, weeding, and gardening. It is helpful to review a site, remove the competition of non-native plants where possible, and wisely add native plants that both fit the conditions and work together. The judicious inclusion of native trees, shrubs, and herbaceous plants provides a ready seed source that can set the successional stage for natural development of the landscape.

Tennessee Plant Communities

The following plant community lists describe the characteristics particular to each community type and highlight many common species. An asterisk (*) denotes an indicator species.

Mixed Mesophytic Forest Communities— Diverse Plants, Moist Soil

Mixed mesophytic forest communities exhibit great diversity in the number of different species present, a rich variety of deciduous woody and herbaceous plants. There is a stunning display of wildflowers in spring and an abundance of ferns in summer. The soil is deep, dark, loaded with organic matter (humus), and nearly neutral in pH. Mixed mesophytic communities require cooler temperatures, reliably moist but well-drained soil, and protection from drying winds. The Cumberland Mountains, dipping into Tennessee on the northeastern edge of the Cumberland Plateau, contain excellent examples of the mixed mesophytic forest type. Spreading out from this center, other fine examples can be found in the protected cove forests of the Unaka Mountains and the deep gorges and ravines dissecting the plateau and the Eastern Highland Rim. Other sites may be found throughout the state when the favorable conditions of moisture, temperature, and protection combine.

Canopy:

> *Acer saccharum* ssp. *saccharum*—sugar maple
> *Aesculus flava*—yellow buckeye*
> *Carya cordiformis*—bitternut hickory
> *Fagus grandifolia*—American beech

Fraxinus americana—white ash
Prunus serotina—black cherry
Quercus alba—white oak
Quercus rubra—northern red oak
Tilia heterophylla—white basswood*
Tsuga canadensis—eastern hemlock

Understory and Shrub:

Acer pensylvanicum—striped maple
Amelanchier arborea—downy serviceberry
Asimina triloba—pawpaw
Carpinus caroliniana—American hornbeam
Cornus alternifolia—pagoda dogwood
Cornus florida—flowering dogwood
Hamamelis virginiana—witch hazel
Magnolia acuminata—cucumber tree
Magnolia tripetala—umbrella tree
Ostrya virginiana—American hophornbeam
Clethra acuminata—cinnamon clethra
Euonymus americanus—strawberry bush
Hydrangea arborescens—smooth hydrangea
Lindera benzoin—spicebush
Vaccinium corymbosum—highbush blueberry
Viburnum acerifolium—mapleleaf viburnum
Aristolochia macrophylla—Dutchman's pipe

Herbaceous:

Actaea pachypoda—doll's eyes
Ageratina altissima—white snakeroot
Arisaema triphyllum—jack-in-the-pulpit
Aster cordifolius—blue wood aster
Aster divaricatus—white wood aster
Caulophyllum thalictroides—blue cohosh
Delphinium tricorne—dwarf larkspur
Dicentra canadensis—squirrel corn
Dicentra cucullaria—Dutchman's breeches
Disporum maculatum—spotted mandarin
Erythronium americanum—trout lily
Gentiana saponaria—soapwort gentian
Phacelia bipinnatifida—purple phacelia

Phlox divaricata—wild blue phlox
Solidago caesia—blue-stemmed goldenrod
Thalictrum thalictroides—rue anemone
Tiarella cordifolia—foamflower
Trillium grandiflorum—large-flowered trillium
Uvularia grandiflora—great merrybells
Viola blanda—sweet white violet
Viola canadensis—Canada violet
Adiantum pedatum—maidenhair fern
Deparia acrostichoides—silvery spleenwort
Diplazium pycnocarpon—narrow-leaved spleenwort
Dryopteris goldiana—Goldie's woodfern
Osmunda claytoniana—interrupted fern
Thelypteris hexagonoptera—broad beech fern

Mesic Forest Communities—Moist Soil

Mesic (moist) forests have many species in common with mixed meso-phytic communities and produce an equally lush spring wildflower and summer fern display. The soils are moisture retentive year-round, well drained, and deep with lots of humus. These upland communities are most likely to be found on north- or northeast-facing slopes, which are usually shadier, a bit cooler, and more moist.

Canopy:

Acer saccharum ssp. *saccharum*—sugar maple*
Carya cordiformis—bitternut hickory
Celtis laevigata—sugarberry
Cladrastis kentukea—yellowwood
Fagus grandifolia—American beech*
Fraxinus americana—white ash
Ilex opaca—American holly
Juglans nigra—black walnut
Liquidambar styraciflua—sweetgum
Liriodendron tulipifera—tulip tree*
Prunus serotina—black cherry
Quercus alba—white oak
Quercus muhlenbergii—chinkapin oak
Quercus rubra—northern red oak
Quercus shumardii—Shumard oak
Sassafras albidum—sassafras

Understory and Shrub:

Asimina triloba—pawpaw
Carpinus caroliniana—American hornbeam
Cercis canadensis—redbud
Cornus florida—flowering dogwood
Nyssa sylvatica—blackgum
Ostrya virginiana—American hophornbeam
Euonymus americanus—strawberry bush
Hydrangea arborescens—smooth hydrangea
Lindera benzoin—spicebush
Rhododendron prinophyllum—roseshell azalea
Staphylea trifolia—American bladdernut
Celastrus scandens—American bittersweet
Decumaria barbara—climbing hydrangea
Parthenocissus quinquefolia—Virginia creeper

Herbaceous:

Arisaema triphyllum—jack-in-the-pulpit
Asarum canadense—wild ginger
Aster shortii—Short's aster
Claytonia virginica—spring beauty
Dentaria laciniata—cut-leaved toothwort
Dicentra cucullaria— Dutchman's breeches
Elephantopus carolinianus—Carolina elephant's foot
Erythronium americanum—trout lily
Hydrophyllum appendiculatum—waterleaf
Pachysandra procumbens—Allegheny spurge
Phlox divaricata—wild blue phlox
Podophyllum peltatum—may-apple
Polemonium reptans—Jacob's ladder
Sanguinaria canadensis—bloodroot
Solidago flexicaulis—zigzag goldenrod
Trillium recurvatum—prairie trillium
Adiantum pedatum—maidenhair fern
Athyrium filix-femina—ladyfern
Cystopteris protrusa—lowland bladderfern
Deparia acrostichoides—silvery spleenwort
Diplazium pycnocarpon—narrow-leaved spleenwort
Polystichum acrostichoides—Christmas fern
Thelypteris hexagonoptera—broad beech fern
Chasmanthium latifolium—river oats

Xeric Forest Communities—Dry Soil

In xeric communities the plants are adapted to soils that are rocky or shallow and often dry. Moisture levels will vary from season to season with periodic dry spells. These communities are found on ridges, bluffs, and south- or southwest-facing slopes with warmer air and soil temperatures. The soils are well drained, some excessively so, with a lower pH (acid). Oaks and hickories dominate the canopy and are often joined by pines. Despite its drier nature the soil has a humus layer and still supports numerous herbaceous species.

Canopy:

Carya glabra—pignut hickory*
Carya ovata—shagbark hickory*
Carya tomentosa—mockernut hickory*
Diospyros virginiana—persimmon
Fraxinus quadrangulata—blue ash
Juniperus virginiana—eastern red cedar
Pinus echinata—shortleaf pine*
Pinus taeda—loblolly pine
Pinus virginiana—Virginia pine*
Quercus muhlenbergii—chinkapin oak
Quercus montana—chestnut oak*
Quercus stellata—post oak*
Quercus velutina—black oak*

Understory and Shrub:

Amelanchier arborea—downy serviceberry
Aralia spinosa—devils-walkingstick
Cercis canadensis—redbud
Cornus florida—flowering dogwood
Nyssa sylvatica—blackgum
Ostrya virginiana—American hophornbeam
Oxydendrum arboreum—sourwood
Rhamnus caroliniana—Carolina buckthorn
Rhus copallina—shining sumac
Viburnum rufidulum—rusty blackhaw viburnum
Ceanothus americanus—New Jersey tea
Hydrangea quercifolia—oakleaf hydrangea
Hypericum frondosum—golden St. John's-wort
Kalmia latifolia—mountain laurel

Rhododendron alabamense—Alabama azalea
Rhododendron periclymenoides—pinxterbloom azalea
Vaccinium arboreum—farkleberry
Vaccinium stamineum—deerberry
Vitis vulpina—frost grape

Herbaceous:

Antennaria plantaginifolia—plantain-leaved pussytoes
Asclepias variegata—white milkweed
Aster patens—late purple aster
Coreopsis major—large tickseed
Euphorbia corollata—flowering spurge
Heuchera americana—alumroot
Heuchera villosa—hairy alumroot
Mitchella repens—partridgeberry
Opuntia humifusa—prickly-pear cactus
Oxalis violacea—violet wood sorrel
Porteranthus stipulatus—Indian physic
Ruellia humilis—wild petunia
Sedum ternatum—woodland stonecrop
Silene virginica—fire pink
Solidago ulmifolia—elm-leaved goldenrod
Asplenium platyneuron—ebony spleenwort
Polystichum acrostichoides—Christmas fern
Woodsia obtusa—blunt-lobed cliff-fern

Hydric Forest Communities—Wet Soil

Swamps, marshes, bottomlands, alluvial floodplains, and streamsides often experience year-round or seasonal standing water due to flooding, poor drainage, or a high water table. Plants inhabiting these areas either prefer or possess the ability to tolerate saturated soil.

Canopy:

Acer rubrum—red maple*
Betula nigra—river birch
Fraxinus pennsylvanica—green ash
Liquidambar styraciflua—sweetgum*
Nyssa aquatica—water tupelo
Platanus occidentalis—sycamore
Populus deltoides—cottonwood

Hydric Forest Community: Huge stands of *Taxodium distichum* (bald cypress), *Nelumbo lutea* (American lotus), *Pontederia cordata* (pickerelweed), and *Typha latifolia* (common cattail) can be found at Reelfoot Lake in Lake and Obion counties.

Quercus lyrata—overcup oak*
Quercus michauxii—swamp chestnut oak
Quercus nigra—water oak
Quercus pagoda—cherrybark oak
Quercus palustris—pin oak
Quercus phellos—willow oak*
Salix nigra—black willow
Taxodium distichum—bald cypress*

Understory and Shrub:

Hamamelis virginiana—witch hazel
Alnus serrulata—tag alder
Aronia arbutifolia—red chokeberry
Calycanthus floridus—sweetshrub
Cephalanthus occidentalis—buttonbush
Cornus amomum—silky dogwood
Ilex decidua—possumhaw
Ilex verticillata—winterberry
Itea virginica—Virginia sweetspire
Rosa palustris—swamp rose
Viburnum dentatum—arrowwood viburnum
Viburnum nudum—possumhaw viburnum
Wisteria frutescens—American wisteria

Emergent herbaceous:

Nelumbo lutea—American lotus
Orontium aquaticum—golden club
Peltandra virginica—arrow arum
Sagittaria latifolia—arrowhead
Typha latifolia—cattail

Water's edge herbaceous:

Chelone glabra—turtlehead
Conoclinium coelestinum—mist flower
Hibiscus moscheutos—swamp rose-mallow
Impatiens capensis—spotted jewelweed
Iris virginica—southern blue flag
Lobelia cardinalis—cardinal flower
Mimulus ringens—monkey flower
Saururus cernuus—lizard's tail

Equisetum hyemale—scouring rush
Arundinaria gigantea—river cane
Juncus spp.—rush

Wet meadow herbaceous:

Bidens aristosa—tickseed sunflower
Doellingeria umbellata—flat-topped aster
Eupatorium fistulosum—Joe-Pye-weed
Phlox maculata—meadow phlox
Rhexia mariana/R. virginica—meadow beauty
Vernonia gigantea—tall ironweed
Xyris torta—slender yellow-eyed grass
Osmunda cinnamomea—cinnamon fern
Osmunda regalis—royal fern
Thelypteris noveboracensis—New York fern
Woodwardia areolata—netted chain fern
Carex grayi—Gray's sedge
Panicum virgatum—switch grass

Barrens Communities—Grasslands

Barrens are natural grassland openings "barren" of trees and bear a strik-ing similarity to midwestern prairies. Perennial grasses dominate these areas (constituting over 50 percent of the plant species) with significant contributions from composites (Asteraceae—Aster Family) and legumes (Fabaceae—Pea Family). These natural openings occur throughout the Southeast from Texas and Florida as far north as Arkansas, Kentucky, and Virginia. Barrens are found virtually throughout Tennessee: on gen-tle, loess slopes in West Tennessee; in loess soils around the Highland Rim; in shallow, sandy soils on the Cumberland Plateau; and in shallow clay soils in both the Central Basin and Valley and Ridge Region. Fire and grazing/browsing historically have maintained these sites, perhaps with the assistance of Native Americans. Periodic drought on shallow soils contributes, too. Today mowing and controlled burns help prevent the invasion of woody species. Some sites with deeper loess soils have a fragipan, or hard layer of clay, that retards drainage of surface water and creates a wet meadow in winter and spring. This fragipan also prevents water from moving up from the lower soil, which keeps the same area droughty in summer and autumn. This natural phenomenon favors the barrens community.

George W. Hornal.

Barrens Community: Periodic controlled burns deter woody species and help maintain the diverse collection of native grasses, orchids, and other wildflowers found at May Prairie, a State Natural Area in Coffee County.

Grasses:

Andropogon gerardii—big bluestem
Andropogon glomeratus—bushy bluestem
Panicum spp.—switch grass
Schizachyrium scoparium—little bluestem
Sorghastrum nutans—Indian grass

Wildflowers:

Aster spp.
Baptisia australis—blue wild indigo
Euphorbia corollata—flowering spurge
Helianthus spp.—sunflower
Manfreda virginica—false aloe
Oenothera spp.—sundrops/primrose
Opuntia humifusa—prickly-pear cactus

Rhexia virginica—Virginia meadow beauty
Rudbeckia spp.—black-eyed Susan
Silphium spp.—rosinweed
Solidago spp.—goldenrod

Shrubs and Vines:

Berchemia scandens—Alabama supplejack
Rosa carolina—Carolina rose
Rosa setigera—prairie rose

Cedar Glade Communities—Thin Soil on Limestone

Like the barrens, cedar glades are naturally sunny openings in the more typically forested landscape of Tennessee, and like the barrens, cedar glades have shallow, drier soils. However, a very different plant community establishes itself in the cedar glades. Several factors influence this. The soil is often very shallow, usually no greater than eight inches and sometimes an inch or less, which makes it highly susceptible to temperature extremes. Flat limestone bedrock lies directly underneath the soil. Soil moisture is quite variable, ranging from standing water in

George W. Hornal.

late winter to cracked and bone dry in summer. Cedar glades are often a mosaic of shrubby thickets and glade woodlands interwoven among the true open glades which support a mix of grasses (less than 50 percent of the plant species) and other herbaceous plants. Many of these plants are endemic to these areas and endangered. The Central Basin has the highest concentration of cedar glade endemics. Cedar glade communities are also found in other areas of the Mid-South, especially the Valley and Ridge Region, northern Alabama, northwestern Georgia, northern Arkansas, southern Missouri, and Kentucky.

Trees and Shrubs:

Celtis spp.—hackberry/sugarberry

Juniperus virginiana—eastern red cedar

Quercus stellata—post oak

Forestiera ligustrina—glade privet

Rhus aromatica—fragrant sumac

Symphoricarpos orbiculatus—coralberry

Grasses:

Andropogon spp.—bluestem

Bouteloua curtipendula—side oats grama

Schizachyrium scoparium—little bluestem

Wildflowers:

Allium cernuum—nodding onion

Dalea gattingeri—Gattinger's prairie-clover

Echinacea tennesseensis—Tennessee coneflower

Leavenworthia spp.—mustards

Manfreda virginica—false aloe

Phlox bifida—glade phlox

Ruellia humilis—wild petunia

Sedum pulchellum—lime stonecrop

Verbena canadensis—rose verbena

Viola egglestonii—Eggleston's violet

Opposite page: Cedar Glade Community: In the spring cedar glades become a colorful tapestry of blooming species, many found only in these thin soil, flat limestone areas. Off Interstate 24 in Rutherford County, *Sedum pulchellum* (lime stonecrop), *Dalea gattingeri* (Gattinger's prairie-clover), and *Lobelia appendiculata* var. *gattingeri* (Gattinger's lobelia) create a lively carpet with *Senecio* sp. (ragwort) in the background.

Unaka Mountain Peak Communities—Northern Viewpoint

Beginning at about 4,500 feet above sea level, the plant communities found in the Unaka Mountains assume the look and characteristics of forests usually found much farther north. There are three distinct types: the spruce-fir forest, the northern hardwoods forest, and the balds.

1. Spruce–Fir Forest (above 5,500 feet):

Abies fraseri—Fraser fir
Betula alleghaniensis—yellow birch
Picea rubens—red spruce
Prunus pensylvanica—fire cherry
Rhododendron catawbiense—Catawba rhododendron
Sorbus americana—mountain ash

2. Northern Hardwoods Forest (4,500 to 5,500 feet):

Acer pensylvanicum—striped maple
Acer saccharum ssp. *saccharum*—sugar maple
Acer spicatum—mountain maple
Aesculus flava—yellow buckeye
Fagus grandifolia—American beech
Prunus serotina—black cherry
Sorbus americana—mountain ash

Spruce and fir remain in protected sites.

Herbaceous:

Caltha palustris—marsh marigold
Clintonia borealis—Clinton's lily
Hedyotis michauxii (*Houstonia serphyllifolia*)—prostrate bluets
Maianthemum canadense—Canada mayflower, false lily of
    the valley
Phacelia fimbriata—fringed phacelia
Sanguisorba canadensis—Canada burnet
Streptopus roseus—rosy twisted-stalk
Symplocarpus foetidus—skunk cabbage
Trillium undulatum—painted trillium
Vaccinium macrocarpon—cranberry

3. Balds (4,500 to 6,600 feet):

There are three types of balds: orchard, grass, and heath. Orchard balds have sparse trees, dwarfed and twisted from the harsh exposure, amid various grasses, ferns, and other herbaceous plants. Grass balds do not have

George W. Hornal.

Unaka Mountain Peak Community: Round Bald, a grassy bald near Roan Mountain in Carter County, also features blooming rhododendrons in the background.

trees. Heath balds (laurel slicks) are almost exclusively populated with plants in the Ericaceae or Heath Family.

> *Leiophyllum buxifolium*—mountain myrtle
> *Rhododendron calendulaceum*—flame azalea
> *Rhododendron catawbiense*—Catawba rhododendron
> *Rhododendron minus*—Carolina rhododendron
> *Vaccinium corymbosum*—highbush blueberry
> *Viburnum cassinoides*—northern witherod
> *Carex pensylvanica*—Pennsylvania or high meadow sedge
> *Danthonia compressa*—mountain oat grass

Sources for Further Reading

(Full citation information can be found in the bibliography.)

Deciduous Forests of Eastern North America, E. Lucy Braun

Natural Landscaping: Designing with Native Plant Communities,
John Diekelmann and Robert Schuster

Conserving Natural Communities: Inventory and Classification, Daryl Durham,
et al.

*The Book of Forest and Thicket: Trees, Shrubs, and Wildflowers of Eastern North
America*, John Eastman

*The Book of Swamp and Bog: Trees, Shrubs, and Wildflowers of Eastern
Freshwater Wetlands*, John Eastman

The Flora of Tennessee and a Philosophy of Botany, Augustin Gattinger

Landscape Restoration Handbook, Donald Harker, et al.

A Field Guide to Ecology of Eastern Forests, North America, John C. Kricher

American Plants for American Gardens, Edith A. Roberts and Elsa Rehmann

Nature's Design: A Practical Guide to Natural Landscaping, Carol A. Smyser

      The following useful articles are from the *Journal of the Tennessee Academy
of Science*:

"Preliminary Check-list of the Herbaceous Vascular Plants of Cedar Glades,"
Jerry M. Baskin, Elsie Quarterman, and Carole Caudle, July 1968

"Plant Communities of Northwestern Middle Tennessee," Edward W. Chester
and William H. Ellis, July 1989

"Forest Communities of Montgomery and Stewart Counties, Northwestern
Middle Tennessee," Edward W. Chester, Richard J. Jensen, and Joe Schibig,
July–October 1995

"Vegetation of the Appalachian Mountains of Tennessee East of the Great
Valley," Edward E. C. Clebsch, July 1989

"The Barrens of Tennessee," H. R. DeSelm, July 1989

"Upland Swamps of the Highland Rim of Tennessee," William H. Ellis and
Edward W. Chester, July 1989

"Forest Composition, Environment and Dynamics at Land Between the Lakes
in Northwest Middle Tennessee," James S. Fralish and Fred B. Crooks,
July 1989

"A Floristic and Vegetational Overview of Reelfoot Lake," Milo Guthrie,
July 1989

"Plant Communities and Flora of West Tennessee Between the Loess Hills
and the Tennessee River," Thomas E. Heineke, July 1989

"Forest Communities of the Cumberland Plateau of Tennessee," Ross C.
Hinkle, July 1989

"A Floristic Study of Wetlands on the Cumberland Plateau of Tennessee,"
Ronald L. Jones, July 1989

"Forest Patterns in the Great Valley of Tennessee," William H. Martin, July 1989

"Vegetation of the Eastern Highland Rim of Tennessee," Landon E. McKinney, July 1989

"A Plant Community Study of the Third Chickasaw Bluff, Shelby County, Tennessee," Neil A. Miller and John Neiswender, July 1989

"Structure and Dynamics of the Limestone Cedar Glade Communities in Tennessee," Elsie Quarterman, July 1989

"Some Changes in the Vegetation of the Great Smoky Mountains," George S. Ramseur, July 1989

"The Vegetation of Chilhowee Mountain, Tennessee," R. Dale Thomas, July 1989

"Changes in the Spruce-Fir Forest of Roan Mountain in Tennessee Over the Past Fifty Years as a Result of Logging," John C. Warden, July 1989

"The Aquatic Vascular Flora and Plant Communities Along Rivers and Reservoirs of the Tennessee River System," David H. Webb and A. Leon Bates, July 1989

"Floristic Elements of the Tennessee Blue Ridge," B. Eugene Wofford, July 1989

3

Tennessee Wildlife

This world . . . is furnished with an

infinite variety of animated scenes,

inexpressibly beautiful and pleasing,

equally free to the inspection and

enjoyment of all [H]is creatures.

—William Bartram,
Travels, 1791

The surface of the earth is portioned out

among them. By a beautiful law

of distribution, one creature does

not too much interfere with another.

—Henry David Thoreau,
Journal XII, 1859

Southern leopard frog.

Susan Felts.

$\mathcal{A}$LL LIVING THINGS ARE INTERCONNECTED. THIS VAST ARRAY OF CONNECTIONS IS ABSOLUTELY DEPENDENT UPON DIVERSITY. A GREAT variety of plant species growing in an area will attract a great variety of insects, birds, and other animal species, each in its turn predator and prey. Variety is the spice of life. Nature abhors sameness. Left to her own devices, she turns an old cornfield into a jumble of hundreds of different plant species accompanied by various animal and insect friends and enemies.

Bluebirds increasingly depend on humans for their nesting sites.

Monoculture can be as bad as it is boring. A large, single crop becomes dependent on chemicals (pesticides, fertilizers, and herbicides) for survival. Even in the home landscape the same old lineup of foundation plantings and ornamentals (many non-native) will likely attract more pests than desirable wildlife. However, a gardener with a rich and varied native landscape, who refrains from chemicals, will find few pest problems. Those that do occur can be easily resolved using the least toxic means. Allowed to function in the way she has perfected over millions of years, nature strikes a balance protecting all her children by spreading the bounty. Ladybugs will help control aphids; birds will help control caterpillars. Bats will hold down the mosquito population; in less urban areas predators such as hawks, owls, and foxes will keep mice, chipmunks, and squirrels in check.

Diversify and think native. The reward will be a landscape alive with the colors, movements, and sounds of Tennessee's flora and fauna living in concert. Programs such as the National Wildlife Federation's Backyard Wildlife Habitat promote the development of individual properties into mini-sanctuaries, offering food, water, cover, and nesting opportunities to neighboring wildlife. It's not a one-way street. In return these creatures offer genuine beauty, entertainment, and science lessons, as well as the more practical benefits of pest control and plant pollination. Their mere presence adds a certain *joie de vivre*.

Attracting Wildlife: What to Do, What Not to Do

Use the following guidelines to examine and evaluate landscapes.

- Vegetation size and type: Offer a variety of nesting sites for wildlife preference by including canopy and understory trees, shrubs of differing heights, a mix of evergreen and deciduous plants, and herbaceous ground covers, grasses, and flowers.
- Food: A wide variety of trees, shrubs, flowers, and grasses produces an open-air market of nuts, berries, seeds, nectar, and foliage.
- Water: A constant source of clean water is an essential component.

- Cover: Tangles, brambles, thickets, and hedgerows are not for the neat freak, but many of nature's other animals love the sense of security derived from brushpiles, vine tangles, fall leaves, dead stalks standing through winter, and even dead trees if not a hazard. These areas provide escape from danger, respite from storms, and nursery accommodations for young.

There are several books available, including *National Wildlife Federation's Guide to Gardening for Wildlife* by Craig Tufts and Peter Loewer, that offer suggestions on attracting wildlife, especially butterflies and birds. Establishing a haven for these two groups will likely attract most of the others, too. Many of these books recommend specific plants to attract wildlife. One word of caution: often these plant lists include invasive exotics, non-native plants that reproduce prolifically in wild areas and devastate native plant populations. It is often the attractiveness these exotics hold for wildlife that unfortunately contributes to their uncontrolled spread.

The following exotic plants are listed by the Tennessee Exotic Pest Plant Council (TN-EPPC) as being either a severe or significant threat to invade and displace native plant communities in Tennessee, yet they sometimes appear on wildlife friendly lists:

Albizia julibrissin—mimosa
Berberis thunbergii—Japanese barberry
Daucus carota—Queen Anne's lace
Elaeagnus umbellata—autumn olive
Hedera helix—English ivy
Hesperis matronalis—dame's rocket
Lonicera fragrantissima—winter honeysuckle or
    January jasmine
Lonicera japonica 'Halliana'—Japanese honeysuckle
    vine or Hall's honeysuckle
Lonicera maackii—Amur bush honeysuckle
Lonicera morrowii—Morrow's bush honeysuckle
Lythrum salicaria (all varieties and cultivars)—
    purple loosestrife
Tussilago farfara—coltsfoot

Do a little research before buying a plant. If it is not native to Tennessee, make sure a particular exotic will be a well-behaved guest. An invasive exotic will do far more harm to the natural environment than its limited food value to wildlife could ever justify. (See chapter 4 for more information on exotic pest plants.)

Another word of caution. Wildlife has an uncanny ability to search out prime habitat. Build it, and they will come. Therefore, it is unnecessary to purchase insects or animals. Such introduced species may not be native and could harm local species.

Tennessee Wildlife

Here is a partial list of some of our vibrant Tennessee fauna.

Butterflies

Pipevine Swallowtail, Zebra Swallowtail, Eastern Black Swallowtail, Giant Swallowtail, Eastern Tiger Swallowtail, Spicebush Swallowtail, West Virginia White, Falcate Orangetip, Clouded Sulphur, Orange

James F. Snyder.

Gray hairstreak.

Sulphur, Southern Dogface, Great Purple Hairstreak, Gray Hairstreak, Red-banded Hairstreak, Eastern Tailed Blue, Spring Azure, Gulf Fritillary, Variegated Fritillary, Great Spangled Fritillary, Pearly Crescentspot, Baltimore Checkerspot, Question Mark, Comma, Mourning Cloak, American Painted Lady, Red Admiral, Common Buckeye, Red-spotted Purple, Viceroy, Hackberry Emperor, American Snout, Carolina Satyr, Common Wood-nymph, Monarch, Silver-spotted Skipper, Golden-banded Skipper, Northern Cloudywing, Horace's Duskywing, Checkered Skipper, Common Sootywing, and Fiery Skipper.

Moths

Tulip Tree Beauty, Cecropia Moth, Regal Moth, Luna Moth, Ilia Underwing, Hummingbird Clearwing, Virginian Tiger Moth or Yellow Bear Moth, Isabella Tiger Moth or Woolly Bear, Io Moth, Imperial Moth, Polyphemus Moth, Promethea Moth or Spicebush Silkmoth, Painted Lichen Moth, Twin-spotted Sphinx, Oak Beauty, Cloaked Marvel, Red Groundling, Pearly Wood-nymph, Moonseed Moth, Decorated Owlet, American Dagger Moth, and American Idia.

Other Insects, Spiders, and Worms

There are innumerable bees, wasps, worms, ants, spiders, beetles, bugs, and flies in the state. Many provide beneficial services, such as preying on damaging pests, pollinating flowers, and aerating and enriching the soil. Others at least provide lunch to wildlife further up the food chain. Desirable beneficial insects include the ladybug, praying mantis, damsel bug, assassin bug, Ichneumon wasps, and giant cicada killer.

Birds

Year-round residents. Black-crowned Night-Heron, Canada Goose, Black Vulture, Turkey Vulture, Red-shouldered Hawk, Red-tailed Hawk, American Kestrel, Ruffed Grouse, Wild Turkey, Northern Bobwhite, Killdeer, Rock Dove, Mourning Dove, Eastern Screech Owl, Great Horned Owl, Barred Owl, Belted Kingfisher, Red-headed Woodpecker, Red-bellied Woodpecker, Downy Woodpecker, Hairy Woodpecker, Northern Flicker, Pileated Woodpecker, Eastern Phoebe, Horned Lark, Blue Jay, American Crow, Carolina Chickadee, Tufted Titmouse,

Susan Felts.

Mockingbird.

White-breasted Nuthatch, Carolina Wren, Eastern Bluebird, American Robin, Northern Mockingbird, Brown Thrasher, Cedar Waxwing, Loggerhead Shrike, Northern Cardinal, Eastern Towhee (Rufous-sided Towhee), Field Sparrow, Song Sparrow, Red-winged Blackbird, Eastern Meadowlark, Common Grackle, Brown-headed Cowbird, House Finch, and American Goldfinch.

Winter residents and migrants. Pied-billed Grebe, Great Blue Heron, American Black Duck, Mallard, Blue-winged Teal, Bald Eagle, Sharp-shinned Hawk, Broad-winged Hawk, American Coot, Spotted Sandpiper, Yellow-bellied Sapsucker, Least Flycatcher, Tree Swallow, Cliff Swallow, Red-breasted Nuthatch, Brown Creeper, House Wren, Winter Wren, Golden-crowned Kinglet, Ruby-crowned Kinglet, Hermit Thrush, Tennessee Warbler, Nashville Warbler, Magnolia Warbler, Yellow-rumped Warbler, Blackburnian Warbler, Palm Warbler, Rose-breasted Grosbeak, Savannah Sparrow, Swamp Sparrow, White-throated Sparrow, Dark-eyed Junco, Baltimore Oriole, Purple Finch, and Pine Siskin.

Summer residents. Green-backed Heron, Wood Duck, Least Tern, Yellow-billed Cuckoo, Common Nighthawk, Chuck-will's-widow, Whip-poor-will, Chimney Swift, Ruby-throated Hummingbird, Eastern Wood-pewee, Acadian Flycatcher, Great Crested Flycatcher, Eastern Kingbird, Purple Martin, Northern Rough-winged Swallow, Barn Swallow, Blue-gray Gnatcatcher, Veery, Wood Thrush, Gray Catbird, White-eyed Vireo, Solitary Vireo, Yellow-throated Vireo, Red-eyed Vireo, Blue-winged Warbler, Northern Parula, Yellow Warbler, Chestnut-sided Warbler, Black-throated Blue Warbler, Black-throated Green Warbler, Yellow-throated Warbler, Pine Warbler, Prairie Warbler, Cerulean Warbler, Black-and-white Warbler, American Redstart, Prothonotary Warbler, Worm-eating Warbler, Ovenbird, Louisiana Waterthrush, Kentucky Warbler, Common Yellowthroat, Hooded Warbler, Yellow-breasted Chat, Summer Tanager, Scarlet Tanager, Blue Grosbeak, Indigo Bunting, Dickcissel, Chipping Sparrow, Grasshopper Sparrow, and Orchard Oriole.

Amphibians and Reptiles

Frogs and toads. Cricket Frog, Western Chorus Frog, Mountain Chorus Frog, Upland Chorus Frog, Spring Peeper, Eastern Gray Treefrog, Western Bird-voiced Treefrog, Green Treefrog, Bullfrog, Pickerel Frog, Northern Crayfish Frog, Green Frog, Leopard Frog, Eastern Wood Frog, Narrow-mouthed Toad, Eastern Spadefoot Toad, American Toad, and Fowler's Toad.

Turtles. Box Turtle, Common Snapping Turtle, Alligator Snapping Turtle, Painted Turtle, Musk Turtle, Map Turtle, False Map Turtle, Mud Turtle, Saw-toothed Slider, Elegant Slider, and Smooth and Spiny Soft-shelled Turtles.

Lizards. Fence Swift, Ground Lizard, Broad-headed Skink, Five-lined Skink, Southeastern Five-lined Skink, Anole, Coal Skink, Glass Lizard, and Racerunner.

Salamanders. Mudpuppy, Waterdog or Hellbender, Spotted Salamander, Marbled Salamander, Tiger Salamander, Newt, Dusky Salamander or Spring Lizard, Red-backed Salamander, Slimy Salamander, Red Salamander, Texas Salamander, Two-lined Salamander, Four-toed Salamander, Purple Salamander, Green Salamander, Long-tailed Salamander, Cave Salamander, Siren, and Congo or Lampers eel.

George W. Hornal.

Rough green snake—the closest thing to cute in reptiles.

Poisonous snakes. Timber Rattlesnake, Canebrake Rattlesnake, Pygmy Rattlesnake, Copperhead, and Cottonmouth (water-based).

Non-poisonous snakes. Common Garter, Ribbon Snake, Smooth Earth Snake, Midland Brown Snake, Mud Snake, Worm Snake, Hognosed Snake, Black Racer, Black Kingsnake, Scarlet Kingsnake, Prairie Kingsnake, Mole Kingsnake, Red Milk Snake, Eastern Milk Snake, Black Rat Snake, Gray Rat Snake, Corn Snake, Ringneck Snake, Crowned Snake, and Rough Green Snake. Water-based—Common Water Snake, Green Water Snake, Diamond-backed Water Snake, Plain-bellied Water Snake, and Queen Snake.

Raccoon.

Mammals

Black Bear, White-tailed Deer, Bobcat, Red Fox, Gray Fox, Coyote, Mink, River Otter, Striped Skunk, Spotted Skunk, Raccoon, Woodchuck, Eastern Cottontail Rabbit, Swamp Rabbit, Eastern Chipmunk, Gray Squirrel, Fox Squirrel, Flying Squirrel, Deer Mouse, Eastern Woodrat, Vole, Shrew, Eastern Mole, Opossum, Beaver, Muskrat, Big Brown Bat, Little Brown Bat, and several other bat species.

Sources for Further Reading

(Full citation information can be found in the bibliography.)

Eyewitness Handbooks Butterflies and Moths, David Carter
A Field Guide to the Moths of Eastern North America, Charles V. Covell Jr.
The Naturalist's Garden, Ruth Shaw Ernst
Tennessee Wildlife Viewing Guide, Paul Hamel
Native Trees, Shrubs, and Vines for Urban and Rural America,
   Gary L. Hightshoe

The Bird Garden, Stephen W. Kress

Atlas of the Breeding Birds of Tennessee, Charles P. Nicholson

Birds of the Nashville Area, Henry E. Parmer

A Field Guide to the Birds of Eastern and Central North America, Roger Tory Peterson

National Audubon Society Field Guide to North American Butterflies, Robert Michael Pyle

The Wildlife Garden, Charlotte Seidenberg

Amphibians and Reptiles of Tennessee, Ralph Sinclair, Will Hon, and Robert B. Ferguson

Noah's Garden and *Planting Noah's Garden*, Sara Stein

The Butterfly Garden, Mathew Tekulsky

The Journal of Henry D. Thoreau, Bradford Torrey and Francis H. Allen, editors

National Wildlife Federation's Guide to Gardening for Wildlife, Craig Tufts and Peter Loewer

North American Wildlife, Susan J. Wernert, editor

4

Endangered Native Plants and Exotic Pest Plants in Tennessee

Hast thou named all the

birds without a gun?

Loved the wood-rose,

and left it on its stalk?

—Ralph Waldo Emerson
"Forbearance," 1847

Echinacea tennesseensis (Tennessee coneflower) blooming at Couchville Cedar Glade, a State Natural Area in Davidson County.

The Rare

Why Some Plants Are Endangered, and What Is Being Done to Help Them

THE DIVERSITY OF TENNESSEE'S LANDSCAPE PRESENTS US WITH AN AMAZINGLY BOUNTIFUL PLANT AND ANIMAL HERITAGE. AN INTERESTING corollary is the fact that we can also claim more federally rare species than any other non-coastal state in the United States. The reasons for this distinction are twofold. Our wide-ranging topography—from mountains to cedar glades to the Mississippi River—means a greater variety of plants and animals adapted to specialized conditions. This is compounded by our central positioning north to south, making Tennessee a crossroads for southern and northern species hitting, respectively, the upper and lower reaches of their ranges. These are natural factors contributing to our high number of rare species. Human factors account for the rest—habitat destruction brought about by residential and commercial development, lumbering, impoundment of land for dams, commercial exploitation of species, and environmental pollution.

The Federal Endangered Species Act of 1973 focused attention on plants and animals that were being pushed toward extinction. Tennessee's vanishing species received state protection through the adoption of legislation on behalf of non-game and rare wildlife species in 1974 and plants in 1985. The Natural Heritage Program, a division of the Tennessee Department of Environment and Conservation (TDEC), maintains lists of the rare plants and wildlife in the state. The Rare Vertebrates List (May 1997, including amphibians, birds, fish, mammals, and reptiles) and the Rare Invertebrates List (April 1998, including crustaceans, molluscs, insects, and spiders) combine to identify 421 species. Of these, 190 species are given an official state status (Endangered, Threatened, or Deemed in Need of Management) under the authority of the Tennessee Wildlife Resources Agency (TWRA). The Rare Plant List (October 1999) tracks 486 species, about 17 percent of the approximately 2,850 plant species in Tennessee, and classifies all but two of them into three categories under the authority of TDEC in accordance with the Rare Plant Protection and Conservation Act of 1985.

- Special Concern (170 species): These plants are uncommon in Tennessee or growing in unique or highly specific habitats.
- Threatened (130 species): These plants are deemed likely to become endangered within part or all of their range in Tennessee.
- Endangered (184 species): The continued existence of these plants in Tennessee is judged to be in jeopardy.

Only the 184 species designated Endangered receive protection under the 1985 state law. This law makes it illegal to dig endangered plants on private property without the owner's permission or on public land without a state permit. No one may sell endangered plants without a state license. Public works projects, such as highways, that imperil endangered plants can be exempted from the law. Private landowners, guided only by knowledge and conscience, are under few, if any restrictions regarding endangered species on their property.

Rare plants are under pressure from several different sources. Proliferating development, having outgrown the most accessible sites, is now spilling into places once deemed unsuitable, which are often the last bastions for rare species. Off-road recreation and illegal dumping trample specialized environments. Wild collecting disrupts the immediate ecosystem (soil, water runoff, etc.,) and threatens the ability of species to maintain stable populations, especially plants thought to have some medicinal value. Encroaching development disturbs stable native plant populations by allowing exotic (non-native) plants to invade an area. Some of these are so invasive as to completely take over, depriving many different native species of water, nutrients, and light. As exotics and garden species get nearer their wild cousins, hybridizing can occur, contaminating the genetic purity of rare plant populations. Lengthy climatic extremes, such as drought, can be devastating.

Efforts are being made to combat and ease these pressures. Government agencies, such as TDEC and TWRA, monitor and inventory plant and animal populations throughout the state and take all possible measures to identify and protect rare species. Research into the life history of a plant helps botanists understand its habitat requirements, reproductive methods, and genetic makeup and thus develop appropriate maintenance programs, such as periodic controlled burns. Genetically similar plants are reintroduced to enhance the population at an existing site or establish a new site to maintain diversity. Tennessee's Natural Heritage Program works with interested gardeners and nurseries in the collection of seed and propagation of rare plants. The state and other groups, such as the Tennessee chapter of The Nature Conservancy, purchase sensitive sites. Concerned citizens often donate their land or provide for conservation easements.

Designated Rare Plants in Tennessee

The Rare Plant List is compiled by TDEC's Natural Heritage Program and is updated every three years as botanists evaluate a plant's distribution, the size and number of its populations, known threats, and biological factors. Several of the plants featured in this book are designated

Division of Natural Heritage, Tennessee
Department of Environment and Conservation.

Lilium canadense (Canada lily) is one of the many beautiful, but rare plants in Tennessee.

rare. Even though some of these plants may be common elsewhere in the United States, be sure to purchase only nursery-propagated stock.

> *Acer saccharum* ssp. *leucoderme*—chalk maple
> *Allium stellatum*—prairie or glade onion
> *Castanea dentata*—American chestnut
> *Chrysogonum virginianum*—green-and-gold

Clethra alnifolia—sweet pepperbush
Collinsia verna—blue-eyed Mary
Conradina verticillata—Cumberland rosemary
Diervilla lonicera—northern bush honeysuckle
Echinacea pallida—pale purple coneflower
Echinacea tennesseensis—Tennessee coneflower
Fothergilla major—large fothergilla
Gelsemium sempervirens—yellow jessamine
Hydrastis canadensis—goldenseal
Iris fulva—copper iris
Lonicera flava—yellow honeysuckle
Panax quinquefolius—American ginseng
Phlox pilosa ssp. *ozarkana*—Ozark downy phlox

The following three plants are listed as commercially exploited rare plants in Tennessee. They are being dug from the wild and sold for profit as nursery and medicinal plants.

Cypripedium acaule—pink lady's-slipper
Hydrastis canadensis—goldenseal
Panax quinquefolius—American ginseng

Other rare plants in Tennessee can often be found in the nursery trade:

Anemone canadensis—Canada anemone
Aster ericoides—white heath aster
Baptisia bracteata var. *leucophaea*—cream wild indigo
Caltha palustris—marsh marigold
Clintonia borealis—Clinton's lily
Comptonia peregrina—sweet fern
Cymophyllus fraserianus—Fraser's sedge
Cypripedium reginae—showy lady's-slipper
Dryopteris carthusiana—spinulose shield-fern
Hexastylis virginica—heartleaf ginger
Hydrophyllum virginianum—waterleaf, John's cabbage
Iris prismatica—slender blue flag
Leucothoe racemosa—fetterbush
Lilium canadense—Canada lily
Lilium grayi—Gray's lily
Lilium michiganense—Michigan lily
Lilium philadelphicum—wood lily

Linnaea borealis—twinflower
Lysimachia fraseri—Fraser's loosestrife
Magnolia virginiana—sweetbay magnolia
Marshallia grandiflora—large-flowered Barbara's buttons
Meehania cordata—heartleaf meehania, creeping mint
Neviusia alabamensis—Alabama snow-wreath
Phlox subulata—moss phlox
Prenanthes aspera—rough rattlesnake-root
Prunus virginiana—choke cherry
Sanguisorba canadensis—Canada burnet
Silene regia—royal catchfly
Silphium laciniatum—compass plant
Smilacina stellata—starflower false Solomon's seal
Spiranthes odorata—sweetscent ladies'-tresses
Streptopus roseus—rosy twisted-stalk
Symplocarpus foetidus—skunk cabbage
Talinum calcaricum, T. mengesii, T. teretifolium—fame-flower
Trientalis borealis—northern starflower
Trillium decumbens—trailing trillium
Trillium pusillum var. *ozarkanum*—Ozark least trillium
Trillium pusillum var. *pusillum*—least trillium
Woodwardia virginica—Virginia chainfern

The Rowdy

Why Some Plants Become Pests, and What Is Being Done to Control Them

Exotic plants, those that are introduced and not native to Tennessee, are an important part of gardens, home landscapes, and the nursery trade. Most are well-behaved, welcome additions that stay within their managed environments. A few, however, are not so restrained. Invasive exotic (pest) plants have the ability to escape from the garden and take hold within wild habitats, such as forests, cedar glades, barrens, wetlands, etc., where their rapid growth may overwhelm the native plants. Exotic pest plants steal nutrients, water, and light, outcompeting and eventually displacing the native plants who have so patiently evolved with the landscape over millions of years.

Lonicera maackii (Amur bush honeysuckle) has invaded parts of the Warner Parks in Davidson County. Seeding itself prolifically, it leafs out unusually early to outcompete and eventually displace the vast array of native shrubs, spring wildflowers, and summer ferns that should grace the forest floor.

Invasive exotics share several strong traits:

- fit well within the environment
- grow rapidly
- mature to produce flowers and seed at an early age
- produce great quantities of seed
- effectively disperse their seed (via birds, etc.)
- rampantly spread vegetatively
- have no major pest or disease problems

Horticulturally, some of these characteristics are considered quite desirable. Thus there is the absurd irony of various governmental and environmental groups trying hard to control and eradicate in the wild some of the very same species being sold to gardeners all over the United States in nurseries and plant catalogs. Reseachers have found that the vast majority (85 percent) of the invasive woody plants (vines, shrubs, and trees) in North America were originally introduced here for use as ornamental or landscape plants.

Before humans began shifting plants and animals around the globe, nature had spent eons evolving a symbiotic flora and fauna, where each species could survive without causing or sustaining undue harm. We began bringing outside components into this closed system. In a friendly environment away from their co-evolved biological controls (pests, disease, competition), exotics can experience explosive growth against which native species cannot defend and often suffer harm, perhaps irreparably.

Few laws addressing exotic pest plants currently exist, and those that do usually pertain to noxious weeds that affect agriculture. However, changes are occurring. Under a newly amended state rule, the Tennessee Department of Agriculture now has the authority to ban the sale of exotic pest plants in Tennessee. The first horticultural species to be banned under this rule is purple loosestrife (*Lythrum salicaria*) and its cultivars. Once established, the lightning spread of this ornamental plant is impossible to stop. Untouched, however, are a number of other pernicious species that have invaded the state's forests, parks, and other wild areas and have replaced our native plant diversity with a homogenized palette stripped of all local color and form.

Through research and experimentation, botanists and forestry officials are searching for appropriate controls, such as natural predators (biological control), controlled use of fire, selective application of herbicides, and physical removal, to slow the spread of invasive exotics and reclaim land for native plants. Identifying potential problem plants before they get out of hand allows preventative measures.

Exotic Pest Plants in Tennessee

The Tennessee Exotic Pest Plant Council (TN-EPPC), a state chapter of the Southeast Exotic Pest Plant Council (SE-EPPC), is a nonprofit organization whose mission is to raise public awareness regarding invasive exotics, explore measures for eradication and control, and identify and prevent the appearance and spread of potential problem plants. TN-EPPC appoints a committee of natural resource managers (national, state, and local officials, both public and private, charged with managing wild areas) and botanists to compile a list of those exotic plants that are threatening native plant populations in our area. Revisions are planned every three or four years.

The following is a partial list of exotic pest plants recognized in Tennessee. Many of these plants can be found for sale and are often used as ornamental landscape plants. Avoid them and, if possible, work to eradicate any located on your property. A complete list of exotic pest plants in Tennessee is available from TN-EPPC. See appendix B.

Severe Threat. These plants will spread easily into native plant communities (natural areas) and displace native vegetation; they possess invasive characteristics.

> *Ailanthus altissima*—tree of heaven
> *Albizia julibrissin*—mimosa
> *Celastrus orbiculatus*—Oriental bittersweet
> *Elaeagnus umbellata*—autumn olive
> *Euonymus fortunei*—climbing euonymus, winter creeper
> *Hedera helix*—English ivy
> *Ligustrum sinense* and *L. vulgare*—Chinese and
>   common privet
> *Lonicera japonica*—Japanese honeysuckle vine
> *Lonicera maackii*—Amur bush honeysuckle
> *Lythrum salicaria*—purple loosestrife (all varieties and
>   cultivars)
> *Paulownia tomentosa*—princess tree
> *Polygonum cuspidatum*—Japanese knotweed, bamboo
> *Pueraria lobata (P. montana)*—kudzu
> *Rosa multiflora*—multiflora rose
> *Spiraea japonica*—Japanese spiraea

Significant Threat. These species will invade native plant communities (natural areas) adjacent to disturbed areas, but possess fewer invasive characteristics.

> *Berberis thunbergii*—Japanese barberry
> *Clematis terniflora (C. paniculata, C. maximowicziana)*—
>   sweet autumn or leatherleaf clematis
> *Coronilla varia*—crown vetch
> *Daucus carota*—Queen Anne's lace

Dipsacus sylvestris—fuller's teasel
Euonymus alata—burning bush
Hesperis matronalis—dame's rocket
Hydrilla verticillata—hydrilla, water thyme
Ligustrum japonicum—Japanese privet
Lonicera fragrantissima—January jasmine
Lonicera morrowii—Morrow's bush honeysuckle
Lonicera tatarica—Tartarican honeysuckle, twinsisters
Lonicera x bella—bush honeysuckle
Lysimachia nummularia—moneywort, creeping Jenny
Mahonia bealei—Chinese leatherleaf grapeholly
Miscanthus sinensis—zebra grass
Myriophyllum aquaticum—parrot's-feather, water-milfoil
Nandina domestica—nandina, heavenly bamboo
Populus alba—white poplar
Tussilago farfara—coltsfoot
Verbascum thapsus—common mullein
Vinca minor—common periwinkle
Wisteria floribunda and *W. sinensis*—Chinese wisteria

Lesser Threat. These will spread and remain primarily in disturbed areas but do not readily invade natural areas.

Arundo donax—giant reed, elephant grass
Centaurea cyanus—bachelor's button, cornflower
Chrysanthemum leucanthemum (Leucanthemum vulgare)—
    ox-eye daisy
Cichorium intybus—chicory
Elaeagnus angustifolia—Russian olive
Eschscholtzia californica—California poppy
Iris pseudacorus—yellow flag iris
Melia azedarach—chinaberry
Ornithogalum umbellatum—star of Bethlehem
Pinus taeda—loblolly pine (native in southern tier of counties)
Polygonum persicaria—lady's thumb

Another group of plants, *Ampelopsis brevipedunculata* (Amur pepper-vine, porcelain ampelopsis), *Cosmos bipinnatus* and *C. sulphureus* (cosmos), *Echium vulgare* (viper's bugloss), *Hibiscus syriacus* (rose of Sharon), *Hypericum perforatum* (goatweed or St. John's-wort), *Mentha spicata* and

M.x piperita (spearmint and peppermint), *Muscari neglectum* and *M. botryoides* (grape hyacinth), *Rhamnus cathartica* (European buckthorn) and *R. frangula* (alder buckthorn), and *Senecio vulgaris* (ragwort), are being watched closely by the state since they are troublesome plants elsewhere.

What Gardeners Can Do

Gardeners as educated consumers wield tremendous power. Nurseries will only stock what they can sell. Know which exotics are harmful, refuse to buy them, and be vocal about why. Learn more about our rare species and question anyone selling them. Sellers of our endangered plants are supposed to do so only with a state license. Verify that they have one. Buyers of endangered plants are under certain obligations, too. These plants may only be placed in private gardens and may not be planted in the wild. The reason for this is genetics—naturally occurring populations of these plants must have their genetic purity protected. Horticulturally grown plants might be too genetically distinct and contaminate wild stands.

Guard against purchasing wild-collected plants, those dug from wild habitats and sold for profit to nurseries and gardeners. Many nurseries operate under strong, personal philosophies protective of nature and abhorrent to this practice of wild collecting. These businesses offer plants that have been nursery-propagated—the key word is *propagated*—meaning that existing nursery plants were used to increase stock through division or planting seeds. Check out any seller of native plants. Those who sell nursery-propagated stock are proud to say so. Avoid any seller who will not provide this assurance. There are a few red flags that might indicate wild collecting:

- selling plants in quantities of hundreds
- very low prices for quantity, especially spring ephemerals such as spring beauty (*Claytonia virginica*) and Dutchman's breeches (*Dicentra cucullaria*)
- bare-root plants
- plants in real soil instead of potting soil
- tree roots or rocks in the plant's rootball or other plants growing in the pot
- big plants for low prices

- hard to propagate, slow-growing, or difficult plants, such as trilliums (*Trillium* spp.), trailing arbutus (*Epigaea repens*), and trout lily (*Erythronium* spp.)
- orchids (Species of *Cypripedium, Spiranthes, Platanthera,* etc.) and lilies (*Lilium canadense, L. grayi, L. michiganense, L. philadelphicum*)

Good sources do sell some of the plants mentioned above, but they won't mind your questions.

Genetic Diversity

Another point worthy of mention is the choice between a cultivar, a plant commercially bred and selected as desirable, and a species, the natural botanical designation for similar plants. All plants of one species are going to possess certain characteristics that distinguish them from other species within that same genus. Smooth asters (*Aster laevis*) can be distinguished from white wood asters (*Aster divaricatus*). Individual plants of one species may demonstrate slight variations from one another: greater drought tolerance, different flower color, more compact form, etc. Plants that exhibit superior traits in terms of size, form, bloom, or leaf attract the attention of plant breeders looking for bigger and better garden plants. Since seeds are not reliable in producing plants like the parent, the best way to maintain the desired trait is to vegetatively propagate (clone) the individual plant exhibiting the trait through cuttings, division, or tissue culture. This is a cultivar (short for cultivated variety), and it is given a name appearing in single quotes after the botanical name, e.g., *Aster laevis* 'Bluebird'. All plants of *Aster laevis* 'Bluebird' are genetically identical.

Botanists recognize the importance of genetic diversity, which holds the potential to produce plants with enough variations to cope with different pressures exerted by a changing and often hostile environment. It is the coping power of these variations that perpetuate the species via the slowly turning wheel of evolution. Maintaining a large gene pool for a species gives it a better opportunity to successfully meet any challenges nature or humans might present. Therefore, as wild populations of many of our species diminish, every genetically distinct individual becomes more valuable. Sometimes gardens are the last safe haven for these plants. Plus, gardeners who always opt for the flash of new and improved cultivars often miss out on the subtle beauty inherent in the species. This is not meant to imply that cultivars of native plants should not be used, but rather to point out that the species have value and charm equally worthy of a gardener's interest.

Sources for Further Reading

(Full citation information can be found in the bibliography.)

"A Method for Evaluating Plant Invasiveness," Sarah H. Reichard,
   Public Garden, Apr. 1999

Materials are available from these agencies and organizations (see appendix B for address, phone, and website information):

Tennessee Department of Environment and Conservation, Division of
   Natural Heritage

Tennessee Exotic Pest Plant Council

Tennessee Wildlife Resources Agency

Spring is especially beautiful when gardening with native plants. *Halesia tetraptera* (silverbell) is the centerpiece in this garden, tying together an array of herbaceous plants including *Osmunda cinnamomea* (cinnamon fern), *Polemonium reptans* (Jacob's ladder), *Stylophorum diphyllum* (wood poppy), *Phlox divaricata* (wild blue phlox), *Asarum canadense* (wild ginger), *Hepatica acutiloba* (sharp-lobed liverleaf), *Trillium sulcatum* (Barksdale's trillium), *Sanguinaria canadensis* (bloodroot), *Delphinium tricorne* (dwarf larkspur), *Geranium maculatum* (wild geranium), *Jeffersonia diphylla* (twinleaf), *Cimicifuga racemosa* (black cohosh), *Dodecatheon meadia* (shooting star), and the non-natives *Dicentra spectabilis* 'Alba' and *Hosta sieboldiana* 'Elegans'. Woody native plants *Itea virginica* (Virginia sweetspire), *Tsuga canadensis* (eastern hemlock), and *Ilex opaca* (American holly) provide a backdrop.

J. Paul Moore.

5

Native Plant Gardening

First and last, the wild-flower

gardener works with nature.

—Frances Tenenbaum
Gardening with
Wild Flowers, 1973

A mulch of shredded leaves is ideal for a native woodland garden. Leaves recycle nutrients, improve soil texture, modify soil pH, retain soil moisture, and retard weeds without inhibiting delicate ferns or spring ephemerals. Fallen twigs, branches, and even limbs can be easily worked into this natural setting.

The Basics of Native Plant Gardening

Caring for Native Plants

*G*ARDENING WITH NATIVE PLANTS BLENDS THE BEST ASPECTS OF TWO DISCIPLINES—ECOLOGY AND HORTICULTURE. IT IS AN EXCITING challenge to observe the favored conditions of various local plants in the wild and use that knowledge to grow them advantageously in a garden.

Native plants do grow unaided in the wild, but in a garden they benefit from the same care given other ornamental plants. Amend the soil as needed, provide extra water the first year or two, control weeds, and divide crowded plants. Properly sited native plants in a garden setting are low care, not no care.

Soil Profile

As discussed in chapter 1, there is no substitute for good soil. Some native plants will grow just fine in poor soil; a few actually prefer it. Most plants, however, grow much better in loam soil, rich with decayed organic matter (humus). Woodland plants, especially the spring ephemerals, virtually demand a loose, organically rich soil that stays moist while allowing excess water to drain away.

Check your soil carefully. Many residential plots have been stripped of the darker, rich topsoil during construction and severely compacted. Subsoil usually contains little of the microorganisms, nutrients, oxygen, and moisture holding capacity of good topsoil. Work in compost, leaf mold, rotted manure, or bagged soil conditioners if necessary. Heavy, wet, clay soil, porous, dry, sandy soil, and compacted soil will each benefit greatly from these organic additions.

Soil fertility hinges upon the delicate balance of macronutrients and micronutrients. These two nutrient categories are essential to both plant growth and the health of vital soil organisms that work with plant roots to facilitate nutrient absorption. Mother Nature's organic recycling of nutrients strikes this balance. Chemical fertilizers, dependent upon mathematical computation, often do not. Too much of one nutrient can interfere with a plant's ability to access other nutrients. Some nutrients become toxic in too large concentrations and can adversely affect soil organisms. Natural, organic sources of nutrients, such as compost, manures, etc., form the basis for healthy soil. Healthy soil produces healthy plants that resist pests and diseases, further reducing a gardener's need for any chemical interventions.

Growing Ferns

Here are a few general tips on the culture of ferns:

- Do not plant ferns too deep. Crowns should be just above soil level with runners about one inch deep.

- With most ferns, the soil needs to be loose and rich with lots of organic matter.
- Maintaining even soil moisture is very important throughout the year. A mulch of shredded leaves holds moisture, enriches the soil, and deters weeds without inhibiting young frond development.

Grasses in the Garden

The primary garden maintenance task for ornamental grasses is cutting them back to three or four inches above the ground in early spring before new growth begins. Larger expanses, such as meadows, require the development of a planting scheme that mixes grasses and forbs, herbaceous wildflowers, and a maintenance regimen of mowing or burning. Meadow maintenance is particularly important during the first three years in order to minimize weeds. Mowing can be done in spring or fall. Fall mowing eliminates important winter wildlife cover, which is one of the primary benefits of a grassland or meadow. Controlled burns are usually done in the spring and will be strictly regulated by municipal ordinances. Two good references on the more complex establishment of a grassland or meadow are *Natural Landscaping: Designing with Native Plant Communities* by John Diekelmann and Robert Schuster and *Planting Noah's Garden* by Sara Stein. Grasses are very wildlife friendly, providing nesting, cover, and food for a wide variety of creatures. When grasses bloom, close examination of the spikelets (flowers) will often reveal brightly colored stigmas and stamens in rich reds, purples, and yellows. Sedges and rushes, despite appearances, are not true grasses.

Woody Plants and the Provenance Factor

Woody plants—vines, shrubs, and trees—develop bark and remain viable above ground over the winter. These plants can live several decades to several centuries. Potential longevity of this nature raises the importance of provenance, the concept of buying plants propagated locally using seed or cuttings from successful area plants. The advantage lies in genetic evolution. For plants with a broad native range, differences in climate, soil, and other conditions can become very pronounced from one end of that range to the other. Plants best adapted to local conditions are most likely to survive and set seed carrying these same adapted traits.

J. Paul Moore.

Shrubs and trees are important components in the native plant garden. A grouping of *Tsuga canadensis* (eastern hemlock), *Rhododendron periclymenoides* (pinxterbloom azalea), *Aesculus pavia* (red buckeye), and *Itea virginica* (Virginia sweetspire) adds height and mass to the *Polemonium reptans* (Jacob's ladder), *Stylophorum diphyllum* (wood poppy), and *Hydrophyllum* sp. (waterleaf) underneath.

As an example, sugar maple (*Acer saccharum* ssp. *saccharum*) grows from southern Canada to the southern border of the eastern half of Tennessee. West Tennessee and a large chunk of southwestern Middle Tennessee are not included on most range maps. Therefore, many of us are right on the southernmost edge of the sugar maple's range. Since our weather differs significantly from that of Vermont, it is reasonable to expect that northern sugar maples have evolved to display greater cold hardiness in a shorter growing season while their southern sisters have moved in the other direction to display greater tolerance to long, hot

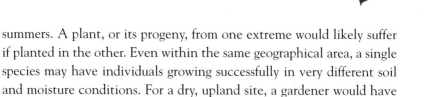

summers. A plant, or its progeny, from one extreme would likely suffer if planted in the other. Even within the same geographical area, a single species may have individuals growing successfully in very different soil and moisture conditions. For a dry, upland site, a gardener would have greater success using seed or cuttings from healthy individuals growing in similar conditions rather than one from the moist, rich soil of lowlands.

Any habitat that is marginal or potentially stressful requires consideration not only of appropriate genera and species but also the provenance factor within a species. It could mean the difference between a stunted or dead tree and one that thrives. Provenance can be an important consideration with herbaceous plants, too, yet this idea is employed most effectively with larger, longer-lived plants such as trees and shrubs. Suitable habitats can often be established and maintained for many herbaceous plants, but this is not a practical alternative for the larger, woody species. Besides, one of the main advantages of native plants is their ability to produce an attractive landscape without a lot of special attention and fuss. Therefore, look for plants propagated locally or start your own using seed or cuttings from successful area plants.

Difficult Natives

In addition to ecology and horticulture, native plants often require a third discipline, conservation. Threats to wild habitats leave the garden as one of the last defenses for the survival of some plants. There are a few native species, however, that resist the best cultivation efforts of gardeners. They often require specialized conditions that are hard to duplicate, such as low soil pH (acid), cool temperatures, or the presence of host-specific bacterial or fungal soil organisms necessary for the plant's survival. These conditions make it very difficult to successfully grow certain desirable species outside of their wild habitats.

The native Tennessee plants listed below are universally recognized as very difficult to cultivate. Several are rare plants, and Tennesseans must work to ensure the preservation of dwindling natural habitats. Do not seek to grow these plants unless certain that your garden can successfully meet their needs.

> *Botrychium dissectum*—common grape fern (possible soil
>   associate; statewide in woodlands)
> *Botrychium virginianum*—rattlesnake fern (same)

Chimaphila maculata—striped wintergreen, pipsissewa
(dry, acid soil and possible soil associate; East Tennessee
and Highland Rim oak-pine woods)

Cymophyllus fraserianus—Fraser's sedge (cool, moist, acid soil
and shade; Unaka Mountains)

Epigaea repens—trailing arbutus (cool, dry, rocky or sandy, acid
soil and possible soil associate; East Tennessee)

Lilium canadense—Canada lily (cool, moist soil and sun;
East Tennessee and Highland Rim)

Lilium michiganense—Michigan lily (same)

Orchid family—*Cypripedium* spp.—lady's-slippers (soil
associate; East Tennessee and elsewhere); *Platanthera*
(Habenaria) spp.—fringed orchids; *Spiranthes* spp.—
ladies'-tresses; *Calopogon* spp.—grass pink; and others

Shortia galacifolia—Oconee bells (cool, moist, acid soil and
shade; Unaka Mountains, Native to North Carolina,
not Tennessee)

Trillium undulatum—painted trillium (cool, moist, acid soil
and shade; Unaka Mountains)

Top Trial Garden Native Plants

The Tennessee native plants below were selected as choice perennials
based on their performance under Tennessee's climatic conditions as
observed in the University of Tennessee Trial Gardens. Criteria for selection include low maintenance, flower and foliage integrity, profuse
blooming, and insect and disease resistance. The four trial gardens are
located in Jackson (University of Tennessee West Tennessee Experiment
Station), Nashville (Cheekwood Botanical Garden), Knoxville (University of Tennessee Agriculture campus), and Johnson City (East Tennessee
State University campus). There are other plants native to North America that also performed well in the trial gardens.

Remember to check all plant lists carefully. There are invasive
exotics on the trial gardens' choice perennials list, too, including *Mis-*
canthus sinensis 'Zebrinus' (zebra grass) and *Lythrum salicaria* 'Happy',
'Morden's Pink', and 'Pink Spires' (purple loosestrife). The latter
species and all its cultivars are now illegal to sell in Tennessee. Horti-
culturists may love a plant, but that does not indicate a clean bill of
health ecologically. The complete Choice Annuals and Perennials for

Tennessee Landscapes is available from the University of Tennessee's Department of Ornamental Horticulture and Landscape Design in Knoxville.

Amsonia tabernaemontana—blue star
Asclepias sp. 'Silky Gold'—butterfly-weed
Baptisia australis—blue wild indigo
Boltonia asteroides 'Pink Beauty' and 'Snowbank'—boltonia
Chasmanthium latifolium—river oats (grass)
Chrysogonum virginianum—green-and-gold
Conoclinium coelestinum (*Eupatorium coelestinum*)—mist flower
Coreopsis lanceolata 'Early Sunrise'—lanceleaf tickseed
Coreopsis verticillata 'Zagreb' and 'Moonbeam'—
    threadleaf tickseed
Echinacea purpurea 'Bravado', 'Magnus', and 'White Swan'—
    purple coneflower
Heuchera americana 'Eco Magnififolia', 'Ruby Veil', and
    'Chocolate Ruffles'—alumroot
Hibiscus moscheutos 'Disco Belle Mix'—swamp rose-mallow
Liatris spicata 'Kobold'—blazing star, gayfeather
Lobelia x *speciosa* 'Compliment Scarlet', 'Compliment Blue',
    and 'Pink Flamingo'—cardinal flower
Lysimachia ciliata var. *purpurea*—fringed loosestrife
Monarda didyma 'Croftway Pink', 'Cambridge Scarlet',
    'Blaustrumpf Deep Lilac', and 'Blue Stocking'—bee balm
Monarda punctata—dotted horsemint
Panicum virgatum 'Heavy Metal' and 'Hanes Herms'—
    switch grass
Penstemon digitalis 'Husker Red'—white beard-tongue
Phlox divaricata—wild blue phlox
Physostegia virginiana 'Rose Queen'—false dragonhead
Rudbeckia fulgida 'Goldstrum'—black-eyed Susan
Rudbeckia hirta 'Becky Mix', 'Goldilocks', 'Marmalade', 'Toto',
    and 'Indian Summer'—black-eyed Susan
Solidago rugosa 'Fireworks' and 'Crown of Rays'—
    wrinkle-leaved goldenrod
Sorghastrum nutans—Indian grass
Stokesia laevis 'Bluestone' and 'Omega Skyrocket'—
    Stokes' aster

Large drifts of *Phlox divaricata* (wild blue phlox), *Senecio aureus* (golden ragwort), and *Geranium maculatum* (wild geranium) weave among *Lindera benzoin* (spicebush), *Carex grayi* (Gray's sedge), *Phlox paniculata* (summer phlox), and the still leafless *Ptelea trifoliata* (hoptree).

Tradescantia virginiana 'Zwanenburg Blue'—spiderwort
Verbena canadensis 'Homestead Purple'—rose verbena
Veronicastrum virginicum 'Album'—culver's root

Definitions

Botany is a very complex science chock full of specialized terms; it is very hard to adequately describe some plants without using a few of them. Simple explanations of some terms found in the text are provided.

Soil pH

Whether a soil is acid (sour), neutral, or alkaline (basic, sweet) is really just a matter of positively charged hydrogen ions versus negatively charged OH ions. More of the former provide azaleas with an optimum soil pH (acid); more of the latter are good for cacti (alkaline). A plant's ability to take up nutrients is influenced by soil pH. Plants have adapted to their own ideal soil pH somewhere between 4 and 8 on the 0 to 14 scale. Most plants will grow best between 6 and 7 because the availability of soluble nutrients is highest at this pH. A few exceptions, like the *Rhododendron* (azalea) and *Vaccinium* (blueberry) genera, prefer a more acid soil. Earthworms and other soil organisms thrive best in a slightly acid to neutral soil. Use home kits or the Agricultural Extension Service to test your soil's pH.

There are a few general rules of thumb regarding soil pH. Deeper soils are more acid at the surface and less near the bedrock. Upland soils have a lower pH due to the leaching of alkalis by rainfall. Soils in the lowlands are closer to neutral due to this downward leaching. Thin soils in flat areas are also usually closer to neutral, especially if limestone bedrock lies below. Since several factors influence soil pH, individual environments will differ. Testing is the only sure way to know.

- Strongly acid soil is 4–5 pH
- Moderately acid soil is 5–6 pH
- Slightly acid soil is 6–7 pH
- Neutral soil is 7 pH
- Slightly alkaline soil is 7–8 pH

Soil pH can be altered with the use of certain organic materials. To increase soil acidity, work in peat moss, cottonseed meal, needles of pines and hemlocks, and oak leaves. Beech, birch, red maple, chestnut, tobacco, blueberry, and azalea leaves are also acidic. Ground sulfur, ferrous sulfate, and aluminum sulfate are chemical additions that work quickly to lower soil pH, but do not last long. Organic materials provide a longer-term solution.

To neutralize an acid soil, add lawn clippings, hay, composted animal manure, and the leaves of hickory, ash, elm, dogwood, poplar, basswood, willow, tulip, and most maple trees. Wood ashes add a lot of calcium carbonate, the same chemical component of ground limestone, as well as other nutrients. Wood ashes are very potent; use them sparingly. Dolomitic limestone will also add magnesium.

Plant Life Cycle

Most wildflowers, ferns, and grasses are perennials. They live a few to several years and typically die back annually to dormancy, some in winter, some in summer. A few plants are biennials. These sprout from seed and establish themselves the first year, then actively grow, flower, and fruit the second year before dying. Annuals germinate, grow, flower, fruit, and die within one year's time leaving future offspring (seed) to carry on the

Flower Parts

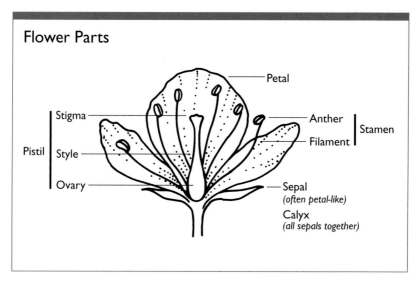

tradition next year. Removing faded blossoms on some plants, called deadheading, prevents them from setting seed and can encourage longer bloom or rebloom later in the season. It also keeps prolific self-sowing plants under control.

Light Requirements

The following explanations provide some clarity to highly subjective light terms:

- full sun—at least six hours of direct sun per day
- part shade—a little shade but more direct sun
- part sun—a little direct sun but more shade
- light shade or open shade—shade from tall trees or a shifting mosaic of dappled sun and shade filtered through tall trees
- medium shade—constant shade below canopy and understory layers

Plant Parts

Flowers:

Some flowers are referred to as perfect, meaning they have both male and female reproductive parts. Some flowers are unisexual and only have functional stamens (staminate, or male flowers) or functional pistils (pistillate, or female flowers). If staminate and pistillate flowers are both present on the same plant, as with oaks, the plant is monoecious

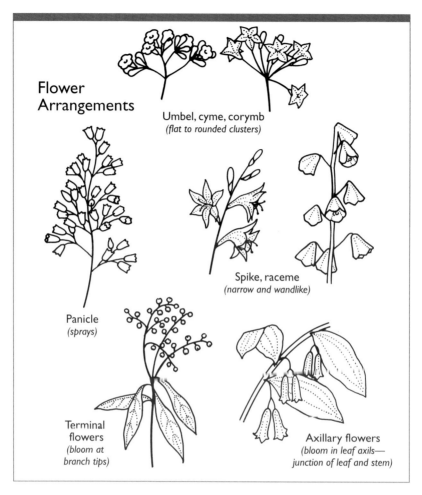

Flower Arrangements

Umbel, cyme, corymb
(flat to rounded clusters)

Spike, raceme
(narrow and wandlike)

Panicle
(sprays)

Terminal flowers
(bloom at branch tips)

Axillary flowers
(bloom in leaf axils—junction of leaf and stem)

(mah-'nee-shus). If the differently sexed flowers are only found on separate plants, as with hollies, the plants are dioecious (die-'ee-shus). Cleistogamous (kly-'stog-ah-mus) flowers, also called blind flowers, look like unopened buds and self-pollinate, setting seed without opening. Some plants, such as violets, employ this backup method to normal, cross-pollinated seed production. A few plants, such as jack-in-the-pulpit, produce tiny flowers massed together on a thickened spike called a spadix, which is usually enclosed within a large, leaflike bract called a spathe.

Underground Structures:

- Bulb—a modified bud or shoot with fleshy scales that stores food
- Corm—bulb-like, but without scales, the enlarged base of a stem that stores food

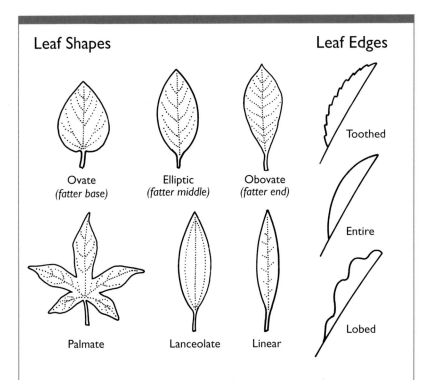

Leaf Shapes

Ovate
(fatter base)

Elliptic
(fatter middle)

Obovate
(fatter end)

Palmate

Lanceolate

Linear

Leaf Edges

Toothed

Entire

Lobed

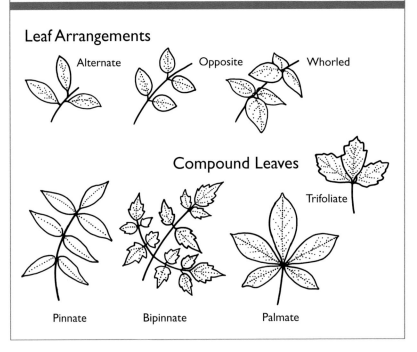

Leaf Arrangements

Alternate

Opposite

Whorled

Compound Leaves

Trifoliate

Pinnate

Bipinnate

Palmate

- Tuber—a short, fleshy, underground stem
- Rhizome—an underground, horizontal, root-like stem that produces other shoots (suckers) and roots.
- Stolons—a runner that can root and send up shoots (suckers)
- Rhizomatous, stoloniferous, suckering—as the definitions above indicate, these terms refer to the tendency of a plant to send out underground stems and spread vegetatively to colonize an area. Plants that employ this trait aggressively would be undesirable in small or very neat gardens, yet can be useful in large, semi-wild areas or where erosion is a concern.

Leaves:

- Basal—foliage at the base of a plant (as opposed to leaves on stems)
- Rosette—a cluster of foliage emerging from one point, often at the plant's base
- Whorled—three or more leaves encircle the stem at the same point
- Petiole—leaf stalk
- Sessile—leaf base attaches directly to the stem, no leaf stalk
- Clasping—the base of the leaf wraps around the stem

Ferns:

- Crozier—the tightly coiled leaf bud that expands in spring. It is often covered with hairs or scales that drop off as it grows. It is also called a fiddlehead as it begins to elongate and unroll.
- Frond—the entire leaf including the petiole
- Petiole—the portion of the central stalk from the ground to the start of the leaf blade
- Rachis—the portion of the central stalk in the leaf blade
- Pinna—primary division of the leaf blade (plural pinnae)
- Pinnule—secondary division of the leaf blade
- Pinnatifid—deeply cut leaf blade, but not all the way to the rachis

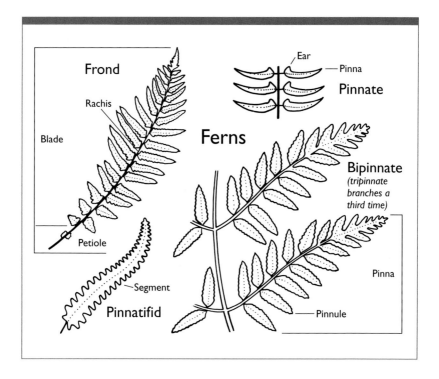

- Segment—a lobe on a pinnatifid leaf
- Sterile fronds—leaves that have no sporangia
- Fertile fronds—leaves with sporangia
- Sporangia—tiny capsules containing dustlike spores that produce new ferns
- Sori—clusters of sporangia often arranged in patterns under leaves

Nomenclature and Plant Distribution

Scientific or botanical names are the bane of many gardeners. They are hard to remember and often even harder to pronounce. Further, once a name is finally committed to memory there is no guarantee that botanists won't discover a reason to change it. However, scientific names are the best way to ensure that the plants you are getting are the plants you want. Common names leave too much to chance. Many plants have several different common names, and some share the same common name. *Cimicifuga racemosa*, for instance, is called black cohosh, black snakeroot, bugbane, or fairy candles. *Manfreda virginica* and *Eryngium yuccifolium* are both called rattlesnake-master. The shrubs *Ilex decidua* and *Viburnum nudum* have possumhaw in their common names.

The first word in a scientific name is the genus or generic name. It is a noun. The second word is the species or specific epithet, an adjective modifying or describing the genus. The genus is capitalized, and the species is not. Both are italicized or underlined. The species name often refers to

- descriptive feature of the plant (*hirsutus*, hairy; *altissima*, very tall; *diphylla*, two leaves)
- where it was found (*carolinianus*, the Carolinas; *virginica*, Virginia; *novae-angliae*, New England)
- great botanists (*michauxii*, Andre Michaux; *grayi*, Asa Gray; *gattingeri*, Augustin Gattinger)

A plant's name can change over time as botanists learn more, and authorities can differ on a plant's classification. The scientific names used in this book follow the "Checklist of the Vascular Plants of Tennessee," *Sida, Botanical Miscellany*, No. 10 (1993), by B. Eugene Wofford and Robert Kral. If a plant is or has been widely known by another scientific name, that name appears in parentheses. A pronunciation guide is included based on L. H. Bailey's *Standard Cyclopedia of Horticulture* and *Gray's Manual of Botany*. Sources and experts sometimes differ on pronunciation, too. Another valuable reference used to sort through complex plant families, genera, and species is the *Manual of Vascular Plants of Northeastern United States and Adjacent Canada* by Henry Gleason and Arthur Cronquist.

Distribution of plants in Tennessee was judged from map data in the *Atlas of Tennessee Vascular Plants*, vols. 1 and 2, by Edward W. Chester, et al. All plants found in Tennessee are listed, and accompanying each plant name is a county map of the state. Each county from which a plant has been documented is marked, providing a guide (though not absolute) to the plant's natural occurrence in Tennessee. These map data were collated from several in-state and out-of-state herbaria collections. Additions to these collections are ongoing to fill information gaps and reflect the dynamic nature of the plant world.

Different sources can present widely differing information on the same plant. Until an effort is made to describe accurately the appearance, growth habit, and needs of a particular plant, it is impossible to fully appreciate how frustrating such an attempt can be. As habitats shift in myriad combinations of light, moisture, elevation, orientation, temperature, and soil, so may a plant's response. Leaving the dog-eat-dog world of the wild for the pampered luxury of a tended garden can have a real impact on bloom time and quality, height and form, and aggressiveness. Bloom time can vary up to a month from one end of Tennessee to the other. Weather variations from year to year also affect a plant's performance. Therefore, while a sincere effort has been made to tailor this information to Tennessee gardens, your experience with a plant in your environment might be somewhat different.

Sources for Further Reading

(Full citation information can be found in the bibliography.)

Growing Woodland Plants, Clarence and Eleanor G. Birdseye

How to Grow Wildflowers and Wild Shrubs and Trees in Your Own Garden, Hal Bruce

The Nature and Properties of Soil, Harry O. Buckman and Nyle C. Brady

Botany for Gardeners: An Introduction and Guide, Brian Capon

Landscaping with Nature, Jeff Cox

Natural Landscaping: Designing with Native Plant Communities, John Diekelmann and Robert Schuster

Wildflowers in Your Garden, Viki Ferreniea

The Gardener's Fern Book, F. Gordon Foster

The Soul of Soil: A Soil-Building Guide for Master Gardeners and Farmers, Grace Gershuny and Joe Smillie

The Encyclopedia of Ornamental Grasses, John Greenlee

Wild Flowers to Know and Grow, Jean Hersey

Taylor's Guide to Natural Gardening, Roger Holmes, editor

Wild Flowers for Your Garden, Helen S. Hull

Gardening with Native Wild Flowers, Samuel B. Jones Jr. and Leonard E. Foote

The Rodale Book of Composting, Deborah L. Martin and Grace Gershuny, editors

Gardener's Latin: A Lexicon, Bill Neal

Growing Wildflowers: A Gardener's Guide, Marie Sperka

Wild Flowers and How to Grow Them, Edwin F. Steffek

Planting Noah's Garden, Sara Stein

Landscaping with Native Trees, Guy Sternberg and Jim Wilson

The Wild Garden: Making Natural Gardens Using Wild and Native Plants,
Violet Stevenson

Handbook of Wild Flower Cultivation, Kathryn S. Taylor and
Stephen F. Hamblin

Wild Flower Gardening, Norman Taylor

Gardening with Wild Flowers, Frances Tenenbaum

Landscaping with Wildflowers, Jim Wilson

6

The Native Plants of Tennessee

Summary, Description, Culture, and Distribution

Although the cultivation of [native plants] is in no way a substitute for their preservation in their natural habitats, it does give to the care of the amateur gardener, the expert, and the nurseryman a small piece of the American wilderness and keeps before us living treasures of our natural heritage.

—Marie Sperka
*Growing Wildflowers:
A Gardener's Guide*, 1973

Osmunda cinnamomea (cinnamon fern) seems to float in a sea of *Tiarella cordifolia* (foamflower), *Geranium maculatum* (wild geranium), and *Tradescantia virginiana* (spiderwort).

Wildflowers

Ornamental Interest and Site Summary

THIS SUMMARY PROVIDES A QUICK REFERENCE TO THE DISTINCTIVE HORTICULTURAL CHARACTERISTICS AND SITE PREFERENCES OF THE wildflowers featured in this book. A complete description, cultural information, and state distribution for each plant follow the summary. The following abbreviations appear in the summary.

Flower Season and Color:

Sp—Spring

Su—Summer

A—Autumn

W—Winter

Wh—White

Y—Yellow

O—Orange

P—Pink

R—Red

Pr—Purple

Bl—Blue

GBM—Green, brown, maroon

Distinctions:

Fr—Fruit

Lf—Leaf (shape or color)

Gc—Groundcover

Ev—Evergreen

Ar—Aromatic, fragrant

UF—Unique form

TH—Tall herbaceous, over 4 feet

AB—Annual or biennial

Site Preferences:

S—Full sun to part shade

Sh—Part sun to medium shade

Alk—Tolerates slight alkalinity

PS—Poor soil, low fertility

WS—Wet soil

MS—Moist soil

DS—Dry soil

Wildflowers	Flower	Distinctions	Site
Actaea pachypoda (doll's eyes)	Sp Wh	Fr	Sh, MS
Ageratina altissima (white snakeroot)	A Wh	TH	Sh, MS
Allium cernuum & A. stellatum (nodding & prairie onion)	Su Wh/P	UF	S, DS Alk
Amsonia tabernaemontana (blue star)	Sp Bl		S/Sh MS
Anemone quinquefolia (wood anemone)	Sp Wh		Sh, MS
Anemone virginiana (thimbleweed)	Su Wh	Fr	S/Sh PS, DS
Antennaria plantaginifolia (plantain-leaved pussytoes)	Sp Wh	Ev, Gc	Sh, DS PS
Aquilegia canadensis (wild columbine)	Sp R/Y		Sh MS/DS
Aralia racemosa (spikenard)	Su Wh	Fr, TH	Sh, MS
Arisaema dracontium (green dragon)	Sp GBM	Fr, Lf, UF	Sh, MS
Arisaema triphyllum (jack-in-the-pulpit)	Sp GBM	Fr, UF	Sh, MS
Aruncus dioicus (goat's-beard)	Sp Wh	TH	Sh, MS
Asarum canadense (wild ginger)	Sp GBM	Gc, Ar	Sh, MS
Asclepias incarnata (swamp milkweed)	Su P	Fr	S WS/MS
Asclepias quadrifolia (four-leaved milkweed)	Sp/Su P/Wh	Fr	S, DS
Asclepias tuberosa (butterfly-weed)	Su O	Fr	S, DS
Asclepias variegata (white milkweed)	Su Wh/Pr	Fr	S MS/DS
Aster cordifolius (blue wood aster)	Su/A Bl		Sh MS/DS
Aster divaricatus (white wood aster)	Su/A Wh		Sh MS/DS

(Continued next page)

Wildflowers	Flower	Distinctions	Site
Aster dumosus (bushy aster)	Su/A Bl/Wh		S, DS
Aster laevis (smooth aster)	Su/A Bl		S, MS
Aster lateriflorus (calico aster)	Su/A Wh/Pr		S, DS
Aster linariifolius (stiff-leaved aster)	Su/A Bl		S, DS
Aster novae-angliae (New England aster)	Su/A Pr/P/Wh	TH	S MS/WS
Aster oblongifolius (aromatic aster)	Su/A Pr	Ar	S, DS
Aster patens (late purple aster)	Su/A Pr		S, DS
Aster shortii (Short's aster)	Su/A Bl		Sh MS/DS
Aster undulatus (wavy-leaved aster)	Su/A Bl/Pr		S, DS
Astilbe biternata (false goat's-beard)	Sp Wh	TH	Sh, MS
Baptisia alba (white wild indigo)	Sp Wh	Fr	S MS/DS
Baptisia australis (blue wild indigo)	Sp Bl	Fr	S, Alk MS/DS
Baptisia tinctoria (yellow wild indigo)	Sp Y	Fr	S MS/DS
Bidens aristosa & *B. polylepis* (tickseed sunflower)	Su/A Y	AB	S WS/MS
Blephilia ciliata (downy wood-mint)	Sp Bl	UF	Sh MS/DS
Blephilia hirsuta (hairy wood-mint)	Sp Bl	UF	Sh, MS
Boltonia asteroides (boltonia)	Su/A Wh	TH	S WS/MS
Camassia scilloides (wild hyacinth)	Sp Bl		S, MS
Campanula americana (tall bellflower)	Su Bl	TH, AB	Sh, MS

(Continued next page)

Wildflowers	Flower	Distinctions	Site
Campanula divaricata (southern harebell)	Su Bl		Sh, DS PS
Caulophyllum thalictroides (blue cohosh)	Sp GBM	Fr	Sh, MS
Chamaelirium luteum (devil's-bit)	Sp Wh		S/Sh WS/MS
Chelone glabra & C. lyonii (turtlehead)	Su Wh & P		S WS/MS
Chrysogonum virginianum (green-and-gold)	Sp Y	Ev, Gc	Sh, MS
Cimicifuga racemosa (black cohosh)	Su Wh	TH	Sh MS/DS
Claytonia caroliniana & C. virginica (spring beauty)	Sp Wh/P		Sh, MS
Collinsia verna (blue-eyed Mary)	Sp Bl/Wh	AB	Sh, MS
Conoclinium coelestinum (mist flower)	Su/A Bl		Sh WS/MS
Coreopsis auriculata (eared tickseed)	Sp Y		S/Sh MS
Coreopsis lanceolata (lanceleaf tickseed)	Sp/Su Y		S, DS
Coreopsis major (large tickseed)	Sp/Su Y	Lf	S/Sh DS
Coreopsis tripteris (tall tickseed)	Su Y	TH	S WS/MS
Coreopsis verticillata (threadleaf tickseed)	Sp/Su Y	Lf	S, DS
Delphinium tricorne (dwarf larkspur)	Sp Pr		Sh, MS
Dentaria diphylla & D. laciniata (two-leaved & cut-leaved toothwort)	Sp Wh	Lf	Sh, MS
Dicentra canadensis (squirrel corn)	Sp Wh		Sh, MS
Dicentra cucullaria (Dutchman's breeches)	Sp Wh	UF	Sh, MS

(Continued next page)

Wildflowers	Flower	Distinctions	Site
Dicentra eximia (wild bleeding heart)	Sp/Su P		Sh MS/DS
Disporum lanuginosum (yellow mandarin)	Sp Y/GBM	Fr	Sh, MS
Disporum maculatum (spotted mandarin)	Sp Wh/Pr	Fr	Sh, MS
Dodecatheon meadia (shooting star)	Sp Wh/P		Sh, MS
Doellingeria umbellata (flat-topped aster)	Su Wh	TH	S WS/MS
Echinacea pallida & *E. purpurea* (pale & purple coneflower)	Su Pr		S MS/DS
Echinacea tennesseensis (Tennessee coneflower)	Su Pr		S Alk, DS
Elephantopus carolinianus & *E. tomentosus* (Carolina & woolly elephant's foot)	Su P/W		Sh, DS
Enemion biternatum (false rue anemone)	Sp Wh		Sh, MS
Erigenia bulbosa (harbinger-of-spring)	W Wh		Sh, MS
Erigeron pulchellus (robin's plantain)	Sp Bl/P/Wh		Sh, MS
Eryngium yuccifolium (rattlesnake-master)	Su Wh	UF	S MS/DS
Erythronium albidum & *E. americanum* (trout lily)	Sp Wh & Y	Lf	Sh, MS
Eupatorium fistulosum & *maculatum* (Joe-Pye-weed)	Su P/Pr	TH	S WS/MS
Eupatorium perfoliatum (boneset)	Su/A Wh	TH, Lf	S WS
Eupatorium purpureum (sweet Joe-Pye-weed)	Su P/Pr	TH, Ar	S, MS
Euphorbia corollata (flowering spurge)	Su Wh	Lf	S, DS

(Continued next page)

Wildflowers	Flower	Distinctions	Site
Fragaria virginiana (wild strawberry)	Sp Wh	Fr	S MS/DS
Galax urceolata (galax)	Sp/Su Wh	Lf, Ev	Sh, DS
Gaultheria procumbens (wintergreen)	Su Wh	Fr, Gc, Ev, Ar	Sh MS/DS
Gentiana andrewsii & G. saponaria (bottle & soapwort gentian)	A Bl		Sh, MS
Gentiana villosa (striped gentian)	A GBM/Wh/Bl		Sh, MS
Geranium maculatum (wild geranium)	Sp P	Lf	Sh, MS
Hedyotis caerulea (bluets)	Sp Bl		S, MS
Hedyotis purpurea (large houstonia, summer bluets)	Sp Wh/Pr		Sh MS/DS
Helenium autumnale & H. flexuosum (sneezeweed)	Su Y		S, MS
Helianthus angustifolius (narrow-leaved sunflower)	A Y	TH	S WS/MS
Helianthus atrorubens (dark-eyed sunflower)	Su Y	TH	S, DS
Helianthus microcephalus (small-headed sunflower)	Su Y	TH	S, MS
Helianthus mollis (ashy sunflower)	Su Y		S, DS
Hepatica acutiloba & H. americana (sharp- & round-lobed liverleaf)	Sp Wh/Bl		Sh MS/DS
Heterotheca graminifolia & H. mariana (silkgrass & Maryland golden aster)	Su Y		S, DS
Heuchera americana & H. villosa (alumroot)	Sp Wh	Ev, Lf	Sh MS/DS

(Continued next page)

Wildflowers	Flower	Distinctions	Site
Hexastylis arifolia & H. shuttleworthii (heartleaf ginger)	Sp GBM	Lf, Ev, Gc	Sh, MS
Hibiscus moscheutos (swamp rose-mallow)	Su Wh/R	TH	S WS/MS
Hydrastis canadensis (goldenseal)	Sp Wh	Fr	Sh, MS
Hydrophyllum appendiculatum (waterleaf)	Sp Bl	AB	Sh, MS
Hymenocallis occidentalis (spider lily)	Su Wh		S WS/MS
Hypoxis hirsuta (yellow star-grass)	Sp/Su Y		S/Sh DS
Impatiens capensis & I. pallida (spotted & pale jewelweed)	Su O & Y	AB	Sh WS/MS
Iris cristata (crested iris)	Sp Bl		Sh MS/DS
Iris fulva (copper iris)	Sp R		S, WS
Iris verna (dwarf iris)	Sp Pr/Bl		Sh, DS
Iris virginica (southern blue flag)	Sp Bl		S WS/MS
Jeffersonia diphylla (twinleaf)	Sp Wh	Fr	Sh, MS
Liatris aspera, L. microcephala, L. scariosa, L. squarrosa, & L. squarrulosa (blazing star)	Su Pr		S, DS
Liatris spicata (blazing star)	Su Pr		S, MS
Lilium michauxii & L. superbum (Michaux's & turk's cap lily)	Su O/R	TH	S/Sh MS
Lobelia cardinalis (cardinal flower)	Su R		S/Sh WS/MS
Lobelia siphilitica (great blue lobelia)	Su/A Bl		S/Sh MS

(Continued next page)

Wildflowers	Flower	Distinctions	Site
Lysimachia ciliata (fringed loosestrife)	Su Y		Sh WS/MS
Lysimachia quadrifolia (whorled loosestrife)	Sp Y		Sh MS/DS
Manfreda virginica (false aloe)	Su GBM	UF	S, DS PS, Alk
Medeola virginiana (Indian cucumber-root)	Sp Y	Fr, UF	Sh, MS
Mertensia virginica (Virginia bluebells)	Sp Bl		Sh, MS
Mimulus alatus & *M. ringens* (monkey flower)	Su Bl	TH	Sh, WS
Mitchella repens (partridgeberry)	Sp Wh	Fr, Ev, Gc	Sh, MS
Mitella diphylla (bishop's cap)	Sp Wh	Gc	Sh, MS
Monarda clinopodia (basil balm)	Su Wh	Ar	S/Sh MS/DS
Monarda didyma (bee balm)	Su R	Ar	S/Sh MS
Monarda fistulosa (wild bergamot)	Su P/Pr	Ar	S/Sh MS/DS
Monarda punctata (dotted horsemint)	Su Y/P	Ar	Sh DS
Nelumbo lutea (American lotus)	Su Y	Fr, Lf	S, WS
Nymphaea odorata (fragrant waterlily)	Su Wh	Lf, Ar	S, WS
Oenothera fruticosa (sundrops)	Sp Y		S, DS
Opuntia humifusa (prickly-pear cactus)	Sp Y	Fr, UF, Ev, Gc	S, DS
Orontium aquaticum (golden club)	Sp Y	UF	S, WS
Oxalis violacea (violet wood sorrel)	Sp Pr		Sh, DS
Pachysandra procumbens (Allegheny spurge)	Sp Wh	Ev, Gc, Lf, Ar	Sh, MS

(Continued next page)

Wildflowers	Flower	Distinctions	Site
Panax quinquefolius & P. trifolius (American & dwarf ginseng)	Sp/Su Y/GBM & Wh	Fr	Sh, MS
Peltandra virginica (arrow arum)	Sp/Su Y/GBM	Lf	S/Sh WS
Penstemon calycosus, P. hirsutus, P. laevigatus, P. smallii (beard-tongue)	Sp Pr		S MS/DS
Penstemon digitalis (white beard-tongue)	Sp Wh		S MS/DS
Phacelia bipinnatifida (purple phacelia)	Sp Pr	AB	Sh, MS
Phacelia purshii (Miami mist)	Sp Pr/Wh	AB	S, DS
Phlox divaricata (wild blue phlox)	Sp Bl	Ar, Ev	Sh, MS
Phlox glaberrima & P. paniculata (smooth & summer phlox)	Su Pr/P/Wh	Ar	S/Sh MS
Phlox maculata (meadow phlox)	Su Pr/P/Wh	Ar	S/Sh WS
Phlox pilosa (downy phlox)	Sp P	Ar	S, DS
Phlox stolonifera (creeping phlox)	Sp Bl/P/Wh	Ar, Gc	S/Sh MS
Physostegia virginiana (false dragonhead)	Su Pr		S, MS
Podophyllum peltatum (may-apple)	Sp Wh	Fr	Sh, MS
Polemonium reptans (Jacob's ladder)	Sp Bl		Sh, MS
Polygonatum biflorum & P. pubescens (Solomon's seal)	Sp Wh	Fr	Sh, MS
Pontederia cordata (pickerelweed)	Su/A Bl		S, WS
Porteranthus stipulatus & P. trifoliatus (Indian physic & bowman's root)	Sp Wh		Sh MS/DS

(Continued next page)

Wildflowers	Flower	Distinctions	Site
Pycnanthemum incanum (silverleaf mountain mint)	Su Pr	Lf, Ar	S MS/DS
Pycnanthemum tenuifolium (slender mountain mint)	Su Wh	Lf, Ar	S MS/DS
Ratibida pinnata (prairie coneflower)	Su Y	Ar, TH	S, DS
Rhexia mariana & R. virginica (Maryland & Virginia meadow beauty)	Su P		S WS/MS
Rudbeckia fulgida (black-eyed Susan)	Su Y		S MS
Rudbeckia laciniata (green-headed coneflower)	Su Y	TH	S, MS
Rudbeckia triloba (three-lobed coneflower)	Su Y	TH, AB	S/Sh DS
Ruellia caroliniensis (wild petunia)	Sp/Su Pr		Sh, MS
Ruellia humilis (wild petunia)	Sp/Su Pr		S MS/DS
Sabatia angularis (rose-pink)	Su P	AB	S, MS
Sagittaria latifolia (arrowhead)	Su Wh		S, WS
Sanguinaria canadensis (bloodroot)	Sp Wh	Lf	Sh, MS
Saururus cernuus (lizard's tail)	Su Wh	TH, Ar	S/Sh WS
Saxifraga virginiensis (early saxifrage)	Sp Wh		Sh, MS
Scutellaria incana & S. integrifolia (downy & large-flowered skullcap)	Su Bl		Sh, MS
Sedum pulchellum (lime stonecrop)	Sp P	AB	S, DS Alk
Sedum ternatum (woodland stonecrop)	Sp Wh		Sh, DS Alk
Senecio aureus (golden ragwort)	Sp Y		Sh, MS

(Continued next page)

Wildflowers	Flower	Distinctions	Site
Senecio obovatus (round-leaved ragwort)	Sp Y		Sh, MS Alk
Silene stellata (starry campion)	Su Wh		S/Sh MS/DS
Silene virginica (fire pink)	Sp R		S/Sh MS/DS
Silphium perfoliatum (cup-plant)	Su Y	Lf, TH	S WS/MS
Sisyrinchium albidum & S. angustifolium (blue-eyed grass)	Sp Wh & Bl	Lf	S, PS MS/DS
Smilacina racemosa (false Solomon's seal)	Sp Wh	Fr	Sh, MS
Solidago caesia (blue-stemmed goldenrod)	A Y		Sh, MS
Solidago canadensis (Canada goldenrod)	A Y	TH	S, DS
Solidago flexicaulis (zigzag goldenrod)	Su/A Y		Sh, MS
Solidago nemoralis (gray goldenrod)	Su Y		S, DS
Solidago odora (sweet goldenrod)	A Y	Ar	S, MS
Solidago rugosa (wrinkle-leaved goldenrod)	A Y		S WS-DS
Solidago speciosa (showy goldenrod)	Su/A Y	TH	S, MS
Solidago sphacelata (false goldenrod)	A Y		S, MS
Solidago ulmifolia (elm-leaved goldenrod)	Su/A Y		Sh, DS
Spigelia marilandica (Indian pink)	Sp/Su R/Y		Sh, MS
Stellaria pubera (star chickweed)	Sp Wh	Gc	Sh, MS
Stokesia laevis (Stokes' aster)	Sp/Su Bl	Ev	S, MS
Stylophorum diphyllum (wood poppy)	Sp Y		Sh, MS

(Continued next page)

Wildflowers	Flower	Distinctions	Site
Thalictrum dioicum (early meadow rue)	Sp Y/GBM		Sh, MS
Thalictrum pubescens (tall meadow rue)	Su Wh	TH	S WS/MS
Thalictrum revolutum (waxy-leaf meadow rue)	Sp Wh		Sh, DS
Thalictrum thalictroides (rue anemone)	Sp Wh		Sh, MS
Thermopsis villosa (Carolina bushpea)	Sp Y		S, MS
Tiarella cordifolia (foamflower)	Sp Wh	Ev, Gc	Sh, MS
Tradescantia virginiana (spiderwort)	Sp/Su Bl		S MS/DS
Trillium catesbaei (Catesby's trillium)	Sp P/Wh	Fr, UF	Sh, MS
Trillium cuneatum & *T. sessile* (toadshade)	Sp GBM	Lf, Fr, UF	Sh, MS
Trillium erectum & *T. sulcatum* (red & Barksdale's trillium)	Sp GBM	Fr, UF	Sh, MS
Trillium flexipes & *T. grandiflorum* (drooping white & large-flowered trillium)	Sp Wh	Fr, UF	Sh, MS
Trillium luteum (yellow trillium)	Sp Y	Lf, Fr, UF	Sh, MS
Trillium recurvatum & *T. stamineum* (prairie & twisted-petal trillium)	Sp GBM	Lf, Fr, UF	Sh, MS
Triodanis perfoliata (Venus' looking-glass)	Sp Pr	AB	S, DS
Typha angustifolia & *T. latifolia* (narrow-leaved & common cattail)	Sp/Su GBM	TH, UF	S, WS Alk
Uvularia grandiflora & *U. sessilifolia* (great merrybells & wild oats)	Sp Y	Lf	Sh, MS Alk
Uvularia perfoliata (perfoliate bellwort)	Sp Y	Lf	Sh, MS

(Continued next page)

Wildflowers	Flower	Distinctions	Site
Verbena canadensis (rose verbena)	Sp/Su Pr/P		S, DS PS
Vernonia gigantea & V. noveboracensis (tall & New York ironweed)	Su Pr	TH	S WS/MS
Veronicastrum virginicum (culver's root)	Su Wh	TH	S, MS
Viola blanda (sweet white violet)	Sp Wh		Sh WS/MS
Viola canadensis (Canada violet)	Sp/Su Wh/Pr		Sh, MS
Viola cucullata (marsh blue violet)	Sp Bl		Sh, WS
Viola hastata & V. pubescens (halberd-leaf & downy yellow violet)	Sp Y		Sh, MS
Viola palmata & V. rostrata (early blue & long-spurred violet)	Sp Bl		Sh, MS
Viola pedata (birdfoot violet)	Sp Pr		S, DS PS
Viola striata (cream violet)	Sp Wh		Sh, MS
Waldsteinia fragarioides (barren strawberry)	Sp Y	Ev,Gc	Sh, MS
Yucca filamentosa (Adam's needle)	Sp/Su Wh	Ev, UF	S, DS
Zizia aptera & Z. aurea (heartleaf & golden Alexanders)	Sp Y		Sh, MS

Description, Culture, and Distribution

Actaea pachypoda (doll's eyes).

Actaea pachypoda
Doll's Eyes, White Baneberry
[ack-'tee-uh puh-'kih-pah-duh]
Ranunculaceae (Buttercup Family)

This bushy, 1- to 2½-foot plant has large compound leaves with 3 to 5 leaflets that are lobed and toothed. Small, bright white flowers are composed mainly of a thickened style and numerous anthers radiating outward and appear on a terminal raceme in April and May. White berries, each marked with a purple spot, are arranged along a thickened, reddish stalk in August and September. The berries are poisonous. Doll's eyes grow in rich, moist, neutral soil and light to medium shade. Propagate by division or seed. Statewide, lightly in West Tennessee.

Actaea pachypoda—fruit (doll's eyes).

Ageratina altissima (Eupatorium rugosum)
White Snakeroot
[uh-jer-uh-'ty-nuh al-'tih-sih-muh]
Asteraceae (Aster Family)

Growing in branched and bushy clumps 2 to 5 feet high, white snakeroot features showy clusters of white flowers in September and October. Large, opposite, toothed leaves are broad at the base and taper to a point. White snakeroot prefers moist soil, but will accept drier soil, in part sun to light shade. Soil should be humus rich and slightly acid to neutral. It will develop colonies by rhizomes and self-sowing. Propagate by division or seed. Cultivar 'Chocolate' has deep purple stems and leaves suffused with purple. Statewide.

Ageratina altissima (white snakeroot).

Allium cernuum

Nodding Onion
['al-ee-um 'sir-new-um]
Liliaceae (Lily Family)

Allium cernuum (nodding onion).

A slender bulb sends up foot-long, linear basal foliage along with leafless flowering stems 12 inches or more tall. These stems are abruptly bent over at the top and bear an umbel of numerous white to pinkish flowers in July. The nodding onion likes dry, rocky, neutral soil in full sun to part shade. It does not produce bulblets on the stem, but can be propagated by division of underground bulb offsets or seed. Butterflies enjoy the flower nectar. Middle and East Tennessee.

A. stellatum [steh-'lay-tum], prairie or glade onion, is similar with a straight flower stalk and pinkish lavender flowers. Both species tolerate slightly alkaline soil. Central Basin.

Amsonia tabernaemontana

Blue Star
[am-'soh-nee-uh tay-ber-nee-mon-'tay-nuh]
Apocynaceae (Dogbane Family)

Amsonia tabernaemontana (blue star).

Blue star grows in a shrubby clump up to 3 feet in height. Clusters of small, pale blue, star-shaped flowers bloom in May and attract butterflies. The plant continues to grow; erect seedpods blend into the alternate, lanceolate leaves. Foliage turns pale yellow in the fall.

This hardy plant prefers moist organic soil that is slightly acid. It likes full sun to part shade but does just as well in light shade. Propagate by division or seed. Thick roots complicate division, but the plant handles it well. Statewide.

Anemone virginiana

Thimbleweed
[an-eh-'moh-nee vir-jih-nee-'ay-nuh]
(commonly pronounced uh-'nem-oh-nee)
Ranunculaceae (Buttercup Family)

This 2- to 3-foot, lightly fuzzy plant is narrow in profile. Stout stalks feature progressively smaller whorls of dark green, deeply cut, trifoliate leaves and several long-stemmed, single, greenish white flowers that rise above the top leaf whorl in June and July. The flowers produce oblong, green fruit from which the plant derives its common name. The flowers are not overly showy but the foliage adds textural interest to the garden, and its cottony seed heads can last all winter. It will grow in dry, poor soil, moderately acid to neutral, in full to part sun. Propagate by division or seed. Statewide, lightly in West Tennessee.

A. quinquefolia [kwin-kwih-'foh loo uh], wood anemone, is a dainty and delicate plant, consisting of a single, basal, compound leaf accompanying a 4- to 8-inch flower stalk. A solitary white flower blooms above a whorl of 3 smaller compound leaves, each with 3 to 5 toothed leaflets. It flowers in April and requires the slightly acid, moist, rich soil and light to medium shade found in its sheltered woodland habitat. Spreading via creeping rhizomes, it may be propagated by division or seed. East Tennessee.

Anemone virginiana (thimbleweed).

Anemone quinquefolia (wood anemone).

Antennaria plantaginifolia

Plantain-leaved Pussytoes
[an-teh-'nay-ree-uh plan-tuh-jih-nih-'foh-lee-uh]
Asteraceae (Aster Family)

This tiny, evergreen groundcover has little gray green, paddle-shaped leaves silvered with downy hairs. On 4- to 8-inch stems,

Antennaria plantaginifolia (plantain-leaved pussytoes).

several woolly-looking clusters of very tiny, white, tubular flowers are gathered into a rounded head that imaginatively resembles the little furry toes of a kitten's paw from March to May.

The plant prefers well-drained, dry, rocky areas and part sun in relatively poor, moderately acid soil. It is dioecious (the female plant is a little larger) and allelopathic, producing a growth inhibitor that keeps other plants at bay in order to protect its moisture and nutrient sources. Pussytoes is a butterfly larval plant. Propagate by division. Statewide, lightly in West Tennessee.

Aquilegia canadensis
Wild Columbine
[ack-wih-'lee-jee-uh kan-uh-'den-sis]
Ranunculaceae (Buttercup Family)

Aquilegia canadensis (wild columbine).

Wiry stems, 1 to 2½ feet tall, elevate numerous flowers dangling upside down over a mound of soft, blue green, compound foliage with round-lobed leaflets. The individual flowers are creatively designed, as red sepals alternate with yellow petals. Each funnel-shaped petal has a long, slender red spur with a rounded tip. A tuft of protruding stamens hangs beneath. Turn-of-the-century wildflower writer Mrs. William Starr Dana describes its "jewel-like flowers gleaming . . . with a graceful insouciance." Columbines enjoy a long period of bloom from early April through June and attract hummingbirds and bees. Papery seedpods follow. The foliage is semi-evergreen.

Wild columbine grows best in part sun and slightly acid soil that is a bit dry, not too rich, and well drained. The dainty plants found in the wild perched on rocky woodland ledges differ greatly in growth habit from garden plants, which are more robust in every way and often grow 3 or 4 feet tall. *Nature's Garden* author Neltje Blanchan laments that "it never has the elfin charm in a conventional garden that it possesses wild in Nature's." Wild columbine readily self-sows. Middle and East Tennessee.

Aralia racemosa
Spikenard
[uh-'ray-lee-uh ray-seh-'moh-suh]
Araliaceae (Ginseng Family)

Spikenard is a sizable herb growing 3 to 6 feet tall and spreading 2 to 3 feet. It features few but large, bipinnately compound leaves with toothed leaflets and a large panicle of greenish white flowers in July. Wildlife enjoy the dark purple berries that develop. It grows in woodland conditions and needs rich, moist, slightly acid soil and light shade. Propagate by seed. East Tennessee.

Arisaema triphyllum
Jack-in-the-pulpit
[air-ih-'see-muh try-'fill-um]
Araceae (Arum Family)

One or two long-stemmed, trifoliate leaves, rising 12 inches or more, accompany a spathe that appears from late March to May. Inside the spathe the smooth, slender spadix has tiny greenish yellow flowers at the base that can be all male, all female, or a combination. The gender of this plant can change from year to year. The green spathe, often streaked with maroon and white stripes, enfolds the lower half of the spadix and curves over at the top to form a hood that

Arisaema triphyllum (jack-in-the-pulpit).

protects the enclosed flowers. Female plants produce bright red berries on the spadix in late summer and fall. This hardy plant is long-lived, preferring moist, humus-rich soil, neutral to slightly acid, in light to medium shade. It grows from a corm 4 to 8 inches deep and will self-sow, blooming in 3 years. A substance in the corm, foliage, and berries makes the plant unpalatable to most wildlife, but a few game birds do eat the fruit. Propagate by seed or division of corm off-sets. Statewide, especially Middle and East Tennessee.

A. dracontium [druh-'kon-tee-um], **green dragon,** is taller than jack-in-the-pulpit (sometimes 2 to 3 feet) and produces a long, slender green spadix that emerges from a narrow green spathe in May and June. A single compound leaf, with 7 to 11 horizontal, oblong leaflets, offers an interesting foliar texture. Orange fruits are produced in the fall and eaten by birds. Cool, open shade with constant moisture in a slightly acid soil is best for green dragon. Propagate through corm offsets as it takes years for a plant to bloom from seed. Statewide, a good choice for West Tennessee.

Arisaema dracontium (green dragon).

Aruncus dioicus

Goat's-beard
[uh-'run-kus dy-oh-'eye-kus]
Rosaceae (Rose Family)

In spite of its height (3 to 6 feet), goat's-beard possesses an airy grace due to the large, bipinnately compound leaves and the numerous tiny white flowers clustered in loose, terminal panicles. It blooms in May and June, resembling a large astilbe. The plant is dioecious;

Aruncus dioicus (goat's-beard).

George W. Hornal.

staminate (male) plants are showier. Leaflets are sharply toothed, and flower petals are oval. Bees visit for the nectar.

Goat's-beard prefers cool, light shade but can take a little morning sun in moist, rich, moderately acid soil. Supplemental water may be needed in dry spells. Propagate by seed. East Tennessee, lightly elsewhere.

Asarum canadense
Wild Ginger
['ass-uh-rum kan-uh-'den-see]
(commonly pronounced uh-'sair-um)
Aristolochiaceae (Birthwort Family)

Asarum canadense (wild ginger),

Wild ginger is a dense, creeping, deciduous groundcover with thick, branching stems. Pairs of 4- to 6-inch-tall, roundly heart-shaped leaves are graced with the sheen of fine green velvet. Small flowers lie on the ground under the leaves in April and May. The flower is a cup-shaped calyx with 3 spreading, brownish purple lobes that attract gnats, flies, and beetles for fertilization. Mrs. Dana, author of *How to Know the Wild Flowers*, called wild ginger one of the "'vegetable cranks' . . . whose odd, unlovely flower seeks protection beneath its long-stemmed fuzzy leaves, and hides its head upon the ground as if unwilling to challenge comparison with its more brilliant brethren." The roots are aromatic with a ginger scent.

Wild ginger will grow luxuriantly in moist, rich, humusy, neutral soil and the light shade of deciduous trees. Drier soil will not be a problem with established plants. In droughts, wilted plants rebound immediately after a drink with no ill effects. Propagate by division or cuttings; it self-sows readily. Statewide, lightly in West Tennessee.

Asclepias incarnata (swamp milkweed).

Asclepias incarnata
Swamp Milkweed
[uh-'sklee-pee-us in-kar-'nay-tuh]
Asclepiadaceae (Milkweed Family)

Swamp milkweed grows 3 to 4 feet tall on branched stems with smooth, opposite, lanceolate leaves. In July and August terminal umbels of mauve pink flowers are gathered into large, flat clusters. Each milkweed flower has 5 sharply recurved petals and an elevated central crown in 5 sections called hoods. Large seedpods develop. Found naturally in swampy and wet places, it adapts well to regular garden moisture in full sun and neutral to slightly acid soil. It transplants well and can be propagated by division or seed. Bees and butterflies adore all species of *Asclepias,* visiting for nectar and larval food. Middle and East Tennessee.

A. tuberosa [too-beh-'roh-suh], **butterfly-weed,** has lance-shaped, hairy leaves alternating up hairy 1- to 2-foot stems. It is topped with a compact cluster of brilliant orange flowers, which sometimes shade toward red or yellow, in June through August. A pair of large, green, pointed seedpods on each stem mature and split in the fall to reveal a stable of silky, plumed seeds. Butterfly-weed does not have the milky stem juice typical of the milkweed family. Seen along roadsides, in fields, or on hills, butterfly-weed is drought tolerant. At home in hot, dry gardens with full sun and good drainage, it proves to be hardy, long-lived, and carefree. The thick taproot makes it hard to transplant a mature specimen, but it can be propagated from seed or root cuttings. Statewide.

Asclepias tuberosa (butterfly-weed).

William Hall.

J. Paul Moore.

A. quadrifolia [kwah-drih-'foh-lee-uh], four-leaved milkweed, has ovate to lance-shaped leaves whorled on 1- to 2-foot stems. Dainty, pale pink to cream flowers bloom in late spring or early summer. It prefers dry soil and part shade. Eastern half of the state.

A. variegata [vair-ee-uh-'gay-tuh], white milkweed, has white flowers with purplish centers in June and broad ovate leaves. Give it moist to dry soil and part shade. Statewide.

Asclepias quadrifolia (four-leaved milkweed).

Aster spp.
Aster
['ass-ter]
Asteraceae (Aster Family)

The *Aster* genus has a staggering number of species adapted to a wide range of growing conditions. All asters will perform well in lean soil (low nitrogen), which helps keep the plants in bounds. Pinch them back in late spring for bushier plants. Periodic division renews vigor; they may also be propagated from seed. The nectar attracts bees and butterflies, some as a larval food source. Many *Aster* species have named cultivars.

A. cordifolius [kore-dih-'foh-lee-us], blue wood aster, has branching panicles of numerous ½-inch, pale blue violet flowers on a stem 1½ to 4 feet tall. Leaves are heart shaped, toothed, and stemmed. It blooms in September and October in the light shade of moist to dry woodlands. Rather recumbent in shade, it grows more upright with a little sun. Scattered lightly statewide, heavier in East Tennessee.

A. divaricatus [dih-vair-ih-'kay-tus], white wood aster, has creeping rhizomes that produce 1- to 3-foot, zigzag stems with 1-inch,

Aster cordifolius (blue wood aster).

Aster divaricatus (white wood aster).

Aster laevis 'Bluebird' (smooth aster).

Aster lateriflorus 'Lady in Black' (calico aster) with an eastern tailed blue butterfly.

Aster linariifolius (stiff-leaved aster).

white-rayed flowers in August and September. Yellow disk flowers turn bronzy purple. Lower leaves are stemmed, heart shaped, and toothed, but upper leaves are ovate and sessile. It grows in part sun in a slightly acid to neutral, moist to dry soil. Eastern half of the state.

A. dumosus [doo-'moh-sus], bushy aster, is 3 feet tall with sessile, linear leaves along the stems. Clusters of branches are lined with tiny leaves and many pale lavender, blue, or white flowers ½ to ¾ inch across. Bushy aster is a good choice for dry or moist sandy sites in full sun to part shade and blooms between August and October. Statewide.

A. laevis ['lee-vis], smooth aster, is 1 to 3 feet tall with basal leaves that are thick and smooth and stem leaves that are broadly lanceolate to oblong and clasping. Loose panicles of light violet blue flowers open in August and September. In part shade it prefers fertile, moist soil but tolerates dryness well. Lightly in Middle and East Tennessee.

A. lateriflorus [lat-eh-rih-'flor-us], calico aster, stands about 2 to 4 feet high with obovate basal and lower leaves. Upper leaves are linear and sessile. Many ¼- to ½-inch, white to pale purple flowers appear on 1-sided branches arranged in a panicle from the leaf axils. It blooms in September and October in full sun to part shade and dry soil. Statewide, lightly in West Tennessee.

A. linariifolius [lin-air-ee-ih-'foh-lee-us], stiff-leaved aster, is a dwarf plant, 1 to 1½ feet tall, with numerous wiry stems and lots of stiff narrow leaves. It features lavender blue flowers August to October and prefers dry, sandy, or rocky soil in full sun. It will self-sow. Cumberland Plateau, lightly elsewhere.

George W. Hornal.

A. novae-angliae ['noh-vee 'ang-lee-ee], **New England aster,** is among the best known species and has many commercially bred cultivars. It is variable with purple, pink, lavender, or white ray flowers encircling a cluster of yellow disk flowers August to October. Ranging from 3 to 5 feet tall, it has branching, hairy stems with narrow clasping leaves. A durable and disease-free plant, New England aster prefers a moist to wet habitat, full sun, and a neutral to slightly acid soil. Lightly statewide.

Aster novae-angliae (New England aster).

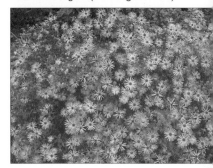

Aster oblongifolius 'Raydon's Favorite' (aromatic aster).

A. oblongifolius [ob-long-ih-'foh-lee-us], **aromatic aster,** is a bushy plant 1 to 3 feet tall with wiry, leafy branches terminating in a cluster of ¾-inch violet flowers in September and October. Leaves are narrowly oblong, sessile, and emit a spicy odor when crushed. It will take dry, rocky soil and full sun. It occurs lightly in Middle and East Tennessee.

A. patens ['pay-tenz], **late purple** or **spreading aster,** is a low plant. Recumbent stems with erect tips are brittle, slender, and hairy and spread out 1 to 3 feet. Leaves are clasping and rough. Deep violet to blue purple, 1-inch flowers bloom in September and October. Late purple aster prefers dry soil and full sun to part shade. Statewide.

Aster patens (late purple aster).

A. shortii ['short-ee-eye], **Short's aster,** is a 2- to 4-foot plant that airily branches into a billow of tiny leaves and pale lavender blue flowers. The yellow disk flowers turn reddish purple with age. Basal and lower stem foliage is broadly lanceolate with heart-shaped bases. It blooms in September and October in part sun and moist to dry soil. Middle Tennessee.

A. undulatus [un-dyew-'lay-tus], **wavy-leaved aster,** has foliage that is heart shaped and rough, often with blunt teeth on a wavy

Aster shortii (Short's aster).

edge. Lower leaf petioles enlarge near the stem and clasp around it; upper leaves are sessile. It grows upright and rather stiff from 1 to 3½ feet tall and produces a narrowly branched panicle of blue violet, ½-inch flowers in September and October. Wavy-leaved aster will take part shade and dry soil. Primarily in East Tennessee, lightly elsewhere.

Astilbe biternata
False Goat's-beard
[uh-'still-bee by-ter-'nay-tuh]
Saxifragaceae (Saxifrage Family)

Astilbe biternata (false goat's-beard).

The similarities between this plant and *Aruncus dioicus*, goat's-beard, prompted the common name. Both plants are 3 to 6 feet tall, have large compound leaves divided 2 or 3 times into sets of 3 ovate leaflets, and produce large, plumelike panicles of small white flowers in May and June. False goat's-beard often has a yellowish cast to its flowers, which have very long filaments and narrow petals. Also like *Aruncus*, *Astilbe* likes cool, rich, moist, moderately acid soil and light shade. Propagate by seed or division. East Tennessee.

Baptisia alba (B. leucantha)
White Wild or False Indigo
[bap-'tih-see-uh 'al-buh]
Fabaceae (Pea Family)

Baptisia alba (white wild indigo).

In its growth habit, this upright plant resembles a shrub 3 feet tall and wide. Stems are a rich charcoal color, and compound leaves have 3 narrow, obovate leaflets that remain attractive all season. On erect racemes smoky-colored buds open to white, pea-shaped flowers in May. Darkened dry pods rattle with seeds. West Tennessee.

B. australis [aw-'stray-lis], blue wild indigo, is showy and bushy in rich soil. Central Basin.

B. tinctoria [tink-'tore-ee-uh], yellow wild indigo, has yellow flowers. East Tennessee.

In general wild indigos are good in average, well-drained soil, tolerate drought, and love full sun. They can take some shade, but do not transplant well. White and yellow wild indigo prefer moderately to slightly acid soil; blue wild indigo does well in neutral to slightly alkaline soil. Wild indigos are a butterfly larval food.

Baptisia australis (blue wild indigo).

Bidens polylepis and B. aristosa
Tickseed Sunflower
['by-denz pah-'lil-eh-pis and air-is-'toh-suh]
Asteraceae (Aster Family)

These two species, both annuals, are virtually identical except for minor differences in the shape of the seeds. Their leaves are pinnately divided into lobed and toothed lanceolate segments, lending a lacy effect to the foliage. The stems branch out into bushy plants 2 to 4 feet in height and are covered in showy yellow blooms nearly 2 inches across in September. Seeds stick to clothing with 2 tiny prongs. These plants are not picky, though wet to moist, sunny sites are preferred. They self-sow prolifically. *B. polylepis* inhabits Middle and East Tennessee, *B. aristosa* Middle and West Tennessee.

Baptisia tinctoria (yellow wild indigo).

Bidens polylepis (tickseed sunflower).

Blephilia ciliata
Downy Wood-mint
[bleh-'fill-ee-uh sih-lee-'ay-tuh]
Lamiaceae (Mint Family)

Pale blue, purple-spotted, lipped flowers encircle the stems in May and June. These whorled clusters sit atop a 1- to 2-foot stem

Blephilia ciliata (downy wood-mint).

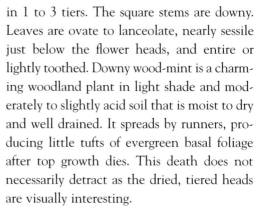

in 1 to 3 tiers. The square stems are downy. Leaves are ovate to lanceolate, nearly sessile just below the flower heads, and entire or lightly toothed. Downy wood-mint is a charming woodland plant in light shade and moderately to slightly acid soil that is moist to dry and well drained. It spreads by runners, producing little tufts of evergreen basal foliage after top growth dies. This death does not necessarily detract as the dried, tiered heads are visually interesting.

B. hirsuta [hir-'sue-tuh], **hairy wood-mint**, has a more hairy stem and serrated, broadly ovate leaves that have longer petioles. It likes moist shade. Both wood-mints are found mostly in Middle Tennessee, lightly elsewhere.

Boltonia asteroides
Boltonia, False Aster
[bowl-'toh-nee-uh ass-ter-oh-'eye-deez]
Asteraceae (Aster Family)

Boltonia asteroides 'Snowbank' (boltonia).

Sprays of white-rayed, yellow-disked flowers billow in profusion around 3- to 4-foot, erect stems throughout August and September. Stems are clothed in thin, narrow, blue green leaves. Popular cultivars, including 'Snowbank' and 'Pink Beauty', are superior to the species in bloom quantity. 'Pink Beauty' is taller and may require staking.

Found naturally in wet to moist soils, boltonia adapts to the garden easily and requires full sun and well-drained, moderately acid soil. Propagate through cuttings or division in early spring, which is periodically recommended to rejuvenate the plant. Scattered lightly in Middle and West Tennessee.

Camassia scilloides
Wild Hyacinth
[kuh-'mass-ee-uh sil-oh-'eye-deez]
Liliaceae (Lily Family)

Linear basal leaves rise from an underground, 1-inch diameter, white bulb. A leafless scape 12 to 18 inches tall is topped with a spire of pale blue, narrow-petaled, starry flowers in April. The plant goes dormant in summer. Wild hyacinths like rich, humusy soil that is slightly acid to neutral, moist in spring, and well drained. Give them full to part sun. Propagate by division of bulb offsets or seed sown immediately after collection. Middle Tennessee.

Camassia scilloides (wild hyacinth).

Campanula americana
Tall Bellflower
[kam-'pan-yew-luh uh-mair-ih-'kay-nuh]
Campanulaceae (Bellflower Family)

This biennial has a leafy flower stalk 2 to 6 feet tall. Violet blue to whitish, 1-inch, star-shaped flowers with curiously protruding and upturned styles appear continuously from the leaf axils during the summer, June through August, and are attractive to bees and butterflies. Leaves are alternate, toothed, and elliptic. It grows in light shade to part sun with moist, rich soil that is slightly acid or neutral. In its first year of growth, the leaves are heart shaped and resemble a violet; take care not to weed it. Tall bellflower propagates easily from seed. Statewide, lightly in West Tennessee.

Campanula americana (tall bellflower).

C. divaricata [dih-vair-ih-'kay-tuh], southern harebell, is 1 to 2 feet tall with lanceolate, toothed leaves. Delicate, loose panicles of tiny, drooping, light blue bells with protruding styles also bloom in August. It likes dry,

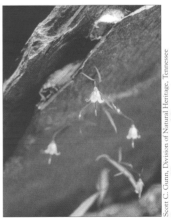

Campanula divaricata (southern harebell).

rocky, poor soil in light shade and is easily overwhelmed by aggressive neighbors. East Tennessee.

Caulophyllum thalictroides (blue cohosh).

Caulophyllum thalictroides
Blue Cohosh
(kaw-loh-'fill-um thuh-lik-troh-'eye-deez]
Berberidaceae (Barberry Family)

An apparent whorl of 3, blue green, bipinnately compound leaves with lobed leaflets is actually 1 large leaf located at midstem. Above this is a smaller leaf and a small panicle of flowers. The dull bronze to yellow green flowers bloom in April. The plant forms a large clump of many stems 1 to 3 feet tall. In July large bright blue berries develop. They are poisonous. In rich, moist, well-drained, slightly acid to neutral soil and moderate shade, blue cohosh pairs well with *Actaea pachypoda*, doll's eyes. Propagate by seed or division. Middle and East Tennessee.

The Center for Field Biology, a Tennessee Center of Excellence at Austin Peay State University.

Chamaelirium luteum (devil's-bit).

Chamaelirium luteum
Devil's-bit, Fairy-wand
(kam-eh-'lih-ree-um 'lew-tee-um]
Liliaceae (Lily Family)

Basal lanceolate leaves surround a flower stem that is 1 to 2 feet tall and studded with smaller leaves or bracts. Dioecious, the male spike of white flowers is a 4- to 10-inch raceme with many yellow and white stamens in each flower. The tip of each spike often curves downward into a crook. The female flower spikes are shorter, more slender, and all white. They elongate as the fruit develops. Devil's-bit blooms in May and prefers rich, moderately acid, wet to reliably moist soil in part shade; increase the shade with drier soil. Propagate by seed. Statewide.

Chelone glabra

Turtlehead
[keh-'low-nee 'glay-bruh]
Scrophulariaceae (Figwort Family)

This 2- to 3-foot plant has opposite lanceolate, toothed leaves and a dense terminal
spike of lipped, tubular white (sometimes
pink-tinged) flowers that bloom from July to
September. Since the upper lip of the flower
closes down over the lower lip, the blossoms
have a fair resemblance to the common
name. It is larval food for some butterflies,
and bumblebees enjoy the nectar.

Preferring moist, low ground and streamsides, turtlehead will last a long time with sufficient moisture. Cutting it back in late spring
produces a bushier plant and later bloom. It
requires moderately acid soil in full sun to
part shade and spreads by rhizomes. Propagate
by seed, cuttings, or division. Statewide.

C. lyonii ['ly-on-ee-eye] is a pink-flowering
species whose lustrous leaves and tighter
growth habit make it an especially good
garden choice. Occurs sporadically in East
Tennessee.

Chelone lyonii (pink turtlehead).

Chrysogonum virginianum

Green-and-gold, Golden Star
[krih-'sah-gah-num vir-jih-nee-'ay-num]
Asteraceae (Aster Family)

This creeping evergreen groundcover of
opposite, hairy, dark green leaves is starred
with small, 5-rayed, golden yellow flowers in
April and May. It can rebloom lightly
throughout the year. Height depends on the
variety. Creeping forms, such as var. *australe*,
are more prostrate and just a few inches tall;
others are clumping and more upright to 1
foot or so.

Chrysogonum virginianum
(green and gold)

It grows in a moist, well-drained garden in part sun or light shade with rich, slightly acid soil. Cultivars exploit the different growth habits. Periodic division is beneficial. It can also be propagated by seed. Lightly in East Tennessee.

Cimicifuga racemosa
Black Cohosh, Bugbane, Black Snakeroot, Fairy Candles
[sih-mee-'sif-yew-guh ray-seh-'moh-suh]
Ranunculaceae (Buttercup Family)

Cimicifuga racemosa (black cohosh).

Large compound leaves, twice divided and sharply toothed, alternate up a 3- to 6-foot stem. A long terminal raceme (6 inches to 2 feet) of small, white, feathery flowers blooms in June and July and attracts bees and butterflies. Moderately acid, rich soil in light shade or part sun is best. The soil should be moist to slightly dry with good drainage. Black cohosh is long-lived, but mature plants do not transplant well. Propagate by seed. Middle and East Tennessee.

Claytonia virginica
Spring Beauty
[klay-'toh-nee-uh vir-'jin-ih-kuh]
Portulacaceae (Purslane Family)

Claytonia virginica (spring beauty).

This tiny spring ephemeral is from 2 to 7 inches tall and due to its weak stem is often found recumbent on the ground. About halfway up the stem are 2 opposite, linear leaves. At the top is a loose terminal raceme of 5-petaled, white to pink flowers veined in deeper pink. It grows from a small, round tuber 2 to 4 inches deep and dies down after flowering in March and April. Statewide.

C. caroliniana [kair-oh-lih-nee-'ay-nuh] is very similar but has broader leaves. Eastern half of the state.

Both species prefer a moist, humus-rich, neutral to slightly acid soil with part sun in spring. They seed readily and transplant well.

Collinsia verna
Blue-eyed Mary
[kah-'lin-zee-uh 'ver-nuh]
Scrophulariaceae (Figwort Family)

Collinsia verna (blue-eyed Mary).

This delightful winter annual, 1 to 2 feet in height, is graced by short-stemmed, 2-lipped, blue and white flowers growing from the axils of clasping, opposite leaves in April. The 2-cleft upper lip is white, while the 3-cleft lower lip is blue.

In the light shade of deciduous woods it loves rich, moist, slightly acid to neutral soil. Seed should be planted in midsummer when ripe. A leaf rosette will develop in the fall, with bloom the following spring. Blue-eyed Mary has been documented in two counties northeast of Nashville and is categorized as Endangered on Tennessee's Rare Plant List.

Conoclinium coelestinum
(Eupatorium coelestinum)
Mist Flower
[kah-nah-'klih-nee-um seh-les-'ty-num]
Asteraceae (Aster Family)

Conoclinium coelestinum (mist flower).

Opposite, triangular, toothed leaves line a 2-foot stem topped by dense terminal flowers, misty lavender blue in hue, during August and September. It spreads by underground stolons and can overstep its bounds in the damp, slightly acid soil it prefers. Drier soil helps keep it in check.

It will grow in part to light shade and is visited by butterflies. Slow to come up, the foliage can fall prey to hungry insects which imparts a ragged look early in the season, but the plant survives to offer its cooling color in the heat of late summer. Propagate by division and seed. Statewide.

Coreopsis auriculata
Eared Tickseed
[kore-ee-'op-sis aw-rik-yew-'lay-tuh]
Asteraceae (Aster Family)

Coreopsis auriculata 'Nana' (eared tickseed).

Stalks of 2-inch, golden yellow flowers float above 12- to 18-inch stems clad with ovate leaves. Each leaf has 2 small lobes flanking its base forming the ears in the common name. A dwarf cultivar, 'Nana', has 4-inch-high foliage and 10- to 12-inch flower stalks. Eared tickseed spreads by stolons to create colonies of rosettes. Primary bloom comes in April and May with some scattered bloom until frost. It grows in moist yet well-drained slightly acid, rich soil and part sun to part shade. Eastern half of the state.

C. lanceolata [lan-see-oh-lay'-tuh], lance-leaf tickseed, is 8 to 20 inches tall with branching stems and narrow leaves mostly at the base. It produces 2-inch flowers from May through July. The 3-lobed rays are bright golden yellow and encircle a yellowish disk. It prefers dry soil and full sun. This potentially weedy tickseed self-sows prolifically and is best naturalized in meadows. West and Middle Tennessee.

C. major ['may-jer], large tickseed, is a 2-foot plant with opposite sessile leaves each composed of 3 leaflets, giving the look of 6 leaves whorled around the stem. Yellow flowers, 1 to 2 inches across, bloom in the upper

Coreopsis major (large tickseed).

leaf axils in June and July, sometimes longer. This tickseed likes dry, well-drained, slightly acid soil in full to part sun. It is a well-behaved and attractive garden plant. East and Middle Tennessee.

C. tripteris ['trip-teh-ris], tall tickseed, is another good meadow species. It grows up to 8 feet tall and blooms in mid- to late summer. Each leaf has 3 lanceolate leaflets. It likes wet to moist soil and can take some shade. Scattered lightly statewide.

C. verticillata [vir-tih-sih-'lay-tuh], thread-leaf tickseed, has leaves that are palmately divided into linear segments and impart a soft, lacy texture. Wiry stems colonize in a dense mat 1 to 2 feet tall. The bright yellow flowers bloom in June and July. Popular cultivars include 'Golden Showers', 'Zagreb', and the hybrid 'Moonbeam', but the species is well worth planting, too. Threadleaf tickseed likes part shade in dry soil. Native to the coastal plain it is not documented in Tennessee, but is an impressive plant in the garden.

Coreopsis verticillata (threadleaf tickseed).

Propagate all *Coreopsis* spp. by division or seed. Butterflies enjoy the nectar.

Delphinium tricorne
Dwarf or Spring Larkspur
[del-'fih-nee-um try-'kore-nee]
Ranunculaceae (Buttercup Family)

In April a 6- to 12-inch, terminal raceme holds spurred, dark blue violet flowers. Flowers can sometimes be white or pale purple. Leaves are palmately cleft into 5 to 7 linear divisions and form a low mound. Three-horned seedpods are visually interesting. In summer the plant goes dormant. The imagined resemblance of the flower buds to dolphins inspired the genus name. Dwarf larkspur

Delphinium tricorne (dwarf larkspur).

is long lived and thrives in open shade with spring sun and rich, moist, neutral soil. It is not tolerant of soil acidity. Middle and East Tennessee.

Dentaria diphylla (Cardamine diphylla)
Two-leaved Toothwort, Crinkleroot
[den-'tay-ree-uh dy-'fill-uh]
Brassicaceae (Mustard Family)

Dentaria diphylla (two-leaved toothwort).

A pair of leaves, each divided into 3 ovate, toothed leaflets, are nearly opposite each other halfway up the 6- to 10-inch flower stem. A loose terminal cluster of 6 to 12 small, white to pinkish lavender flowers opens in April. Trifoliate basal leaves appear in the fall and overwinter, often displaying a striking maroon cast to the undersides. Middle and East Tennessee.

   D. laciniata (C. concatenata) [luh-sih-nee-'ay-tuh], cut-leaved toothwort, has toothed leaves, each deeply cleft into narrow segments and arranged in a whorl of 3. It blooms a little earlier. Statewide.

Dentaria laciniata (cut-leaved toothwort).

J. Paul Moore.

   Both toothworts like the high, open shade and spring sun of deciduous woods in rich, moist, leaf mold. D. diphylla likes a bit more soil acidity. D. laciniata can take a more neutral soil. The rhizomes, which are supposed to be tasty, creep through the humus layer. The plants produce flat, lance-shaped seedpods about 1 inch long and go dormant early. Propagate by division; the rhizomes break apart very easily. Aggressive plants can overwhelm toothwort.

Dicentra eximia

Wild or Fringed Bleeding Heart

[dy-'sen-truh eks-'ih-mee-uh]

Fumariaceae (Fumitory Family)

Narrow, pale pinkish to rose lavender, heart-shaped flowers bloom on 12- to 18-inch stalks all season, April to frost, above a neat mound of ferny, pale green foliage. Seedpods (resembling tiny green bananas) develop and split open to eject shiny black seeds. Needing part sun to light shade, wild bleeding heart grows in moist to slightly dry, humusy soil that is moderately acid. It self-sows, and the rootstock creeps to enlarge the clump. Periodic division keeps the plant strong. A dose of bonemeal or other organic fertilizer helps to encourage flowering all season. Collected seed should be sown immediately. Documented mostly in the Unaka Mountains, it is a good garden plant statewide.

Dicentra eximia (wild bleeding heart).

D. canadensis [kan-uh-'den-sis], squirrel corn, and *D. cucullaria* [kuh-kyew-'lay-ree-uh], Dutchman's breeches, are little spring ephemerals that produce dainty clumps of finely cut, pale gray green foliage and delicate stalks of nodding white flowers in March and April. They both love humus-rich, neutral soil in the filtered spring sun under deciduous trees and die back after flowering. The primary difference is in the shape of the flower. *D. canadensis* more closely resembles *D. eximia*, sporting a small 6- to 8-inch leafless stalk of narrowly heart-shaped, drooping, tubular flowers, greenish white with a rosy tinge and a sweet, faint fragrance. *D. cucullaria*'s 8- to 12-inch stalk carries several double-spurred flowers, each white with a yellow tip, and looks like a fairy washline of tiny pantaloons hung out to air in the spring breeze.

Dicentra cucullaria (Dutchman's breeches).

Kurt Emmanuele.

Both plants grow from tubers. *D. canadensis* has a tiny yellow tuber, suggesting a kernel of corn that the squirrels and chipmunks love, thus its common name. It might be wise to protect the tuber with wire mesh in the ground. *D. cucullaria* has a series of tiny tubers joined together in a rhizome. In the wild it grows on moist, well-drained slopes, and is a hardy, long-lived plant whose delight is all the more precious for its fleeting vernal appearance. Both are found in Middle and East Tennessee.

A bit of trivia—the flowers of *Dicentra* seem designed for long-tongued bees. While probing for the nectar they cross-pollinate the plant. However, some bees cheat and cut a hole in the spur to more easily reach the sweet stuff.

Division of Natural Heritage, Tennessee
Department of Environment and Conservation.

Disporum lanuginosum (yellow mandarin).

Disporum lanuginosum
Yellow Mandarin, Fairy-bells
['dis-pah-rum luh-new-jih-'noh-sum]
Liliaceae (Lily Family)

Yellow mandarin blooms in April and May, producing 1 to 3 flared, greenish yellow flowers drooping at the tips of forked stems. Alternate leaves are oblong and sessile on stems 2 feet tall. Smooth red berries follow the flowers. Rich, moderately acid, rocky soils should be moist but well drained in light shade. Propagate by dividing clumping rhizomes or seed. It is found on the Highland Rim and in East Tennessee.

D. maculatum [mak-yew-'lay-tum], **spotted** or **nodding mandarin**, is a little shorter with white, purple-spotted flowers and yellow, hairy fruit. East Tennessee.

Dodecatheon meadia
Shooting Star
[doh-deh-'kath-ee-on 'mee-dee-uh]
Primulaceae (Primrose Family)

Dodecatheon meadia (shooting star).

A basal rosette of thick, oblong leaves (4 to 6 inches) provides the base for a leafless, hollow, 10- to 20-inch stem topped with several white to pinkish flowers in April and May. The flowers are characterized by sharply reflexed petals. A tight cluster of yellow stamens and the pistil protrude from the flower's center in a sharply pointed projection. Urn-shaped, narrow seedpods split open at the top prior to the plant's summer dormancy.

Shooting star grows best in light shade or spring sun and in humusy, fertile soil that is slightly acid to neutral. Moist, well-drained areas are best, but it can take a little dryness if mulched or tucked among the stones of a rock garden. Rabbits are said to enjoy nibbling this plant. Propagate from seed, root cuttings, or division. Middle and East Tennessee.

Doellingeria umbellata (Aster umbellatus)
Flat-topped Aster
[deh-lin-'jee-ree-uh um-beh-'lay-tuh]
Asteraceae (Aster Family)

Doellingeria umbellata (flat-topped aster).

This aster is 3 to 5 feet tall, sometimes more, with white-rayed, ½-inch flowers arranged in a wide, rather flat cluster. Leaves are narrow and elliptic, almost lanceolate. It blooms in August and September. Flat-topped aster looks its best in full sun and moist soil, moderately to slightly acid and not too rich. It spreads on creeping rhizomes and could be aggressive in damp soil. Propagate by division, cuttings, or seed. Eastern Highland Rim and Cumberland Plateau.

Echinacea purpurea
Purple Coneflower
[ek-ih-nay'-see-uh per-pure'-ee-uh]
Asteraceae (Aster Family)

Echinacea purpurea (purple coneflower).

A popular garden plant, purple coneflower grows 3 to 5 feet tall and branches into several stems, each with a large terminal flower head of long, dull purple ray flowers and a large, orange brown cone. It blooms throughout the summer and into fall with the peak in June and July. Each flower lasts a long time. The ray flowers often reflex or turn downward, and the rough leaves are broadly ovate and alternate. Bees and butterflies are attracted to the flowers, and birds love the seeds in fall.

E. *purpurea* is considered drought tolerant but prefers moist, neutral, well-drained soil. Full sun is best; some shade produces a taller, looser plant. Trimming shaded plants in May will help prevent flopping. Propagate by seed. There are cultivars. *E. pallida* ['pal-ih-duh], pale purple coneflower, has narrower leaves and light purple ray flowers. *E. tennesseensis* [teh-neh-see-'in-sis], Tennessee coneflower, is a rare endemic found in the specialized environment of the Central Basin's cedar glades. It grows 1 to 2 feet tall and has upturned ray flowers. *Echinacea* spp. can hybridize with one another. Middle Tennessee and Valley and Ridge.

Elephantopus carolinianus
Carolina Elephant's Foot
[eh-leh-'fan-tah-pus kair-ah-lih-nee-'ay-nus]
Asteraceae (Aster Family)

Elephant's foot grows 1 to 3 feet tall, and is widely branched with broadly elliptical, toothed leaves along the hairy stems. In mid- to late summer it produces small pinkish lav- ender to white, fringed flowers clustered within a pair of leaflike bracts at the branch tips. The flowers open a few at a time over several weeks, and in autumn the dried brown flower heads are attractive. Statewide.

Elephantopus carolinianus (Carolina elephant's foot).

    E. tomentosus [toh-men-'toh-sus], woolly elephant's foot, is a bit shorter with larger, densely hairy, basal leaves. It is most common in East Tennessee, lightly elsewhere.

    Both species like dry, slightly acid soil and the light shade of a woodland setting. Though not showy, elephant's foot is a tough plant that blooms during the late summer lull.

Enemion biternatum (Isopyrum biternatum)
False Rue Anemone
[eh-'neh-mee-un by-ter-'nay-tum]
Ranunculaceae (Buttercup Family)

In March and April false rue anemone creates a carpet of leaves twice divided into sets of 3 and surmounted by a host of solitary white flowers 4 to 12 inches tall. It closely resembles fellow spring bloomer *Thalictrum thalictroides*, rue anemone, hence its common name. In addition to its foliage, false rue anemone may be identified by its uniformly 5-petaled flow- ers and the large drifts it forms. Filtered spring sun with light to medium summer shade and moist, humusy, slightly acid to neutral soil are basic requirements. Foliage dies back in sum- mer and often emerges in winter. Propagate by seed or division. Middle Tennessee.

Enemion biternatum (false rue anemone).

Erigenia bulbosa (harbinger-of-spring).

Erigenia bulbosa

Harbinger-of-spring, Salt-and-pepper
[eh-rih-jeh-'ny-uh bul-'boh-suh]
Apiaceae (Carrot Family)

A small herb that blooms in late winter, harbinger-of-spring produces a 3- to 4-inch blossom stalk topped by clusters of tiny white flowers with reddish brown anthers in a terminal cyme. It grows from a small tuber, and each plant has 1 or 2 leaves twice divided into tiny leaflets. True to its common name, it blooms in February and March and is gone quickly. It loves the moist, humusy, neutral soil of the deciduous forest. Middle Tennessee, lightly elsewhere.

George W. Hornal.

Erigeron pulchellus (robin's plantain).

Erigeron pulchellus

Robin's Plantain
[eh-'rih-jeh-ron pul-'kell-us]
Asteraceae (Aster Family)

Robin's plantain has a basal rosette of hairy, obovate leaves and sends out runners (though not aggressively) to develop a colony. Each plant produces a hairy stalk, 8 to 20 inches tall, topped with 1 to several flower heads an inch across in April and May. The slender, numerous ray flowers are a pale blue lavender, sometimes white or pink, and the disk flowers are yellow.

Part to light shade and moist, rich soil that is well drained and slightly acid will promote development of a healthy colony. Robin's plantain attracts spring bees and butterflies. Propagate by division. Middle and East Tennessee.

Eryngium yuccifolium
Rattlesnake-master, Button Snakeroot
[eh-'rin-jee-um yuh-kih-'foh-lee-um]
Apiaceae (Carrot Family)

Eryngium yuccifolium (rattlesnake-master).

Not a typical charming wildflower, rattlesnake-master sets itself apart as an unusual and architectural plant. Leathery, basal foliage is linear and long, sometimes 1 to 2 feet, with parallel veins and bristly edges. A rigid, smooth stem is 2 to 4 feet tall and clad with progressively shorter, clasping leaves. At the top is a branching cluster of flower heads in July and August. Each flower head is a spherical cluster of tiny, whitish flowers packed together with spiky bracts.

Rattlesnake-master needs full sun to part shade. It will take soil that is moist or dry as long as it is well drained and slightly acid to neutral. It is drought resistant and can be propagated by seed. Statewide, in the southern half of the state.

Erythronium americanum
Trout Lily, Dogtooth Violet
[eh-rih-'throw-nee-um uh-mair-ih-'kay-num]
Liliaceae (Lily Family)

Erythronium americanum (trout lily).

A leafless 8-inch flower stalk, nestled between 2 green and maroon mottled leaves, carries a solitary, nodding, rusty yellow, bell-shaped flower with recurved petals in March and April. It grows from a small, narrow bulb or corm 3 to 5 inches underground. The corm tends to squirm its way deeper into the soil over time and also produces runners. Colonies form, with young plants sending up a single leaf and no flower. Once old enough the corm sends up 2 leaves and a flower. The foliage dies back by June. Trout lilies love deep, humus-rich, moist soil, moderately acid to neutral, and a little spring sun under deciduous trees. Propagate with seed or young offsets, keeping in mind that it may take a few years to flower. Middle and East Tennessee.

E. albidum ['al-bih-dum], a white flowering species, blooms more freely and has leaves that may or may not be mottled. Its native range extends farther west, and it prefers neutral soil. Scattered lightly in Middle and West Tennessee.

Eupatorium 'Gateway' (Joe-Pye-weed).

Eupatorium fistulosum
Joe-Pye-weed
[yew-puh-'tore-ee-um fis-tyew-'loh-sum]
Asteraceae (Aster Family)

Branched clusters of tiny tubular flowers gather in a large, rounded head at the top of a 5- to 9-foot, hollow stem from July to September. The dusky lilac pink flowers have long, protruding styles. The leaves are thin, rough, toothed, and lanceolate, appearing in whorls of 4 to 7 around the stem. Low, damp thickets and meadows are its favorite sites. Reliably moist, moderately to slightly acid soil in full sun works best, especially for young plants. Once established, though, Joe-Pye-weed grows in regular garden moisture with an extra drink during prolonged dry spells. Cutting it back in early summer will help control the height. Joe-Pye-weed is very attractive to bees and butterflies. Some nurseries also list *E. maculatum* [mak-yew-'lay-tum], spotted Joe-Pye-weed, a very similar species. Propagate by seed, cuttings, or division. Statewide, lightly in West Tennessee.

E. purpureum [per-'pure-ee-um], **sweet Joe-Pye-weed,** another species similar to *E. fistulosum*, differs only in height (3 to 6 feet), number of leaves in the whorl (3 to 4), and its ability to grow in drier sites. The plant exudes a vanilla scent when bruised. State-wide, lightly in West Tennessee. Popular cultivar 'Gateway' is variously attributed to each of these species.

E. perfoliatum [per-foh-lee-'ay-tum], **bone-set,** has dull white flowers similar but inferior to *Ageratina altissima*, white snakeroot. It grows 2 to 5 feet tall, has opposite, lanceolate leaves joined at the base around the stem, and blooms earlier. Boneset needs full sun and is a good choice for damp meadows. Statewide.

Euphorbia corollata
Flowering Spurge
[yew-'fore-bee-uh kore-ah-'lay-tuh]
Euphorbiaceae (Spurge Family)

Euphorbia corollata (flowering spurge).

A multi-stemmed slender herb, flowering spurge grows 1 to 3 feet tall with branched panicles of showy white flowers. In reality, each apparent flower is a very tiny cluster of several true flowers surrounded by white petal-like appendages. Blue green leaves are elliptic to linear and can appear opposite or whorled. They turn red in the fall. It has a long season of bloom through the summer and retains its fresh, cool appearance despite heat and drought. Give it full sun to part shade in well-drained, slightly moist to dry, moderately to slightly acid soil. Flowering spurge is slow to establish and should not be moved. Propagate by seed. Statewide, lightly in West Tennessee.

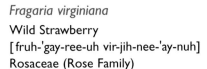

Fragaria virginiana
Wild Strawberry
[fruh-'gay-ree-uh vir-jih-nee-'ay-nuh]
Rosaceae (Rose Family)

Our native wild strawberry has basal leaves, each with 3 oval leaflets and a hairy stem. In April a cluster of white flowers, each ½ to ¾ inch across, opens on a stem 3 to 6 inches tall. The red, egg-shaped fruit is very sweet and flavorful though smaller than cultivated varieties, which are hybrids of this plant and its South American cousin. Wildlife and humans enjoy the fruit. Like all strawberries *F. virginiana* spreads into a colony via runners, but should not be confused with the exotic lawn weed *Duchesnea indica,* Indian or mock strawberry. Give wild strawberry full to part sun, in moist to dry soil that is slightly acid and well drained. Propagate by division. Middle and East Tennessee.

Fragaria virginiana (wild strawberry).

The Center for Field Biology, a Tennessee Center of Excellence at Austin Peay State University.

Galax urceolata (G. aphylla)
Galax, Wand Flower, Beetleweed
['gay-lax ur-see-ah-'lay-tuh]
Diapensiaceae (Diapensia Family)

The evergreen foliage of galax provides year-round interest. Long-stemmed basal leaves, nearly round to broadly heart shaped and very shiny, take on a coppery red glow in winter. In June a leafless 10- to 20-inch stem holds a dense spike of white flowers above the foliage. It spreads slowly via rhizomes. Galax prefers light to medium shade and slightly moist to slightly dry, well-drained, strongly acid, sandy soil mixed with humus. Propagate by division. Unaka Mountains and Valley and Ridge.

Galax urceolata (galax).

Kurt Emmanuele.

Gaultheria procumbens
Wintergreen, Teaberry, Checkerberry
[gawl-'thee-ree-uh proh-'kum-benz]
Ericaceae (Heath Family)

An evergreen groundcover 2 to 6 inches high, wintergreen features leathery, oval leaves that enter the world a rich red before turning dark, shiny green on top and light green below. They mellow to bronze in winter. In the leaf axils small racemes of little urn-shaped, waxy white flowers dangle in June and July. In the fall spicy red berries ripen and reportedly last through the winter, provided birds and other animals restrain themselves.

Gaultheria procumbens (wintergreen).

Wintergreen is happiest in a moist to dry, humusy, moderately acid soil with good drainage and part sun. Some sun assists the leaf coloring, flowering, and berry production. Its favorite spots in the wild are under oaks and evergreens, which is a testament to its love of acidity and need for some shade. It creeps along by underground stems and can be propagated by division or cuttings. The aromatic leaves can be dried and made into a tea. The berries are minty, too. It used to be the source for wintergreen oil until science discovered an artificial substitute. Scattered in East Tennessee, especially Unaka Mountains.

Gentiana saponaria
Soapwort Gentian
[jen-tee(she)-'ay-nuh sap-ah-'nay-ree-uh]
Gentianaceae (Gentian Family)

Our resident gentian grows 8 to 20 inches tall with lanceolate leaves and both terminal and axillary flower clusters. Like the bottle gentian below, soapwort gentian has tubular flowers of a lovely blue about 1½ inches long,

Gentiana saponaria (soapwort gentian).

but these blossoms open near the tip with pleats to allow expansion for pollinating insects, usually bumblebees. It blooms in October and November. Part sun to light shade and rich, consistently moist, moderately acid soil are its basic needs. Eastern Highland Rim and Cumberland Plateau.

G. villosa [vih-'loh-suh], striped gentian, has greenish white tubular flowers striped with blue violet in October and November. Its culture is similar to soapwort gentian, but it will take drier soil. Statewide.

G. andrewsii [an-'drew-zee-eye], bottle or closed gentian, has a range that does not include Tennessee. Yet it is the species most often found in catalogs. Virtually unopened flowers appear in the upper leaf axils of 1- to 2-foot stems between August and October. Pale green leaves are narrowly oval, pointed, opposite, and sessile, turning bronzy in late summer. It will live a long time if it gets the consistently moist soil it needs and some shade. A bit of sunlight will deepen the famed blue. Neutral to slightly acid, rich soil rounds out the requirements. Propagate through division or seed. All gentians can be difficult to grow.

Division of Natural Heritage, Tennessee
Department of Environment and Conservation.

Gentiana villosa (striped gentian).

Geranium maculatum
Wild Geranium, Cranesbill
[jeh-'ray-nee-um mak-yew-'lay-tum]
Geraniaceae (Geranium Family)

Wild geranium forms a large basal clump of long-stemmed leaves that are palmately lobed and toothed. Flower stalks 1 to 2 feet tall sport smaller opposite leaves and a cluster of pinkish lavender, 5-petaled flowers in April and May. Long, pointy seed capsules inspired the common name. The foliage often has a strong

Geranium maculatum (wild geranium).

maroon cast in early spring and in autumn can turn a rich red. Wild geranium likes moist, organically rich soil that is moderately acid to neutral in open shade or part sun. Propagate through division or seed. Statewide.

Hedyotis caerulea (Houstonia caerulea)
Bluets, Quaker Ladies
[heh-dee-'oh-tis seh-'rue-lee-uh]
Rubiaceae (Madder Family)

Hedyotis caerulea (bluets).

Little tufts of ½-inch, yellow-eyed, pale blue flowers on 3- to 6-inch stems form a charming carpet. The tiny leaves are mostly basal. A meadow inhabitant, bluets bloom in April and May in full to part sun and grow in well-drained, moist soil that is moderately to slightly acid. It is a delicate plant whose longevity may be dependent on self-sown seed in a favorable site. It is a good choice for rock gardens and partly sunny, mossy areas.

 H. purpurea (Houstonia purpurea) [per-'pure-ee-uh], **large** or **mountain houstonia, summer** or **purple bluets,** becomes a mound of 10- to 20-inch branched stems with many opposite lanceolate leaves topped by small clusters of tubular flowers, white to pale purple, in May and June. It prefers moist to dry, slightly to moderately acid soil in part sun to light shade. Both *Hedyotis* spp. are found predominately in Middle and East Tennessee.

Hedyotis purpurea (large houstonia, summer bluets).

Helenium autumnale
Sneezeweed
[heh-'leh-nee-um aw-tum-'nay-lee]
Asteraceae (Aster Family)

From 2 to 4 feet in height, sneezeweed branches at the top to produce loose, flat clusters of 1- to 2-inch flowers. Each flower has a yellow, globular disk and yellow, wedge-shaped rays that are cleft into 3 or more lobes and often reflexed. It blooms from July through September. Leaves are narrowly oblong, alternate, and toothed. The stem has little wings that descend from the base of the leaves. Butterflies sip the nectar. The common name refers to the prior use of its leaves as snuff, not allergies. Sneezeweed is a moisture lover that thrives in full sun on low ground, slightly acid to neutral, but can grow in dry soil, too. Division of the clump every 2 to 3 years keeps it vital. It also grows readily from seed. Middle and East Tennessee.

Helenium flexuosum (purple-headed sneezeweed).

H. flexuosum (H. nudiflorum) [fleks-yew-'oh-sum], purple-headed sneezeweed, is 1 to 4 feet tall. The 1-inch flowers have purplish brown disks and branch out airily, radiating about the winged stem. Its smaller leaves are linear and entire, and its culture is the same. Statewide.

Helianthus angustifolius
Narrow-leaved or Swamp Sunflower
[hee-lee-'an-thus an-gus-tih-'foh-lee-us]
Asteraceae (Aster Family)

Tall and erect, the 5- to 7-foot stems have rough, linear leaves that appear opposite one another at the base of the stem and alternate near the top. The 3-inch, yellow-rayed flowers branch out widely and have purplish red disk flowers in September and October. Bees and butterflies seek the nectar, butterfly larvae eat the leaves, and birds eat the seeds. Moist soil is best, but it tolerates both wet conditions and drought. Give it full sun and moderately to slightly acid soil that is not too rich. Staking will likely be necessary; pruning

Helianthus angustifolius (narrow-leaved sunflower).

in July will help. Propagate all sunflowers by division, seed, or cuttings. Statewide.

H. atrorubens [uh-'trah-ruh-bens], **dark-eyed** or **hairy wood sunflower,** is 4 to 6 feet tall and hairy, particularly the lower portion of the plant. The narrowly ovate leaves have winged petioles. At the top are several long-stalked, 2-inch flowers with purplish red disks and yellow rays. It grows in dry, slightly acid soil and part shade and blooms in late summer. East Tennessee and Western Highland Rim.

H. microcephalus [my-kroh-'seh-fuh-lus], **small-headed sunflower,** is 3 to 6 feet in height with smooth stems, lanceolate leaves, and numerous 1¼-inch yellow flowers on thin, branching stems in August and September. This sunflower likes moist soil and part shade. Statewide.

H. mollis ['mah-lis], **ashy sunflower,** has dense, soft hairs on the entire 3-foot plant. Ovate leaves are opposite and clasping with 3-inch yellow flowers from July to September. It likes a dry soil in full sun to part shade and can quickly colonize an area via rhizomes in moist soil. Middle and West Tennessee.

Helianthus mollis (ashy sunflower).

Hepatica acutiloba
Sharp-lobed Liverleaf
[heh-'pat-ih-kuh ack-yew-'tih-lah-buh]
Ranunculaceae (Buttercup Family)

One of the earliest spring flowers, liverleaf sends up plump, fuzzy buds on 3- to 5-inch fuzzy stems in March and April to bravely face unpredictable spring weather. This inspired wildflower author Mrs. Dana to note that "the frail and delicate-looking withstand storm and stress far better than their more robust-appearing brethren." Color worthy of

Hepatica acutiloba (sharp-lobed liverleaf).

fine porcelain in pale blue, lavender, or white graces the little blooms. The flowers protect themselves by closing at night and remaining so on inclement days. After flowering the year-old, 3-lobed foliage gives way to a fresh crop of leaves that were thought to resemble the human liver (hence the name). Morning sun is recommended for spring bloom with full shade in the summer. Moist to dry, slightly acid soil must be organically rich and well drained. Propagate by division. Middle and East Tennessee.

H. americana [uh-mair-ih-'kay-nuh], round-lobed liverleaf, likes a more acid soil (pH 5-6) and has a more northerly range. East Tennessee and lightly on the Highland Rim.

Heterotheca mariana (Chrysopsis mariana)
Maryland Golden Aster
[heh-teh-roh-'thee-kuh mair-ee-'ay-nuh]
Asteraceae (Aster Family)

In August and September, several 1-inch, golden yellow ray and disk flowers crowd the top of 12- to 18-inch stems. Young stems have silky hairs, and the leaves are alternate and oblong on the plant's lower half, smaller and sessile near the top.

H. graminifolia (Chrysopsis graminifolia, Pityopsis graminifolia) [gram-ih-nih-'foh-lee-uh], silkgrass or grass-leaved golden aster, has linear, parallel-veined basal leaves several inches long and a few linear stem leaves that feature soft white hairs. The 1- to 2-foot flowering stem branches out to hold erect numerous ½-inch, bright yellow flowers in August and September.

Both species like dry, well-drained, moderately acid soil in full sun to part shade and

Heterotheca mariana (Maryland golden aster).

Kurt Emmanuele.

benefit from an early summer shearing to produce bushier and more floriferous plants. Propagate by seed. Both *Heterotheca* spp. can be found in East Tennessee, the Western Highland Rim, and West Tennessee Uplands.

Heuchera americana
Alumroot
['hyew-keh-ruh uh-mair-ih-'kay-nuh]
Saxifragaceae (Saxifrage Family)

Heuchera americana (alumroot).

The foliage of alumroot is its primary asset. The basal leaves, scalloped and round lobed, form a mound and are mottled with bronzy veining and edges outlining pale gray green splotches. Leaves are typically evergreen, and 2-foot purplish to pale green flower stems carry loose panicles of insignificant, greenish white flowers from May to June. There are numerous cultivars based on the foliage markings. Statewide.

H. *villosa* [vih-'loh-suh], hairy alumroot, has an 18-inch stalk with tiny white flowers in June and July and bright green sharply toothed and lobed leaves with hairy stems and leaf undersides. There is a form of H. *villosa* with purplish stems and leaves. Middle and East Tennessee.

Heuchera villosa—purple form (hairy alumroot).

Alumroot likes the limestone slopes of moist to dry woods, tolerating relatively poor neutral to moderately acid soil that must be well drained. Part sun (especially morning) to open shade is best; purple-leaved varieties will take more light. Propagate by seed or division. The hybrid x *Heucherella tiarelloides* [hyew-keh-'reh-luh tee-uh-reh-loh-'eye-deez] is a cross between *Heuchera* and *Tiarella (foamflower)*. There are cultivars.

Hexastylis arifolia (heartleaf ginger).

Hexastylis arifolia (Asarum arifolium)
Heartleaf Ginger, Little Brown Jug
[heks-uh-'sty-lis air-ih-'foh-lee-uh]
Aristolochiaceae (Birthwort Family)

This low evergreen groundcover has leathery, mottled leaves. They are triangular to arrow shaped, and fresh leaves replace the previous year's foliage each spring. In April and May a small, vase-shaped flower, fleshy and tan, grows upright in the leaf axils and accounts for the other common name, little brown jug. It is very slow growing. Heartleaf ginger prefers moist, humusy, moderately acid soil and light to medium shade. East Tennessee.

H. shuttleworthii [shuh-tle-'wer-the-eye] is another East Tennessee species with rounded, mottled leaves. Cultivar 'Callaway' is very popular.

Hibiscus moscheutos (swamp rose-mallow).

Hibiscus moscheutos
Swamp Rose-mallow
[hy-'bis-kus mos-'kyew-tos]
Malvaceae (Mallow Family)

Everything about this plant seems oversized. Stems are 4 to 8 feet tall and the large leaves are broadly ovate. From July to September clusters of 4- to 8-inch creamy white or pale pink flowers centered with a dark red eye put on a show.

It likes very moist, rich, nearly neutral soil in full sun but is adaptable to regular garden moisture. These tall plants also have a respectable spread, up to 5 feet, so give them room. They may need staking. Previous year's stalks are sometimes left standing for this purpose. Propagate by seed or cuttings. Collect seeds as soon as the pods split open. Statewide.

Hydrastis canadensis
Goldenseal
[hy-'dras-tis kan-uh-'den-sis]
Ranunculaceae (Buttercup Family)

Goldenseal's thick yellow rhizome sends up a stem with a pair of deeply crinkled, palmately lobed, toothed leaves to a height of 6 to 15 inches. A single white, feathery flower blooms between the leaves in April, and an orange red cluster of berries ripens in late summer. The plant spreads slowly to form a colony.

A comparatively rare find in the wild, goldenseal was once quite common. Its medicinal value has led to commercial exploitation of the plant. It needs light shade with a little spring sun and moist, neutral to slightly acid soil rich in leaf mold. Propagate through seed or division. Statewide.

J. Paul Moore.

Hydrastis canadensis (goldenseal).

Hydrophyllum appendiculatum
Waterleaf
[hy-drah-'fill-um ap-pen-dih-kyew-'lay-tum]
Hydrophyllaceae (Waterleaf Family)

Waterleaf is a biennial. Leaves in the basal rosette are splotched with gray green spots and live through the winter. Basal and lower stem leaves are lobed deeply enough to be considered compound, but upper stem leaves are merely coarsely toothed in a broad maple shape. Loose terminal clusters of blue lavender, cup-shaped flowers bloom on 1- to 3-foot stems in April and May. Waterleaf needs reliably moist, neutral to slightly acid soil with a little spring sun and summer shade. Propagate by seed. Northern Middle Tennessee.

Hydrophyllum appendiculatum (waterleaf).

Hymenocallis occidentalis (spider lily).

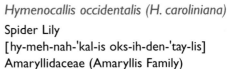

Hymenocallis occidentalis (H. caroliniana)

Spider Lily

[hy-meh-nah-'kal-is oks-ih-den-'tay-lis]

Amaryllidaceae (Amaryllis Family)

Long, narrow straplike petals radiate out from a corona (like the cup on a daffodil) formed from the union of wide stamen bases. These striking, white, fragrant flowers appear in clusters atop a leafless, 1- to 2-foot stalk growing in the midst of broad, daffodil-type foliage in August. Spider lily grows from a bulb in wet meadows and other damp ground and needs moist to wet, slightly acid, fertile soil in full sun to part shade. Propagate by division or seed. The large seeds are round, green, and fleshy. West and Middle Tennessee.

Hypoxis hirsuta

Yellow Star-grass

[hy-'poks-is hir-'sue-tuh]

Amaryllidaceae (Amaryllis Family)

A tiny, round corm or rhizome produces grassy basal foliage 6 to 12 inches tall. In May and June 2- to 6-inch hairy, leafless stalks hold clusters of 1 to 7 bright yellow, starry flowers. It may bloom sporadically throughout the summer. This diminutive native perennial prefers dry, well-drained, sandy soil that is moderately acid in part shade to part sun. Yellow star-grass will tolerate light shade but blooms best with some sun and sufficient moisture. Propagate by division and seed. Middle and East Tennessee, West Tennessee Uplands.

Hypoxis hirsuta (yellow star-grass).

Impatiens capensis
Spotted Jewelweed
[im-'pay-shens kuh-'pen-sis]
Balsaminaceae (Touch-me-not Family)

This annual is 2 to 5 feet tall with alternate ovate to elliptic, round-toothed leaves. In summer deep yellow to orange flowers with reddish brown spots project from the leaf axils on long slender stalks. Like dangling jewels, the flowers attract their primary pollinators, hummingbirds and bees. Jewelweed produces cleistogamous (self-pollinated) flowers. Seed capsules split open quite explosively when touched and fling seeds several feet away.

Impatiens capensis (spotted jewelweed).

In light shade to part sun and moist to wet soil jewelweed will readily self sow to the point of weediness. The shallow-rooted plants are easily pulled if it gets a bit ambitious. The juice of this plant is used as a soothing balm to skin irritations including poison ivy. One interesting note—the leaves never get wet. Microscopic hairs trap air on the leaf surface and repel moisture, even when held under water. Statewide.

I. pallida ['pal-ih-duh], **pale jewelweed**, is yellow in flower and needs more shade. Northern Middle Tennessee and East Tennessee.

Iris cristata
Crested Iris
['eye-ris kris-'tay-tuh]
Iridaceae (Iris Family)

Little 4- to 8-inch fans of iris foliage spread across the ground by means of wiry stems and rhizomes. Pale lavender blue, crested flowers about 2 inches across bloom in April and May on stems 3 to 6 inches tall. Both petals and

Iris cristata (crested iris).

Iris fulva (copper iris).

Scott C. Gunn, Division of Natural Heritage, Tennessee Department of Environment and Conservation.

Iris verna (dwarf iris).

George W. Hornal.

Iris virginica (southern blue flag).

sepals are horizontal. The foliage is deciduous, but keeps its appearance throughout summer.

The ideal environment for crested iris is a well-drained area with morning sun and moist to slightly dry, humusy, slightly acid soil. Periodic division keeps the continually creeping native in place and healthy. There are cultivars of crested iris, including 'Alba', a white flowered form. Statewide, especially Middle and East Tennessee.

I. fulva ['ful-vuh], **copper** or **red iris,** grows naturally in wet, swampy soil. Flower stalks rise above the slender foliage to a height of 3 to 5 feet in May and June. Flowers are a rich, coppery red and very flat topped due to the spreading sepals, petals, and styles. Full sun and reliably moist to damp soil are requirements. It works well potted in a pond with the rhizomes barely submerged. Mississippi River Valley.

I. verna ['ver-nuh], **dwarf iris,** is similar to *I. cristata*. Key differences are erect petals, the absence of a fluted crest on the down-turned sepals, darker flower color, and taller, more slender foliage. It prefers dry, sandy, moderately acid soil and spring sun, blooming in April and May. East Tennessee.

I. virginica [vir-'jin-ih-kuh] **southern blue flag,** has light blue purple flowers splotched with yellow, blooming on a branched stalk 2 feet tall in May and June. Bees and butterflies visit. Foliage is thin and more grasslike in appearance. Southern blue flag needs full sun and reliably moist to damp soil that is moderately to slightly acid. Lightly statewide.

Iris rhizomes benefit from division every few years. Replant rhizomes even with or slightly below the soil surface.

Jeffersonia diphylla
Twinleaf
[jeh-fer-'soh-nee-uh dy-'fill-uh]
Berberidaceae (Barberry Family)

Jeffersonia diphylla (twinleaf).

The foliage is twinleaf's main attraction. Each leaf is deeply cleft into 2 matching leaflets, not unlike bird or butterfly wings. Leaves are pinkish when they first appear. Solitary, 8-petaled, white flowers on 8- to 10-inch leafless stems last only a day or so in March or April. Stems continue to grow to 15 or 20 inches, lifting juglike seed capsules, each equipped with a lid that opens for dispersal.

Twinleaf's preferred habitat calls for light shade and rich, humusy soil that is near neutral in pH. Sufficient moisture in the summer will encourage the foliage to stick around. Protect it from aggressive plants. Propagate by division or seed; fine mesh tied over the pod will collect seed, which must be sown immediately. Middle and East Tennessee.

Liatris spicata
Blazing Star, Gayfeather
[lee-'ay-tris spih-'kay-tuh]
Asteraceae (Aster Family)

Liatris spicata (blazing star).

Blazing star produces a clump of 2- to 5-foot stems clothed in linear foliage and liberally set with compact heads of purple disk flowers attached directly to the stem. The flowering spike accounts for at least half the plant's total height in July and August.

L. squarrulosa [skwah-rue-'loh-suh], southern blazing star, is a bit hairy with flower heads on short peduncles (stems) along the main stem and broader leaves. It blooms in August and September.

Blazing star needs good drainage and moderately acid soil, but *L. spicata* prefers

Liatris squarrulosa (southern blazing star).

Liatris microcephala (small-headed blazing star).

Lilium superbum (turk's cap lily).

moister sites than *L. squarrulosa,* which is happy in dry, rocky soil. Full sun is important for the plants to look their best. *L. spicata* has dwarf varieties, 1 to 2 feet tall, and white varieties. Blazing star grows from a warty-looking corm and can be propagated from seed or corm division. It will self-sow. Bees and butterflies drink the nectar, and birds eat the seeds.

Other locally occurring species are *L. aspera* ['ass-peh-ruh], rough blazing star, 2 to 5 feet; *L. squarrosa* [skwah-'roh-suh], scaly or plains blazing star, 1 to 3 feet; *L. microcephala* [my-kroh-'seh-fuh-luh], small-headed blazing star, 1 to 3 feet; and *L. scariosa* [skair-ee-'oh-suh], northern blazing star, 1 to 3½ feet. All like dry soil. Since there are several species of *Liatris,* a mix of them will provide a longer period of bloom and can be used to fill the gardening niche of the exotic invasive purple loosestrife *(Lythrum salicaria).*

All *Liatris* spp. are found more or less statewide, except *L. microcephala,* which is concentrated primarily on the Eastern Highland Rim and Cumberland Plateau.

Lilium superbum
Turk's Cap Lily
['lih-lee-um sue-'per-bum]
Liliaceae (Lily Family)

This popular lily is a living bouquet, often producing numerous flowers per stem. Flower petals/sepals are strongly reflexed in reddish orange with purple spots and large protruding stamens in June and July. Lanceolate leaves whorl around the stem, which grows 3 to 9 feet tall. *L. michauxii* [mih-'shaw-ee-eye], Michaux's lily, is similar with fewer flowers.

To lilies the critical issue is location. They can be very difficult to grow, and even a seemingly ideal spot can fail to make them happy. However, they are rewardingly beautiful. They need deep, rich, moist, moderately acid soil and part sun. Protect them from wind, mulch to maintain cool soil, and space them about 2 feet apart. Divide bulb offshoots in the fall, but one source advised against disturbing happy plants. Unaka Mountains.

Lobelia cardinalis
Cardinal Flower
[loh-'bee-lee-uh kar-dih-'nay-lis]
Campanulaceae (Bellflower Family)

Lobelia cardinalis (cardinal flower).

The cardinal flower displays a brilliant, clear red that defies comparison. The tubular, lipped flowers adorn a 2- to 4-foot stem in a terminal raceme from July through September. Attractive to hummingbirds, the primary pollinator, the blossoms themselves resemble birds taking flight. Bees can also pollinate the flowers and butterflies visit. The leaves are lanceolate to oblong, alternate, and toothed. Leaf color can vary from a deep bronzy green on a dark stem to a light shining green and adds to the beauty of the plant.

Cardinal flower is a water lover. Right at home on a stream bank, in a wet meadow, or potted in a backyard pond, it will also transition to the regular garden provided consistent moisture is readily available along with slightly acid, rich soil in part shade to part sun. It is a short-lived, shallow-rooted plant susceptible to rot and winter kill, but it grows easily from seed or division of offshoots and cuttings. Keep fallen leaves off the leaf rosettes in winter. There are lots of cultivars. Statewide.

Lobelia siphilitica (great blue lobelia).

Lysimachia ciliata var. *purpurea* (fringed loosestrife).

Lysimachia quadrifolia (whorled loosestrife).

L. siphilitica [sih-fih-'lih-tih-kuh], great blue lobelia, is a bushier, branching plant growing 2 to 3 feet tall. Several terminal racemes of pale to dark violet blue, lipped flowers bloom from August to October. It will take drier sites and is pollinated by bees. Statewide.

Lysimachia ciliata
Fringed Loosestrife
[lih-sih-'mah-kee-uh sih-lee-'ay-tuh]
Primulaceae (Primrose Family)

Fringed loosestrife grows 2 to 3 feet tall, is often unbranched, and has numerous paired ovate leaves. Leaf petioles are lined with tiny hairs. Two slender stalks emerge from the upper leaf pairs and are topped by 2 small, leafy bracts and a cluster of 3 or 4 flowers. The yellow blossoms are ¾ inch across and slightly nodding. Petals have tiny teeth and pointed tips. It blooms in June and July. This loosestrife loves wet to moist soil and light shade. When happy it can display aggressive tendencies, but do not confuse it with the unrelated purple loosestrife, *Lythrum salicaria*, a pink-flowered, exotic pest plant. There is a maroon-leaved variety. Statewide.

    L. quadrifolia [kwah-drih-'foh-lee-uh], whorled loosestrife, is similar in height and form, but has whorls of 4 lanceolate leaves along the stem. From the axil of each leaf springs a single yellow, ½-inch flower on a slender stalk. The flowers have red centers and bloom in May and June. Whorled loosestrife likes moist to dry, slightly acid soil in part to light shade. Middle and East Tennessee. Propagate by division or cuttings.

Manfreda virginica (Agave virginica)
False Aloe, Rattlesnake-master
[man-'free-duh vir-'jin-ih-kuh]
Agavaceae (Agave Family)

False aloe is a succulent, producing a rosette of narrow, fleshy leaves 4 to 12 inches in length. The leaves may be solid green or sprinkled with maroon spots. In June and July it sends up a tall scape (3 to 6 feet) of greenish brown, tubular flowers. They give off a fragrance at night to attract moths. It can grow in dry, poor, thin soil, slightly acid to slightly alkaline and well drained, in full sun to part shade. An unassuming yet unusual plant, false aloe looks best planted in groups. Propagate by seed. Statewide.

Manfreda virginica (false aloe).

Medeola virginiana
Indian Cucumber-root
[meh-'dee-ah-luh vir-jih-nee-'ay-nuh]
Liliaceae (Lily Family)

Indian cucumber-root is a slender plant 1 to 2 feet tall featuring 2 whorls of ovate to lance-olate leaves. The lower whorl, positioned at midstem, has 5 to 9 leaves. The upper whorl of 3 smaller leaves supports an umbel of small greenish yellow flowers, each nodding at the end of a little stalk in May. The sepals, petals, and stigmas of the flowers are recurved. By the end of summer, dark purple berries have developed. The bases of the 3 leaves below the fruit turn red to signal birds that dinner is served.

There is nothing the least bit showy about this wildflower, but its unusual form makes it a neat addition to a woodland garden. It needs rich, reliably moist, moderately acid soil in medium shade. Propagate by

Medeola virginiana (Indian cucumber-root).

Kurt Emmanuele.

dividing the rhizome, which is reported to taste like a cucumber. Eastern half of the state and West Tennessee Uplands.

Mertensia virginica
Virginia Bluebells
[mer-'ten-see-uh vir-'jin-ih-kuh]
Boraginaceae (Borage Family)

Maroon shoots break through the ground in late March or early April. Oblong foliage and stems become a soft bluish green, and terminal clusters of pink buds unfold into porcelain blue, long-necked bells. Some plants will produce flowers that are pale lavender or nearly white. Swaying on leafy stalks 12 to 18 inches tall, the breezy bells last surprisingly well with cooperative weather, but as spring warms they fade quickly. The lanky, ratty, yellowing foliage and soon-to-be bare spot can be disguised and filled by emerging ferns, deciduous groundcovers, or later perennials.

Alluvial streamsides are often home to this enchanting native in the wild. Rich, moist, neutral soil with spring sun and summer shade provides the ideal environment for the fleshy, tuberous rootstock. Propagate through division and seed. It will self-sow. To interplant with ferns or other plants, space bluebells about 18 inches apart. Middle and East Tennessee.

Mertensia virginica (Virginia bluebells).

Susan Felts.

Mimulus alatus
Monkey Flower
['mih-myew-lus uh-'lay-tus]
Scrophulariaceae (Figwort Family)

Solitary, lavender blue, lipped flowers spring out airily on slender stems from the axils of opposite, lanceolate, toothed leaves in July.

Mimulus ringens (monkey flower).

Kurt Emmanuele.

The main stem is angled with narrow wings and grows 2 to 5 feet tall. *Mimulus* is a butterfly larval food. Monkey flowers grow in wet areas—swamps, marshes, pond margins—in part shade to part sun. Propagate by seed. Statewide.

M. ringens ['ring-enz], very similar and much easier to locate in nursery catalogs, is found in East Tennessee and the West Tennessee Uplands.

Mitchella repens
Partridgeberry, Twinberry
[mit-'cheh-luh 'ree-pens]
Rubiaceae (Madder Family)

Mitchella repens (partridgeberry).

The partridgeberry is an evergreen creeping vine that roots along the ground under trees. An attractive groundcover, its small oval to rounded, dark green, white-veined foliage can weave among more delicate plants without causing harm. From April to June it produces tiny pairs of white to pinkish, funnel-shaped, fragrant flowers on erect 3- to 4-inch stalks. Since the paired flowers share an ovary, fertilization results in an odd-shaped red berry with 2 blossom end spots. Berries can persist through winter if not eaten; they are a favorite of game birds.

Moist, humus-rich, moderately acid soil and light to medium shade are important requirements. Division, tip cuttings, and layering are the best propagation methods. Statewide.

Mitella diphylla (bishop's cap).

Mitella diphylla
Bishop's Cap, Miterwort
[my-'teh-luh dy-'fill-uh]
Saxifragaceae (Saxifrage Family)

In foliar appearance, bishop's cap closely resembles its cousin *Tiarella*, the foamflower. Both have hairy, maple-shaped, basal leaves, but in flower they are easily distinguished. In April and May bishop's cap sends up 6- to 12-inch slender racemes of widely spaced, deeply fringed, tiny white flowers. A small pair of opposite leaves is positioned halfway up the flowering stem. The upright calyx of each flower holds tiny black seeds until jarred out by weather or wildlife.

Rich, moist, neutral soil in the light shade of deciduous trees suits bishop's cap quite well. Clumps enlarge slowly on rhizomes, so it makes a good groundcover that tends to stay put. Propagate through seed or division. Middle and East Tennessee.

Monarda fistulosa (wild bergamot).

Monarda fistulosa
Wild Bergamot
[mah-'nar-duh fis-tyew-'loh-suh]
Lamiaceae (Mint Family)

Clusters of pinkish lavender, tubular florets bloom in June and July. Square, 3- to 4-foot stems have opposite, broadly lanceolate, toothed leaves that are aromatic. Pinkish lavender bracts lie just below the flowers. Wild bergamot spreads readily in moist to dry, well-drained, neutral to slightly acid soil and full to part sun. Statewide.

M. clinopodia **[klih-nah-'pod-ee-uh], basil balm,** is a bit taller, with spotted white flowers and white bracts. Old flower heads fade to powdery brown with their own visual appeal.

It blooms along with wild bergamot and likes the same growing conditions. Eastern half of the state.

M. didyma ['dih-dih-muh], **bee balm** or **Oswego tea,** has clusters of scarlet, tubular florets with scarlet bracts. It needs moist soil and full to part sun. Mildew can be a problem, though some cultivars are resistant. It also spreads readily in a favorable site and is sensitive to drought. Unaka Mountains.

M. punctata [punk-'tay-tuh], **dotted horse-mint,** has whorled tiers of yellow florets with purple spots underlain by bracts washed with a soft lilac pink. It is a tad smaller, 2 to 3 feet, and blooms in late July and August. It likes part sun in drier, well-drained, sandy soil and does not spread as much as the other species. It may be short-lived. The *Atlas of Tennessee Vascular Plants* documents it only in the Unaka Mountains, but distribution maps indicate a statewide range.

Monarda spp. attract bees, butterflies, and hummingbirds. Propagate by seed, division, or cuttings.

Monarda didyma (bee balm).

Nelumbo lutea
American Lotus
[neh-'lum-boh 'lew-tee-uh]
Nelumbonaceae (Lotus-lily Family)

The American lotus is a pond plant with large round leaves, often a foot or more across on a centrally positioned stalk, and solitary, many-petaled, 4- to 10-inch pale yellow flowers. Leaves and flowers rise above the water's surface; sometimes leaves float on the water. Blooms in July and August are followed by decorative seedpods, which look something like showerheads. A hard, round seed is in each hole.

Monarda punctata (dotted horsemint).

Nelumbo lutea (American lotus).

Place the rhizomes in a large container of rich soil in 1 to 2 feet of water. Full sun is needed. In the wild it grows in slow streams and ponds, spreading by roots as well as seeds, and may need frequent division when grown in containers. Lightly statewide.

Nymphaea odorata (fragrant waterlily).

George W. Hornal.

Nymphaea odorata
Fragrant Waterlily
[nim-'fee-uh oh-dah-'ray-tuh]
Nymphaeaceae (Waterlily Family)

Smaller scale than the American lotus, the fragrant waterlily produces floating leaves 4 to 12 inches in diameter. Solitary, many-petaled, white flowers are 3 to 5 inches across and either float or rise just above the water's surface. Leaves are round with a triangular notch at the stalk base. As the name implies, the flowers are fragrant and open only in the morning from June to August. Ball-like fruit ripens below the water.

It likes fertile soil and needs lots of sun to bloom well. The quiet waters of a back-yard pond are ideal with the perennial rhizome potted in a container of rich soil about 2 feet below the water's surface. It occurs lightly statewide.

Oenothera fruticosa (sundrops).

Oenothera fruticosa
Sundrops
[ee-nah-'thee-ruh frue-tih-'koh-suh]
Onagraceae (Evening Primrose Family)

Evergreen rosettes of ground-hugging, dark green leaves take on a burgundy hue in winter. This burgundy hue is found in the branched, 18- to 24-inch stems and the alternate stem leaves of summer. Clusters of bright yellow flowers glow like drops of pure sunshine in

May and June. By late summer new rosettes have formed, and the dying stems can be cut back. Another commonly seen sundrop, *O. fruticosa* ssp. *glauca* ['glaw-kuh] *(O. tetragona),* is very similar and blooms a little later.

Regular garden soil, slightly acid and a tad on the dry side, suits drought-tolerant sundrops just fine, along with full-rayed exposure to the source of its name. Sundrops will spread but are not overly aggressive and are easily pulled or divided. You can also propagate with cuttings. Middle and East Tennessee.

Opuntia humifusa (O. compressa)
Prickly-pear Cactus
[oh-'pun-tee-uh hyew-mih-'fyew-suh]
Cactaceae (Cactus Family)

The *Opuntia* genus is quite common in the southwest, but one of the most hardy of its species is found in the eastern United States. *O. humifusa* is a low, slow-spreading, often prostrate plant of branching stems. The stems are flat, oval pads, 2 to 5 inches long, that are joined together. Tiny, awl-shaped leaves are dotted about the pads with a tuft of even tinier yellowish bristles at each leaf base. These leaves often fall off. In May and June large (2 inches or more) yellow flowers with numerous silky petals bloom on the edges of the pads. In August smooth, red, pear-shaped fruit develops. Some birds and small mammals enjoy the fruit; humans can eat it, too. Pads shrivel somewhat in winter, but plump up again in spring.

True to its cactus nature, prickly-pear likes dry, well-drained, sandy or stony soil that is neutral and receives full sun. A spot of

Opuntia humifusa (prickly-pear cactus).

Opuntia humifusa—fruit (prickly-pear cactus).

regular garden soil can be adapted with the addition of gravel or sand. Propagation is easily done by separating the pads at their joints and setting the narrow end, once calloused, in damp sand to root. Protect hands from the bristles. Middle Tennessee, especially the Central Basin.

Orontium aquaticum
Golden Club, Never Wet
[ah-'ron-tee-um uh-'kwah-tih-kum]
Araceae (Arum Family)

Orontium aquaticum (golden club).

Kurt Emmanuele.

Growing from stout rhizomes, the basal, elliptical leaves are 5 to 12 inches long and dark green. They can either rise out of the water or float on the surface. From the midst of this foliage in April and May, slender spadices snake their way out and up about 12 inches. The top 1 to 2 inches of each spadix is bright yellow, crowded with tiny flowers.

Golden club likes deep, loamy, moderately acid soil in 6 to 12 inches of water and full sun. The leaves shimmer when beneath the water and shed the water immediately upon emerging so that they are completely dry. This characteristic prompted another common name, never wet. Propagate by seed or division. Lightly statewide.

Oxalis violacea
Violet Wood Sorrel
['oks-uh-lis vy-oh-'lay-see-uh]
Oxalidaceae (Wood Sorrel Family)

Oxalis violacea (violet wood sorrel).

The Center for Field Biology, a Tennessee Center of Excellence at Austin Peay State University.

The 3 rounded leaflets of the violet wood sorrel fold and droop downward toward the leaf stem at night like the familiar shamrock. These violet-tinged leaves rise directly from an underground tuber. Leafless stalks, 4 to 6 inches tall, bear loosely clustered lavender to violet blossoms in May and June.

With slightly acid, humus-rich soil, a tad on the dry side, and in light shade, O. *violacea* can overstep its bounds. Keep an eye on any delicate neighbors to make sure their rights are not infringed. Statewide.

Pachysandra procumbens
Allegheny Spurge
[pak-ih-'san-druh proh-'kum-bens]
Buxaceae (Box Family)

Allegheny spurge is a low-growing, slow-growing perennial with broadly ovate, toothed leaves closely spaced near the summit of fleshy, erect stems about 6 inches or so high. New stems and leaves of bright green appear in April. The old foliage, which remains if winter is not too severe, becomes beautifully mottled. Old and new grow side by side until the fresh crop matures, at which time the older foliage dies. Appearing with the newly emerging young foliage in April are short (4-inch) terminal spikes of small, white, scented flowers. Allegheny spurge makes an excellent and well-behaved ground-cover in light to medium shade and moist, humus-rich, neutral soil. Propagate by division. Middle and East Tennessee.

J. Paul Moore.

Pachysandra procumbens (Allegheny spurge).

Panax quinquefolius
American Ginseng
['pay-nicks kwin-kwih-'foh-lee-us]
Araliaceae (Ginseng Family)

American ginseng sends up an unbranched stem 8 to 16 inches tall that features a whorl of 3 palmately compound leaves, each with 5 toothed leaflets. At the top of the stem above the foliage is an umbel of yellow green flowers in June and later a cluster of bright red berries. Statewide.

Division of Natural Heritage, Tennessee Department of Environment and Conservation.

Panax quinquefolius (American ginseng).

P. trifolius [try-foh'-lee-us], dwarf ginseng, is only 4 to 8 inches tall with white flowers and yellow berries. Northern counties of the Cumberland Plateau.

Both species of ginseng love moist, humus-rich, moderately acid to neutral soil that is well drained in the cool, medium shade of woodlands. *P. quinquefolius* is a commercially exploited rare plant in Tennessee and is endangered throughout its native range. Used as a Chinese folk medicine, the root is dug and sold as an export. Propagate by seed.

Peltandra virginica (arrow arum).

Peltandra virginica
Arrow Arum
[pel-'tan-druh vir-'jin-ih-kuh]
Araceae (Arum Family)

Arrow arum is grown for its long-stemmed, shiny, arrow-shaped leaves, which reach a height of 18 inches. Its bloom is an unassuming greenish spathe and yellow spadix in late spring that develops green to bronzy berries. The flowering stalk bends over to auger its way into the mud and plant the berries.

A lover of quiet, shallow water with a non-aggressive nature, this native is well suited for small ponds with full sun to light shade. Arrow arum is most commonly found in West Tennessee.

Penstemon laevigatus
Smooth or Eastern Beard-tongue
[pen-'stem-un lee-vih-'gay-tus]
    (commonly pronounced: 'pen-stih-mun)
Scrophulariaceae (Figwort Family)

There are several eastern U.S. species of *Penstemon*. Their differences are slight, which makes positive identification difficult for an amateur; even the experts disagree. Plants produce a basal clump of foliage and 2- to 3-foot stems with opposite, broadly lanceolate, clasping leaves. Atop each stem is a raceme of hairy, purple, tubular flowers, each with a white lip. Bees love them. Beard-tongue blooms in May and June. Lightly in Middle and East Tennessee.

P. hirsutus [hir-'sue-tus], hairy or north-eastern beard-tongue, and P. calycosus [kal-ih-'koh-sus] (listed by one expert as another name for P. laevigatus) are very similar. P. hirsutus occurs in northern Middle Tennessee, while P. calycosus is found throughout Middle Tennessee.

P. digitalis [dih-jih-'tay-lis], white beard-tongue, is taller with pale lavender to white flowers. 'Husker Red' is a popular cultivar. Lightly statewide.

P. smallii ['small-ee-eye], Small's beard-tongue, has reddish purple flowers with striped white throats. Lightly in East Tennessee.

Penstemon hirsutus (hairy beard-tongue).

Beard-tongues like well-drained, average, moist to dry soil that is moderately to slightly acid in full sun or part shade. Periodic division keeps plants strong. They can also be propagated by seed.

Penstemon digitalis (white beard-tongue).

Phacelia bipinnatifida
Purple Phacelia
[fuh-'see-lee-uh by-pin-nuh-'tih-fih-duh]
Hydrophyllaceae (Waterleaf Family)

Deeply lobed basal foliage is mottled with pale grayish blotches, the watermarked characteristic that led to the family name. Stems vary from 8 to 24 inches in height with variously lobed and toothed leaves. In April a tightly recurved coil of ¾-inch lavender blue flowers with white eyes and protruding stamens unwind to put on a lovely display. Purple phacelia is a biennial and will develop

Phacelia bipinnatifida (purple phacelia).

Phacelia purshii (Miami mist).

self-supporting colonies in fertile, moist, slightly acid soil. It needs filtered spring sun or light shade. Middle and East Tennessee.

The annual *P. purshii* ['pursh-ee-eye], Miami mist, forms an 8- to 15-inch plant with hairy, branched stems, deeply cut alternate leaves, and 1-sided coils of small, cupped, pale purple flowers with a white center and lightly fringed petals. Easily grown from seed, it likes moist to dry, neutral soil and full to part sun. Middle Tennessee.

Phlox divaricata
Wild Blue or Woodland Phlox
[flocks dih-vair-ih-'kay-tuh]
Polemoniaceae (Phlox Family)

Phlox divaricata (wild blue phlox) with Senecio aureus (golden ragwort).

In April and May the loose and lovely, not to mention fragrant, clusters of lavender blue flowers swaying gently on thin 12- to 18-inch stems are a classic staple of any woodland, wild or domestic. Low evergreen sterile shoots have small, elliptical leaves. The flowering shoots have oblong to lanceolate opposite leaves. Flower petals are sometimes notched.

Plant wild blue phlox in moist yet well-drained, neutral soil with lots of humus in light shade or part sun. It will root at leaf nodes and self-sow to create gentle drifts. Propagate by division, cuttings, and seed. Rabbits love phlox, so protection may be needed. Butterflies and even hummingbirds visit *Phlox* spp., and most species have cultivars. Statewide.

Phlox paniculata (summer phlox).

P. paniculata [pan-ik-yew-'lay-tuh], summer phlox, is the parent that inspired the garden phlox cultivars in nursery catalogs. Stems are 2 to 4 feet tall with lanceolate leaves and terminate in broad, rounded clusters of magenta, pinkish lavender, or white flowers from July to September. Rich, moist soil is important, and good air circulation will discourage powdery mildew. Light can vary from full sun to light shade, though some sun is best. Statewide.

P. glaberrima *(P. carolina)* **[gluh-'bair-ih-muh], smooth phlox,** is shorter and blooms earlier. Statewide.

P. maculata **[mak-yew-'lay-tuh], meadow phlox,** is also shorter with spotted stems and likes moist to wet soil. Eastern half of the state.

P. pilosa **[pih-'loh-suh], downy** or **prairie phlox,** likes drier soil and full sun and is common in prairie habitats. It spreads slowly and grows 1 to 2 feet tall with narrowly lanceolate leaves and bright pink flowers in May. It will tolerate some shade. Western half of the state.

P. stolonifera **[stoh-lah-'nih-feh-ruh], creeping phlox,** has nearly round leaves along runners that branch out to form a nice ground-cover. Clusters of lavender blue, pink, or white flowers 6 to 8 inches high bloom in April through June. Moist, humus-rich, moderately acid soil in part shade is best. Unaka Mountains.

Phlox pilosa 'Ozarkana' (downy phlox).

Physostegia virginiana *(Dracocephalum virginianum)*
False Dragonhead, Obedient Plant
[fy-sah-'steh-jee-uh vir-jih-nee-'ay-nuh]
Lamiaceae (Mint Family)

The 2- to 5-foot, square stem has opposite, lanceolate, serrated leaves. A tightly packed terminal spike of purplish rose flowers blooms in August and September. The blossoms resemble snapdragons and attract bees.

Moderately acid, moist soil in full sun is all this plant needs to go wild. False dragonhead can be aggressive; drier soil slows it down.

Physostegia virginiana (false dragonhead).

The white-flowered form and other cultivars are reported to be less greedy. The obedient common name refers to the individual flowers, which can be moved around and will retain the new position. Propagate by seed or cuttings. Middle and East Tennessee.

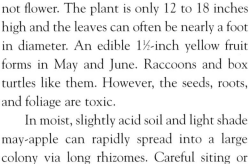

Podophyllum peltatum (may-apple).

Podophyllum peltatum
May-apple, Mandrake
[poh-dah-'fill-um pel-'tay-tum]
Berberidaceae (Barberry Family)

Two large, multilobed leaves emerge in April on a single stem and extend themselves like an umbrella to shield a nodding, waxy, white flower hiding below. Single-leaved stems do not flower. The plant is only 12 to 18 inches high and the leaves can often be nearly a foot in diameter. An edible 1½-inch yellow fruit forms in May and June. Raccoons and box turtles like them. However, the seeds, roots, and foliage are toxic.

In moist, slightly acid soil and light shade may-apple can rapidly spread into a large colony via long rhizomes. Careful siting or containment is advised. It will grow well in dry areas once established. Propagate by division in the fall. Statewide.

Polemonium reptans (Jacob's ladder).

Polemonium reptans
Jacob's Ladder, Greek Valerian
[poh-leh-'moh-nee-um 'rep-tanz]
Polemoniaceae (Phlox Family)

A mounding, foot-high tuft of pinnately compound leaves lined with 5 to 15 leaflets makes a fresh green backdrop for loosely branched, terminal clusters of light blue, bell-shaped flowers in April. The slightly fragrant flowers last well and, with sufficient moisture, the foliage remains attractive into summer. Fresh foliage may emerge in fall. Butterflies sip the nectar. Humus-rich, moist, neutral to slightly acid soil in light shade yields beautiful results. Propagate through division and seed. Lightly statewide, heavier on the Western Highland Rim.

Polygonatum biflorum
(P. commutatum, P. canaliculatum)
Solomon's Seal
[pah-lee-'gah-nuh-tum by-'flor-um]
(commonly pronounced pah-lih-gah-'nay-tum)
Liliaceae (Lily Family)

Polygonatum biflorum (Solomon's seal).

Little creamy white to greenish bells on slender stalks hang singly, in pairs, or in clusters from the leaf axils of 18- to 30-inch stems "forming a curve of singular grace," according to wildflower author Mrs. Dana. The alternate, oval to lanceolate leaves are parallel veined and virtually hide the bells drooping below in April and May as well as the blue black berries in late summer. In autumn the foliage turns a pleasing yellow. Statewide.

The botanical name *P. commutatum* is often listed as giant Solomon's seal, a plant with huge rhizomes and stems up to 6 feet tall. It is a tetraploid, a large form of the regular plant, with no botanical difference beyond size.

P. pubescens [pyew-'bes-ins], hairy Solomon's seal, is similar except for hairs along the veins of leaf undersides. East Tennessee.

Polygonatum biflorum—fruit (Solomon's seal).

Solomon's seal is adaptable but does best in moist, humus-rich soil that is moderately acid to near neutral in light shade. It can tolerate drought. Clumps enlarge slowly on thick creeping rhizomes. Propagate by division or seed.

Pontederia cordata (pickerelweed).

Pontederia cordata
Pickerelweed
[pon-teh-'dee-ree-uh kore-'day-tuh]
Pontederiaceae (Pickerelweed Family)

Amid a colony of glossy, heart-shaped leaves, numerous 2-foot stalks bear dense spikes of violet blue flowers and a lanceolate bract. It flowers throughout the summer and early fall. Pickerelweed likes shallow water and full sun, though it can take some shade. A good potted plant for backyard ponds, its potential for spreading should be considered in any natural pond setting. It occurs lightly statewide.

Porteranthus trifoliatus (Gillenia trifoliata)
Bowman's Root, Indian Physic
[por-ter-'an-thus try-foh-lee-'ay-tus]
Rosaceae (Rose Family)

Bowman's Root is a delightful and easy plant, 2 to 3 feet tall, with leaves divided into 3 narrow, toothed leaflets on slender, branched stems. In May and June the narrowly petaled white flowers spread loosely in terminal panicles. Five little seed capsules form within the reddish calyx. Foliage stays green and attractive throughout the summer and colors in the fall. Found naturally in upland woods, it prefers well-drained, moist to dry, moderately acid soil and high, light shade. A little sun is acceptable, particularly if the soil is moist. East Tennessee.

　　P. stipulatus (G. stipulata) [stih-pyew-'lay-tus], Indian physic or American ipecac, is very similar, appearing 5-leaved due to a pair of large leaflike stipules at the base of each trifoliate leaf. Its culture is similar; propagate either species by division in the spring or seed in the fall. East and Middle Tennessee, West Tennessee Uplands.

Kurt Emmanuele.

Porteranthus stipulatus (Indian physic).

Pycnanthemum incanum
Silverleaf Mountain Mint
[pik-'nan-the-mum in-'kay-num]
Lamiaceae (Mint Family)

A subtle plant, silverleaf mountain mint is not showy in the traditional sense, yet is still an attractive and desirable addition. Tiny, pale purple, spotted flowers are gathered in 1- to 2-inch clusters, which are paired over hairy, whitened upper leaves and leaf bracts at the tips of numerous branches. The square stems are white with downy hairs. The plant is 2 to 4 feet tall and aromatic.

Pycnanthemum incanum (silverleaf mountain mint).

   P. tenuifolium **[ten-yew-ih-'foh-lee-um], slender mountain mint,** is more compact at 18 to 30 inches. Thin stems are well branched and clothed in smooth, linear leaves for a fine texture. Tiny white flowers are packed into small, rounded heads, which are gathered in clusters at branch ends. Bees and butterflies like mountain mints.

   Both flower in July and August taking moist to dry, moderately to slightly acid soil in part shade. Fulfilling a role similar to *Artemesia*, *P. incanum*'s softly whitened greens shine against a dark background and can be used to blend more colorful contemporaries. Propagate by cuttings, division, or seed. Mountain mint is something of a misnomer as both species are found statewide.

Pycnanthemum tenuifolium (slender mountain mint).

Ratibida pinnata
Prairie or Gray-headed Coneflower
[ruh-'tih-bih-duh pih-'nay-tuh]
Asteraceae (Aster Family)

This 3- to 5-foot plant produces long-stemmed, large flowers with drooping yellow rays around elongated, grayish cones from June to August. The cones turn brown as the

Ratibida pinnata (prairie coneflower).

flowers age. Leaves are rough and pinnately divided. Its prairie heritage dictates rich, moist to dry, well-drained soil that is slightly acid to neutral in full sun. Parts of the plant have an anise fragrance. Propagate by seed. Scattered statewide.

Rhexia virginica
Virginia Meadow Beauty
['reks-ee-uh vir-'jin-ih-kuh]
Melastomataceae (Melastome Family)

Rhexia virginica (Virginia meadow beauty).

Inch-wide flowers of bright purplish rose with yellow orange stamens appear in the leaf axils along 4-sided or winged stems, 1 to 2 feet tall, in July. Leaves are lanceolate and in the fall turn red.

R. mariana [mair-ee-'ay-nuh], **Maryland meadow beauty,** often has pale rose pink to white flowers, no wings on the stems, and colony-forming rhizomes. Seed capsules are vase shaped.

Both meadow beauties like full sun to part shade and moist to boggy, moderately acid soil. They will take regular moisture, however, and even tolerate dryness. They naturalize well. Propagate through division, cuttings, or seed. Both *Rhexia* spp. are statewide, except for the Central Basin.

Rudbeckia fulgida
Perennial Black-eyed Susan
[rood-'bek-ee-uh 'ful-jih-duh]
Asteraceae (Aster Family)

Rudbeckia fulgida 'Goldstrum' (black-eyed Susan).

Growing 2 to 3 feet in height, *R. fulgida* produces a multitude of blossoms with deep yellow ray flowers and dark brown disk flowers in July and August. The leaves are rough, ovate, toothed, and primarily basal with a few stem leaves. Full sun in slightly acid, moist soil is all it needs. Divide offsets or plant seed to propagate. Cultivar 'Goldstrum' is widely available and excellent. *R. hirta,* ['her-tuh] **biennial black-eyed Susan,** is not as attractive or reliable as *R. fulgida* and can become a pest, though there are good cultivars.

R. laciniata [luh-sin-ee-'ay-tuh], **green-headed** or **cutleaf coneflower,** varies from 4 to 9 feet tall with large lobed leaves, greenish yellow disk flowers, and long, yellow ray flowers in July and August. It spreads by underground stems in moist soil yet tolerates dry soil in full sun to part shade. Other common names are tall coneflower and wild golden-glow.

R. triloba ['trih-lah-buh], **three-lobed** or **thin-leaved coneflower,** is a biennial growing 2 to 5 feet tall. Its leaves vary in shape, some elliptic and entire, others displaying the 3 lobes of its species name. The branched, bushy plant provides an open display of 1½-inch, yellow-rayed, dark-centered flowers in June and July. Though it can get a bit weedy seeding itself about, it is both drought and shade tolerant, and it is worth keeping a few around. It likes neutral to slightly alkaline soil. Butterflies visit the flowers, and birds eat the seeds. All *Rudbeckia* spp. can be found in Middle and East Tennesee, lightly in West Tennessee.

Rudbeckia triloba (three-lobed coneflower) with *Echinacea purpurea* (purple coneflower).

Ruellia humilis

Wild Petunia
[rue-'el-ee-uh 'hyew-mih-lis]
Acanthaceae (Acanthus Family)

Floppy, 1- to 2-foot, branching stems produce sessile leaves with tubular, violet blue flowers in the upper leaf axils. It blooms in May and June. Wild petunia needs a dry, well-drained

The Center for Field Biology, a Tennessee Center of Excellence at Austin Peay State University.

Ruellia caroliniensis (wild petunia).

soil that is slightly acid to neutral in full sun to part shade. Central Basin and Valley and Ridge.

R. caroliniensis [kair-ah-lih-nee-'in-sis] is a bit taller, with fewer branches and stemmed leaves. It also likes dry soil but will grow in shadier, moister areas. Neither species is very floriferous. Propagate through division, seed, and stem cuttings. Statewide.

Sabatia angularis
Rose-pink
[suh-'bay-shuh ang-yuh-'lay-ris]
Gentianaceae (Gentian Family)

Rose-pink is a biennial that produces an eye-popping cluster of fragrant, bright pink flowers in July and August. It grows about 2 feet tall with a 4-angled stem, opposite clasping leaves, and several flowering branches. Each flower is centered with a greenish yellow, star-shaped eye outlined in red. Growing beautifully along roadsides, it thrives in full sun to part shade and moist or dry, slightly acid soil and will most likely form self-sustaining populations in an open, reliably moist area. Sow seeds where the plants are to grow. Statewide, lightly in West Tennessee.

George W. Hornal.

Sabatia angularis (rose-pink).

Sagittaria latifolia
Arrowhead, Duck Potato
[saj-ih-'tay-ree-uh lat-ih-'foh-lee-uh]
Alismataceae (Water Plantain Family)

Each arrowhead-shaped leaf emerges from the water on a long petiole or leaf stem. From July to September leafless stalks are topped by 3-petaled white male flowers in widely spaced whorls of 3. Female flowers are lower on the stem. Its height is usually 1 to 2½ feet

Sagittaria latifolia (arrowhead).

but can get up to 4 or 5 feet. Growing in shallow water in full sun to part shade, it spreads and colonizes. Waterfowl and snapping turtles feed off this plant, thus keeping it in check. Statewide.

Sanguinaria canadensis
Bloodroot
[sang-gwin-'nay-ree-uh kan-uh-'den-sis]
Papaveraceae (Poppy Family)

Sanguinaria canadensis (bloodroot).

Anticipating the mercurial temperament of spring, bloodroot arrives clothed in layers. Newly emerged tips are protected by papery bracts, which open to allow the tightly curled leaf to continue the journey. Next, to quote Mrs. Dana's poetic description from *How to Know the Wild Flowers*, "When the perils of the way are passed and a safe height is reached, this pale, deeply lobed leaf resigns its precious charge and gradually unfolds itself." The "precious charge" is the flower bud which has been shielded within this "silvery-green leaf-cloak" (*Nature's Garden* author, Neltje Blanchan). Positioned atop its own 6- to 8-inch leafless stalk, a white flower of 8 to 16 petals centered with a tuft of yellow stamens, graces the days of late March or early April but for a short while. To quote Mrs. Dana again, "Its very transitoriness enhances its charm." The leaves are palmately lobed and continue to develop after flowering.

Bloodroot loves well-drained, moist soils that are rich with humus and slightly acid to neutral. Gentle spring sun is acceptable, but protection from the summer sun is a must. In a suitable location the unusual leaves last all summer, but will die down in a dry spell. This could affect the next year's bloom if it occurs too early. Guard against pushy neighbors; bloodroot cannot handle competition. To propagate, divide the thick horizontal rootstock in the fall, or sow seeds when they ripen in June. It can self-sow in good locations. Roots produce a red juice, and flowers attract early bees. Primarily Middle and East Tennessee.

Saururus cernuus
Lizard's Tail
[saw-'rue-rus 'sir-new-us]
Saururaceae (Lizard's Tail Family)

The 2- to 5-foot stems of lizard's tail produce numerous very small white flowers packed in a slender raceme up to 12 inches long. The tip of the raceme crooks into the shape of its common name. The flowers have no petals or sepals, just stamens and a pistil. It blooms throughout the summer, June to August, and is fragrant. Heart-shaped, alternate leaves are dark green and palmately veined.

Lizard's tail grows from creeping rhizomes in wet, marshy areas or shallow water. Its ability to stabilize areas from erosion also means it can be invasive, so containers might be needed in smaller areas. It is adaptable to a wide range of soil pH and shines in light shade. In shallow water it can take full sun. Propagate by division, cuttings, or seed. Statewide, especially West Tennessee.

Saxifraga virginiensis
Early Saxifrage
[sax-'if-ruh-guh vir-jih-nee-'in-sis]
Saxifragaceae (Saxifrage Family)

A small rosette of thick, obovate leaves sends up 1 or more stocky, hairy, 3- to 8-inch stems that branch into little clusters of tiny, starred,

Saururus cernuus (lizard's tail).

George W. Hornal.

white flowers in early April. The stems elongate to a foot or more as the fragrant flowers splay out on their branches.

The generic name means rock breaker. Roots keep cool by burrowing into the cracks and fissures of the rocky hillsides in its native habitat. Good drainage is important, and early saxifrage seems to prefer a site more moist than dry in part sun to light shade. Soil acidity can vary some, but closer to neutral is best. Propagate by seed or division. Middle Tennessee.

Saxifraga virginiensis (early saxifrage).

Scutellaria incana
Downy Skullcap
[skoo-teh-'lay-ree-uh in-'kay-nuh]
Lamiaceae (Mint Family)

The upper portions of this plant are velvety with whitish hairs. In July several short racemes cluster in a tuft at the top of 2- to 3-foot stems. Each raceme is lined with showy, lavender blue flowers. The blossoms are lipped; the upper lip is shaped like a little helmet. Ovate, toothed leaves are opposite. Skullcap likes moist to dry soil that is slightly acid to neutral in part sun to light shade. Statewide.

S. integrifolia **[in-teh-grih-'foh-lee-uh]**, **large-flowered skullcap**, is shorter (1 to 2 feet) with bigger flowers appearing earlier on short terminal and axillary racemes. Leaves are lanceolate, sessile, and entire. It will take more sun. Propagate by seed, cuttings, or division. Eastern half of the state.

Scutellaria incana (downy skullcap).

Sedum ternatum (woodland stonecrop).

Sedum pulchellum (lime stonecrop).

Senecio aureus (golden ragwort).

Sedum ternatum
Woodland Stonecrop
['see-dum ter-'nay-tum]
Crassulaceae (Stonecrop Family)

Woodland stonecrop is a prostrate creeper that sends out sterile shoots with whorls of small, round to oval, fleshy leaves and flowering shoots with narrow, opposite leaves. At the top of the flowering shoots, horizontal branches (usually 3) are lined with small, white, starry flowers in May and June. Overall height is less than 6 inches. As the common name implies, this little succulent grows in the woods on thin, dry soils over limestone and does best in well-drained, neutral to slightly alkaline soil and part sun to light shade. It is very shallow rooted and may be planted among deeper rooted spring ephemerals. Propagate by division, cuttings, or seed. It will self-sow. Middle and East Tennessee.

S. *pulchellum* [pul-'kell-um], lime or pink stonecrop, is a low-growing annual with bluish, cylindrical leaves and rosy purple blossoms lining the horizontal flowering branches in May. It thrives in the full sun and harsh conditions of the cedar glades and readily self-sows. Middle Tennessee.

Senecio aureus
Golden Ragwort
[seh-'nee-see-oh 'aw-ree-us]
Asteraceae (Aster Family)

The leaves on this early blooming composite vary dramatically as you move up the 1- to 3-foot stem. Long-petioled basal leaves are heart shaped and round toothed. The stem leaves are so deeply lobed as to appear nearly pinnate, becoming smaller and more incised near the flattened, terminal cluster of slightly fragrant, golden yellow flowers. It blooms in April and

May. The seeds have long silky hairs. Summer heat and sun can stress the foliage, but in a suitable spot it will spread happily. Plant in moist, fertile, slightly acid soil in light shade to part sun.

S. *obovatus* [oh-bah-'vay-tus], round-leaved ragwort, is very similar and prefers a more alkaline soil. Its peak bloom is a couple of weeks after golden ragwort. Flower nectar draws butterflies. Both *Senecio* spp. are in Middle and East Tennessee.

Silene virginica
Fire Pink
[sih-'lee-nee vir-'jin-ih-kuh]
Caryophyllaceae (Pink Family)

Loose, sparse clusters of rich crimson flowers bloom over a long time from April to June. Each of the 5 narrow, widely spread petals is notched. The leaves are narrow, elliptic, and mostly basal with a few smaller opposite leaves dotting weak 1- to 2-foot stems. Sticky hairs that cover the stem and calyx of *Silene* spp. prompted the common name, catchfly. Fire pink does well in moist to dry, well-drained, moderately acid soil that is not too rich and part shade to light shade. Short-lived, it reseeds itself to the delight of hummingbirds and butterflies. There is a pink variety. Propagate by cuttings or seed. Statewide.

Silene virginica (fire pink).

S. *stellata* [steh-'lay-tuh], starry campion, is another garden worthy species with clusters of white, fringed flowers. Flowers appear in the upper leaf axils on stems 2 to 3 feet tall. Ovate leaves are in whorls of 4. Cultural requirements are similar to fire pink. Though not as showy, it blooms through the summer from June to September and tolerates drought. Statewide.

Silene stellata (starry campion).

Silphium perfoliatum (cup-plant).

Silphium perfoliatum
Cup-plant
['sil-fee-um per-foh-lee-'ay-tum]
Asteraceae (Aster Family)

Cup-plant is a tall prairie species with stout, square stems 5 to 8 feet tall. Large rough, paired leaves join at the base to surround the stem. The upper leaf pairs form a depression that, cuplike, holds rain water. Stems branch near the top displaying several 2- to 3-inch, yellow-rayed flowers in July and August. Cup-plant likes the moist, rich soil of low ground and meadows in full sun to part shade. Once established, drier soil is not a problem. Birds eat the seeds. Propagate by seed. Western half of the state.

Sisyrinchium angustifolium (blue-eyed grass).

Sisyrinchium angustifolium
Blue-eyed Grass
[sis-ih-'rin-kee-um an-gus-tih-'foh-lee-um]
Iridaceae (Iris Family)

Linear blue green leaves form a grasslike tuft of foliage 6 to 10 inches in height. In May and June slightly taller flat stems produce loose clusters of yellow-eyed, violet blue flowers. Each flower lasts only a few hours. Little seedpods are round and green. Blue-eyed grass grows in well-drained, moist to dry, moderately acid to nearly neutral soil in full sun to part shade. In rich soil and shade, the plants become floppy. They will be more attractive in average to somewhat poor soil and full sun. Since individual plants are not very showy, it is best to plant in drifts, which is made easier by the fact that blue-eyed grass self-sows readily and the clumps benefit from periodic division, spring or fall. Statewide.

S. albidum ['al-bih-dum] is a pale blue to white flowered species. Middle and East Tennessee.

Smilacina racemosa
(Maianthemum racemosum)
False Solomon's Seal
[smy-luh-'sy-nuh ray-sih-'moh-suh]
Liliaceae (Lily Family)

The arching 1- to 3-foot stem and alternate, oblong leaves with parallel veins do bear a striking resemblance to Solomon's seal (*Polygonatum biflorum*). The flowers of the 2 plants, however, could hardly be more dissimilar. *S. racemosa* forms a creamy plume of tiny starry flowers on dense terminal panicles that glow in wooded settings in May. After flowering the plant continues its show with a revolving palette of color on the little berries—from green to whitish with red speckles to red with purple speckles. The stem plots a zigzag course from leaf to leaf. False Solomon's seal enjoys rich, moist, humusy soil that is moderately acid in light shade, yet can tolerate drought. Though not the least aggressive, it spreads by rhizomes and will self-seed. Propagate by division. Statewide.

Smilacina racemosa (false Solomon's seal).

Smilacina racemosa—fruit (false Solomon's seal).

Solidago spp.
Goldenrod
[sah-lih-'day-go]
Asteraceae (Aster Family)

There are many different species of goldenrod native to North America lighting up meadows, roadsides, and even shady woodlands from early summer to late fall and displaying a tantalizing variability in height, leaf, stem, and flower appearance. Several species easily

Solidago caesia (blue-stemmed goldenrod).

Solidago flexicaulis (zigzag goldenrod).

Solidago nemoralis (gray goldenrod).

transition to the home garden. Most adapt to any well-drained soil, moist or dry, rich or poor, with a moderately to slightly acid pH. Birds enjoy the seeds; butterflies, bees, and other insects visit; and everyone knows goldenrod is not responsible for allergies. Propagate *Solidago* spp. by division, seed, or cuttings.

S. caesia ['see-zee-uh], blue-stemmed or wreath goldenrod, has branched stems 2 to 3 feet tall with a bluish cast. Clusters of tiny golden flowers bloom in the leaf axils all along the stem and its branchlets in September and October. Leaves are narrowly lance shaped. Blue-stemmed goldenrod is clumping in habit and needs moist, well-drained soil and part sun to light shade. Middle and East Tennessee, Mississippi River Valley.

S. canadensis (S. altissima) [kan-uh-'den-sis], Canada goldenrod, varies from 3 to 6 feet tall with a hairy stem and lance-shaped, toothed leaves. Large, dense, recurved, pyramidal sprays of yellow flowers bloom in September and October in dry soil and full sun. It is recommended for large meadow areas only as it spreads aggressively. Statewide.

S. flexicaulis [fleks-ih-'kaw-lis], zigzag goldenrod, has slightly angled stems that zigzag between the ovate, sharply toothed and pointed leaves. It is 1 to 3 feet tall with clusters of flowers in the leaf axils from late August through September. This goldenrod also likes the rich, moist to dry soil of woodlands, performing well in part sun to medium shade. East Tennessee, northern Middle Tennessee.

S. nemoralis [neh-mah-'ray-lis], gray goldenrod, features a basal clump of gray green, lanceolate leaves and a downy stem 2 to 3 feet tall. One-sided panicles of deep, yellow flowers open in dry soil and part shade in

August and September. It tolerates poor, lean soil. Statewide.

S. odora [ah-'dore-uh], **sweet goldenrod,** is a good garden choice, growing in a clump 2 to 5 feet tall. Linear leaves are dotted and anise scented. The arching terminal panicle has yellow flowers perched in a row atop each branchlet in September and October. Give it moist, well-drained, moderately acid soil and full sun to part shade. Statewide.

S. rugosa [ruh-'goh-suh], **wrinkle-leaved** or **rough-stemmed goldenrod,** features elliptic, sharply toothed, wrinkled leaves on a hairy stem and a curving panicle of branchlets lined with yellow florets in September and October. It grows 2 to 5 feet tall and takes wet or dry soil in full sun to part shade. Wrinkle-leaved goldenrod spreads on rhizomes, but drier soil keeps it in check. Statewide.

S. speciosa [speh-see-'oh-suh], **showy goldenrod,** has a reddish stem with smooth, broadly oval, toothed leaves and, as its name implies, a dense eye-catching panicle of yellow blooms in August and September. It grows 3 to 7 feet tall in full sun and moist soil. Eastern half of the state.

S. sphacelata [spass-eh-'lay-tuh], **false** or **short-pappus goldenrod** is a 2-foot plant with arching stems and narrow wands of yellow flowers above a basal rosette of broadly heart-shaped leaves. It blooms in September and October. Dwarf cultivar 'Golden Fleece' tops out at 18 inches and works well as a groundcover in part shade and rocky, moist, neutral soil. Middle and East Tennessee.

S. ulmifolia [ulm-ih-'foh-lee-uh], **elm-leaved goldenrod,** has dark green, lanceolate, toothed leaves tapering to a point on smooth stems 1 to 4 feet tall. Widely

Solidago odora (sweet goldenrod).

Solidago rugosa (wrinkle-leaved goldenrod).

Solidago speciosa (showy goldenrod).

Solidago sphacelata (false goldenrod).

branched, slender spires of deep yellow flow-ers bloom in dry soil and part sun in August and September. Statewide.

Spigelia marilandica
Indian Pink
[spy-'jee-lee-uh mair-ih-'lan-dih-kuh]
Loganiaceae (Logania Family)

Spigelia marilandica (Indian pink).

This beautiful native produces dense clumps of stems 12 to 24 inches high with pairs of opposite, ovate leaves. In May and June the plant is covered with terminal, 1-sided spikes of deep red to scarlet, tube-shaped flowers. The lobed tips of each blossom flare open to reveal a bright yellow interior. Attractive to hummingbirds, each flower is 2 inches in length, and each spike can have up to a dozen blooms. Indian pink likes rich, moist, slightly acid to neutral soil in part sun to light shade, growing naturally at the edges of open decid-uous woods. Propagate by seed or cuttings. Statewide, lightly in West Tennessee.

Stellaria pubera
Star Chickweed
[steh-'lay-ree-uh pyew-'ber-uh]
Caryophyllaceae (Pink Family)

Stellaria pubera (star chickweed).

Star chickweed is a perennial that forms a weak-stemmed, low carpet of opposite, light green, elliptic leaves with loose clusters of starry white flowers in the upper axils. The apparent 10 narrow petals of the flower are actually 5 deeply-cleft petals. It blooms from March to May.

    This little plant is at home in moist yet well-drained, slightly acid soil in medium shade. Do not let the chickweed name turn you off: this well-behaved cousin of the com-mon lawn-and-garden pest knows its place and is delightful enough to earn a spot in any woodland garden. It spreads through the leaf mold with thin white runners to form a pleasing groundcover yet is easily pinched back. Many birds eat the seeds. Propagate by seed or division. Middle and East Tennessee.

Stokesia laevis
Stokes' Aster
[stoh-'kee-see-uh 'lee-vis]
   (also pronounced 'stokes-ee-uh)
Asteraceae (Aster Family)

Stokes' aster has evergreen basal foliage that is lance shaped with a white, central vein. Stems branch out 12 to 18 inches high with large, showy flower heads of light blue ray flowers in late spring and early summer. It likes moist, moderately acid soil and full sun, tolerating the heat and humidity of the south. There are cultivars based on flower color. Propagate by seed, root cuttings, or division; it will self-sow. Stokes' aster is not native to Tennessee. Its natural range is in the southern coastal plain states, yet it is a popular garden flower that grows well here.

Stokesia laevis (Stokes' aster).

Stylophorum diphyllum
Wood or Celandine Poppy
[sty-'lah-fah-rum dy-'fill-um]
Papaveraceae (Poppy Family)

Wood poppies form leafy clumps of stems 12 to 18 inches tall. Loose clusters of hairy buds open into bright yellow, 2-inch flowers through April and May. Fuzzy drooping seedpods develop. Leaves are grayish green and pinnately cut into several lobes.

The plants appreciate a rich, moist soil with lots of humus that is slightly acid and lightly shaded by high trees. Propagate by

Stylophorum diphyllum (wood poppy).

division, root cuttings, or seed sown fresh. They readily self-sow, and if germination gets out of hand, just snip off the large seedpods before they open. Middle Tennessee, Valley and Ridge.

Thalictrum revolutum (waxy-leaf meadow rue).

Thalictrum dioicum (early meadow rue).

Thalictrum revolutum
Waxy-leaf Meadow Rue
[thuh-'lik-trum reh-vah-'lew-tum]
Ranunculaceae (Buttercup Family)

Meadow rues produce a clump of bluish green compound leaves whose leaflets are small ovals with round-lobed tips. Branched stems grow 2 to 3 feet high and display hanging clusters of feathery, whitish flowers in May. The flowers are really just showy stamens. Dry soil, moderate to slightly acid, in light shade to part sun works best for this meadow rue. Propagate by seed or division of offsets.

T. dioicum [dy-oh-'eye-kum] **early meadow rue**, blooms in April and May in moist, humusy soil and light shade. It is dioecious, and male plants have the showiest bloom with drooping tufts of yellow stamens on branching stems that rise 12 to 30 inches. Female plants have rather inconspicuous greenish purple pistils. Early meadow rue is often grown simply for its ferny foliage.

T. pubescens (T. polygamum) [pyew-'bes-enz], **tall meadow rue**, can grow up to 7 feet in full sun to part shade and wet soil and is very showy with panicles of white blooms in June or July. It will adapt to regular garden moisture. All *Thalictrum* spp. occur in Middle and East Tennessee.

Thalictrum thalictroides
(Anemonella thalictroides)
Rue Anemone
[thuh-'lik-trum thuh-lik-troh-'eye-deez]
Ranunculaceae (Buttercup Family)

The dainty and fragile appearance of this plant belies the reality of its robust constitution. It is just 3 to 8 inches tall on slender and wiry stems. The dark green, compound foliage features 3 round to oval leaflets, lobed like meadow rue. Leaves are grouped in sets of 3 whorled beneath a loose cluster of white flowers with 5 to 7 petals in March and April. It can produce sporadic bloom into the summer. Small tubers or tuberous roots grow in rich, slightly acid, moist to dry soil that is well drained. It does well in filtered spring sun and light to medium shade in summer. Propagate by division or seed; it will self-sow. There are cultivars available. Middle and East Tennessee.

Thalictrum thalictroides (rue anemone).

Thermopsis villosa (T. caroliniana)
Carolina Bushpea
[ther-'mop-sis vih-'loh-suh]
Fabaceae (Pea Family)

Long-lived and stately, Carolina bushpea grows into a large clump of 3- to 5-foot stems clothed in trifoliate leaves and topped by a long spire of yellow flowers in May. Flat seedpods fold up close to the stem. In moist, moderately acid, rich soil and full sun, Carolina bushpea will become a beautiful plant. Give it room to grow (space 2½ feet). Propagate by seed or division. Lightly in Middle and East Tennessee.

Thermopsis villosa (Carolina bushpea).

Tiarella cordifolia var. collina
(foamflower).

Tiarella cordifolia

Foamflower, False Miterwort
[tee-uh-'reh-luh cor-dih-'foh-lee-uh]
Saxifragaceae (Saxifrage Family)

Foamflower is an evergreen groundcover with hairy, maple-shaped, lobed, and toothed leaves that so strongly resembles its cousin, *Mitella diphylla,* miterwort, that another common name is false miterwort. It sends up 6- to 12-inch leafless scapes starred with feathery white flowers and pinkish red anthers from April until June and spreads by runners. Moist, humusy soil, moderately to slightly acid and well drained, is best. A little spring sun should give way to light summer shade.

T. cordifolia var. *collina* **[cah-'ly-nuh]** (*T. wherryi* **['wheh-ree-eye])** grows in a clump and does not produce runners. It is recommended as more floriferous with pinkish buds and burgundy-blushed foliage to enhance its appearance. Propagate by division. It self-sows. There are cultivars. Middle and East Tennessee.

Tradescantia virginiana (spiderwort).

Tradescantia virginiana

Spiderwort
[trad-es-'kan-tee-uh vir-jih-nee-'ay-nuh]
Commelinaceae (Spiderwort Family)

Spiderwort's 3-petaled, purplish blue flowers bloom in clusters 1 to 2 feet high from April through July. Each flower lasts a single day. There are white, pink, purple, and bicolor cultivars. Long, linear, green leaves clasp the thick, round stalk and arch over. Spiderwort likes part to light shade in average (not too rich), well-drained, moist to dry soil that is moderately acid. If the foliage gets a bit ratty, cut it back; it may rebloom. It can self-sow prolifically, but pulls or transplants easily to keep it in check. Clumps may be divided. Valley and Ridge, Western Highland Rim.

Trillium spp.
Trillium, Toadshade, Wake-robin
['trih-lee-um]
Liliaceae (Lily Family)

Trillium cuneatum (toadshade).

From earliest spring to summer the woodlands are graced with a variety of these low-growing, 3-leaved plants. They dot the landscape beneath deciduous trees to take advantage of the early light and moisture that dissipates as the season progresses. Trilliums feature 3 leaves whorled on a stem. A flower with 3 petals, 3 sepals, 6 stamens, and a 3-parted pistil emerges from the center of the leaf whorl. Sometimes the flower is stalked and erect, sometimes nodding; sometimes it is stalkless, sitting directly on top of the leaves. Height varies from 3 to 16 inches. A rather large, 6-sided globular berry is produced in midsummer.

Trilliums love moist, slightly acid to neutral, humus-rich soil with good drainage and deciduous shade. Sufficient soil moisture will keep the foliage from going dormant too soon and possibly affecting the plant's ability to survive. After the plant has ripened in July or August, the tuber may be cut in half. Put damp sphagnum moss on the cut ends and replant in moist humus. If kept moist and fertilized, the portion of the tuber without the growing tip will generate new growth tips, which in a couple of years may be separated. These new plants should bloom in another couple of years. Trilliums propagated by seed (young seedlings have a single ovate leaf)

Trillium luteum (yellow trillium).

Trillium recurvatum (prairie trillium).

Trillium sessile (sessile toadshade).

Trillium stamineum (twisted-petal trillium).

can require 5 years or more to reach blooming size. Plant tubers about 4 to 6 inches deep.

T. cuneatum [kyew-nee-'ay-tum], toad-shade, sweet little Betsy, or whippoorwill flower, has a stalkless flower seated in the midst of the whorled leaves. Flower petals are very narrow, erect, and dark red or maroon. The broadly ovate leaves are heavily mottled with dark green or maroon. Contrary to the impression given by one common name, sweet little Betsy, the flower's perfume is sometimes compared with the sickly sweet odor of rotting meat. It is only detectable if you get your nose right in it, and many people do not find the flower's odor nearly as offensive as the real thing. It blooms in March and April. Middle and East Tennessee.

T. luteum ['lew-tee-um], yellow trillium, features mottled leaves and a yellow, narrow-petaled, erect, stalkless flower. It has a slight lemon fragrance and blooms in April and May. East Tennessee.

T. recurvatum [ree-kur-'vay-tum], prairie trillium, has a stalkless maroon flower with strongly recurved sepals hanging below the leaves. Flower petals are wide in the middle and narrow to a point at each end. Leaves are slightly mottled and narrow at the base to a petiole. It blooms in April. Statewide.

T. sessile ['ses-ih-lee], sessile toadshade, is very similar to *T. cuneatum* though generally smaller with less markings on the leaves. There are other minor botanical differences. Middle Tennessee.

T. stamineum [stuh-'min-ee-um], twisted-petal trillium, also has a stalkless maroon flower whose narrow petals flare out horizon-tally with a 90 degree twist in the middle leaving the stamens and pistil exposed. Leaves are broad and vaguely mottled. Western Highland Rim.

T. catesbaei ['kates-bee-eye], **Catesby's** or **nodding rose trillium**, is a beautifully graceful plant rising to 16 inches with upward arching, petioled, green leaves exposing a stalked white, pink, or rose-colored bloom nodding below. Petals, sepals, and yellow anthers are prominently recurved; petals are ruffled. It likes moderately acid soil. East Tennessee.

T. erectum [eh-'reck-tum], **red** or **purple trillium**, has broadly ovate leaves and a stalked, maroon flower in May with narrow, flaring petals that expose the dark ovary. Sometimes the flower is white, and to a lesser extent, pink or cream. It often has a faint unpleasant odor, which is the source of another common name, stinking Benjamin. This trillium prefers moderately acid soil. Unaka Mountains.

T. flexipes (T. gleasonii) ['fleks-ih-peez], **drooping white** or **bent trillium**, grows to a height of 16 inches or more. Blooming in April, the stalked white flower is large with creamy white anthers and is sometimes held erect above the leaves, sometimes nodding below. The leaves are very broad and solid green. Northwestern Middle Tennessee.

T. grandiflorum [gran-dih-'flor-um], **large-flowered** or **great trillium**, features a pure white, stalked flower with yellow anthers above clear, lighter green leaves. As the flower ages it usually takes on a rose color, and the petals are often crimped. Large-flowered trillium blooms in April. Eastern half of the state.

T. sulcatum [sul-'kay-tum], **Barksdale's trillium**, is very similar to the red trillium, *T. erectum*. However, its petals are ovate and recurve only at the tips, thereby concealing the dark ovary. It blooms in April and is

Trillium catesbaei (Catesby's trillium).

Trillium erectum (red trillium).

Trillium flexipes (drooping white trillium).

Trillium grandiflorum (large-flowered trillium).

often found in a wide variety of petal colors, which earns it the additional common name of rainbow wake-robin. Eastern Highland Rim and Cumberland Plateau.

Triodanis perfoliata (Specularia perfoliata)
Venus' Looking-glass
[try-'od-uh-nis per-foh-lee-'ay-tuh]
Campanulaceae (Bellflower Family)

An annual blooming in May and June, this bellflower is 6 to 18 inches tall. The square stem is lined with clasping, alternate leaves that are short and broadly ovoid in shape. Violet blue, bell-shaped flowers are tucked into each leaf axil. It likes dry soil in full sun to part shade and produces shiny black seeds. Statewide.

George W. Hornal.

Triodanis perfoliata (Venus' looking-glass).

Typha angustifolia
Narrow-leaved Cattail
['ty-fuh an-gus-tih-'foh-lee-uh]
Typhaceae (Cattail Family)

Cattails have tall, grasslike basal foliage that is dull gray green in color. Flower stalks are topped by dense brown spikes of male and female flowers in May and June. The spikes persist as brown, downy seeds throughout the growing season. The male flower spike is slender and usually separated from the thicker female spike below by a small section of bare stem. It grows from 3 to 6 feet tall. Cattails grow in shallow water and increase by creeping rootstocks and self-sown seeds. The narrow-leaved cattail is best suited to a large pond and should be contained in large pots. While not as vigorous as the **common cattail**, *T. latifolia* **[lat-ih-'foh-lee-uh]**, it can

Typha latifolia (common cattail).

still take over. Cattails like full to part sun, and *T. angustifolia* prefers alkaline soil. These plants provide cover and nesting materials for many wetland birds. Scattered statewide.

Uvularia grandiflora
Great Merrybells, Large-flowered Bellwort
[oo-view-'lay-ree-uh gran-dih-'flor-uh]
Liliaceae (Lily Family)

The foliage of great merrybells provides as much interest as the flowers. The bases of the clean, green leaves surround the stem, which appears to pierce each leaf. The stem forks, and from 1 drooping tip dangles a pendant yellow flower 1 to 2 inches long with twisty petals in April and May. A 3-cornered fruit capsule follows. Clumps grow from a thin rhizome and reach a height of 12 to 18 inches. Great merrybells likes neutral to slightly alkaline soil, rich with humus, and part sun to light shade.

Uvularia perfoliata (perfoliate bellwort).

   U. perfoliata [per-foh-lee-'ay-tuh] **perfoliate bellwort** or **merrybells**, is quite similar though a bit shorter and prefers a slightly acid soil.

   U. sessilifolia [seh-sih-lih-'foh-lee-uh], **wild oats**, is a dainty plant under a foot tall with creamy, pale yellow flowers and leaves that clasp the stem.

   Since the foliage of *Uvularia* spp. looks good all season, they are a good choice to interplant with those that die down early, such as *Mertensia*. Propagate by division or seed. All *Uvularia* spp. are statewide, lightly in West Tennessee.

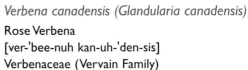

Verbena canadensis (rose verbena).

Verbena canadensis (Glandularia canadensis)
Rose Verbena
[ver-'bee-nuh kan-uh-'den-sis]
Verbenaceae (Vervain Family)

This is a low-growing plant with trailing stems and clusters of small flowers with notched petals. The flowers are often found in various shades of blue, pink, lavender, and white from mid-spring through the summer. The leaves are opposite, pinnately lobed, and toothed. Deadheading encourages a longer period of bloom. Bees and butterflies vie for the nectar, and butterflies use it as a larval food.

Rose verbena is easily grown in areas that pickier plants would refuse, preferring dry, sandy, lean soil that is well drained and in full sun. Pampered with rich garden soil, it can spread quickly. There are numerous cultivars. Propagate by cuttings, seed, and division. It grows especially well in the Central Basin.

Vernonia gigantea (tall ironweed).

Vernonia gigantea (V. altissima)
Tall Ironweed
[ver-'noh-nee-uh jy-gan-'tee-uh]
Asteraceae (Aster Family)

Reaching 7 feet in height, ironweed forms a clump of stems alternately lined with long, lanceolate, dark green leaves that are toothed and downy underneath. Stems terminate in a large, loose cluster of rich red purple disk flowers rising from the upper leaf axils to create a broad cyme in August and September. Ironweed provides food for butterflies in both adult and larval stages. Moist to wet meadows are the natural habitat, but ironweed adapts well to a regular garden in full sun or part shade with moderately acid soil. Propagate by seed or cuttings. It can self-sow. Cut it back early in the summer to reduce the height. Statewide.

V. noveboracensis [noh-veh-bore-uh-'sen-sis], **New York ironweed,** with larger flowers and an often shorter stature, has a native range that is more coastal. Lightly in East Tennessee.

Veronicastrum virginicum
Culver's Root
[veh-ron-ih-'kas-trum vir-'jin-ih-kum]
Scrophulariaceae (Figwort Family)

Veronicastrum virginicum (culver's root).

Culver's root is a stately plant 4 to 6 feet tall with dark green, lance-shaped, toothed leaves in whorls around the stem. Several long, slender spires of densely packed white flowers rise from the top leaf whorls between June and August. The flowers sometimes carry a blue or pink tinge.

Found naturally in moist meadows, culver's root takes well to the garden if given an extra drink during dry spells. It prefers full sun but will tolerate some shade in moderately acid soil. Propagate by seed, division, or cuttings. Scattered statewide, especially the Western Highland Rim.

Viola spp.
Violet
['vy-oh-luh]
   (commonly pronounced vee-'oh-luh)
Violaceae (Violet Family)

Everyone is familiar with the common blue violet, *V. papilionacea* (*V. sororia)*, and its associate the Confederate violet, *V. priceana.* Their ubiquitous presence in lawns and gardens may be attributed to the production of cleistogamous flowers, which resemble closed flower buds but are in reality 3-parted seedpods that spill forth a quantity of self-fertilized seed. However, there are other native violets that one might actually desire in a native or woodland garden.

Most violets prefer cool shade, but can handle more sun if there is sufficient moisture. Neutral to slightly acid soil in a rich deciduous setting is best. All will self-sow. They can blend well around other plants and make a nice groundcover. Some violets produce flowers and leaves each on its own independent stem directly from the roots or tubers below ground; others produce tall stems clad with alternate leaves, in addition to some basal foliage. On these leafy stems the flowers emerge from the upper leaf axils. Violet blossoms make tasty candy, jam, jelly, syrup, and wine. Edible leaves are rich in vitamins A and C. The flower juice is also a quick pH test, turning red when exposed to an acid, green for an alkali. Violets provide larval food for butterflies.

V. canadensis [kan-uh-'den-sis], **Canada violet,** and *V. blanda* ['blan-duh], **sweet white violet,** prefer cooler temperatures and higher elevations. *V. canadensis* has a leafy stem a foot or so tall with heart-shaped, pointed leaves and white flowers with a yellow eye and purple veins. Backs of the petals are often tinted with a purplish blush. It blooms over a long period from April to July. *V. blanda* is a charming miniature, offering tiny white flowers with purple veins and a sweet scent on 3- to 5-inch, leafy stems in April. It is cleistogamous and likes low, wet areas. Both are found in the eastern half of the state.

V. palmata (V. triloba) [pol-'may-tuh], **early blue** or **wood violet,** and *V. cucullata* [kuh-kyew-'lay-tuh], **marsh blue violet,** flower on

Kurt Emmanuele.

Viola canadensis (Canada violet).

stems rising directly from the tuber, have purple blossoms, and produce cleistogamous flowers. The first leaves of *V. palmata* are heart shaped; subsequent ones vary from 3 lobed to palmate. It blooms in April. *V. cucullata* has rounder leaves, blooms in May, and loves wet places. Both are found statewide.

V. pedata [peh-'day-tuh], birdfoot violet, breaks most all the rules that apply to others of its kind. Springing directly from fleshy roots, the leaves are deeply lobed into several linear segments that are often variously toothed. The lovely flowers are large (1 to 1½ inches across) and pansylike in purple or light lilac. A bicolored variety is deep velvety purple on the 2 upper petals and lighter lilac on the 3 lower petals. It blooms in April or May and can rebloom later in the season. Do not pick the blossoms as this species does not produce cleistogamous flowers. Birdfoot violet needs well-drained, dry, sandy, lean (not fertile), moderately acid soil in full sun. In the wild it grows happily perched in thin, poor soil atop rocky ledges and can be difficult to successfully establish in a garden. Middle and East Tennessee.

V. pubescens [pyew-'bes-enz], downy yellow violet, has a leafy stem, 4 to 10 inches high, blooming in April and May. Downy seedpods droop coyly over the stem leaves. Downy yellow violet often has hairy leaves and stems, but this trait can vary. Smoother plants are sometimes called *V. pensylvanica* [pen-sil-'van-ih-kuh], smooth yellow violet, but are simply a less hairy *V. pubescens*. Sources do not mention cleistogamous flowers. Statewide.

Viola palmata (early blue violet).

Viola pedata (birdfoot violet).

Scott C. Gunn, Division of Natural Heritage, Tennessee Department of Environment and Conservation.

Viola pubescens (downy yellow violet).

Viola rostrata (long-spurred violet).

Viola hastata (halberd-leaf violet).

Viola striata (cream violet).

Waldsteinia fragarioides (barren strawberry).

V. rostrata [rah-'stray-tuh], long-spurred violet, is a leafy-stemmed species whose pale blue flowers have slender spurs about a ½ inch in length. They bloom in April and May at a height of 6 inches, and stems continue to elongate to nearly 12 inches. The leaves are broadly ovate. East Tennessee.

V. hastata [hah-'stay-tuh], halberd-leaf violet, is also leafy stemmed with yellow blossoms in April. The long, triangular leaves have a heart-shaped base and are often highlighted with silvery markings. East Tennessee.

V. striata [stry-'ay-tuh], cream violet, has leafy stems that grow nearly a foot tall with ovate, toothed leaves. Small creamy white petals are veined with purple near the base and bloom in April and May. It produces cleistogamous flowers in summer. Middle and East Tennessee.

Waldsteinia fragarioides
Barren Strawberry
[wald-'sty-nee-uh fruh-gair-ee-oh-'eye-deez]
Rosaceae (Rose Family)

While it tends to clump as often as it creeps, barren strawberry spreads slowly. Basal trifoliate leaves are evergreen, wedge shaped, and toothed. Yellow, ½-inch flowers bloom in April and May. It does resemble the true strawberry plant in general appearance, but bears dry, not fleshy, fruit and has no runners. It grows 4 to 8 inches tall in light shade and in humus-rich, moist, slightly acid soil. Propagate by division. *W. ternata*, often seen in catalogs, is a native of Europe and Japan. Eastern half of the state.

Yucca filamentosa
Adam's Needle, Bear-grass
['yuh-kuh fih-luh-men-'toh-suh]
Agavaceae (Agave Family)

Providing a bold, textural accent, this plant has evergreen basal foliage 1 to 2 feet tall. Each leaf is stiff, sword shaped, thick, and leathery with loose, curly threads peeling down the edges and a stout spine at the tip. In May and June it sends up a 4-foot spike of 2-inch, waxy white, bell-shaped flowers. Plant in a well-drained location with dry, slightly acid, sandy soil in full sun. It will tolerate some shade and is pollinated by moths. Propagate by offsets that develop. Its native range is primarily along the East Coast, but it grows quite well in Tennessee.

Yucca filamentosa (Adam's needle).

Zizia aurea
Golden Alexanders
['zih-zee-uh 'aw-ree-uh]
Apiaceae (Carrot Family)

Foliage is once or twice compound with sets of 3 elliptical to lanceolate, toothed leaflets. Stems are 1 to 2 feet tall with small umbels of tiny yellow flowers gathered in dainty flat-topped clusters in April or May.

Zizia aurea (golden Alexanders).

    Z. aptera ['ap-teh-ruh], heartleaf Alexanders, has long-stalked basal leaves that are narrowly heart shaped. Stem leaves have shorter stalks and are divided into 3 leaflets. Flowering is the same. Both species like part sun or light shade and moist, well-drained, slightly acid soil and serve as a butterfly larval food. *Z. aptera* tolerates dryness well. Propagate by seed, cuttings, or division. Both species occur in East and Middle Tennessee.

Zizia aptera (heartleaf Alexanders).

Ferns

Ornamental Interest and Site Summary

This summary provides a quick reference to the distinctive horticultural characteristics and site preferences of the ferns featured in this book. A complete description, cultural information, and state distribution for each plant follow the summary. The following abbreviations appear in the summary.

Distinctions:

Fr—Fruit
Lf—Leaf (shape or color)
Gc—Groundcover
Ev—Evergreen
Ar—Aromatic, fragrant
UF—Unique form
TH—Tall herbaceous, to 4 feet or more

Site Preferences:

S—Full sun to part shade
Sh—Part sun to medium shade
Alk—Tolerates slight alkalinity
WS—Wet soil
MS—Moist soil
DS—Dry soil

Ferns	Distinctions	Site
Adiantum pedatum (maidenhair fern)	Lf, UF	Sh, MS
Asplenium platyneuron (ebony spleenwort)	Lf, Ev	Sh MS/DS
Asplenium rhizophyllum (walking fern)	Lf, Ev, UF	Sh, MS Alk
Athyrium filix-femina (ladyfern)	Lf, Gc	Sh, MS

(Continued next page)

Ferns	Distinctions	Site
Cystopteris protrusa (lowland bladderfern)	Lf	Sh, MS
Dennstaedtia punctilobula (hay-scented fern)	Lf, Ar, Gc	Sh, MS
Deparia acrostichoides (silvery spleenwort)	Lf	Sh, MS
Diplazium pycnocarpon (narrow-leaved spleenwort)	Lf	Sh, MS
Dryopteris goldiana (Goldie's woodfern)	Lf, TH	Sh, MS
Dryopteris intermedia & *D. marginalis* (common & marginal woodfern)	Lf, Ev, Gc	Sh, MS
Equisetum hyemale (scouring rush)	Fr, Ev, UF, TH	S/Sh WS/MS
Onoclea sensibilis (sensitive fern)	Fr, Lf	S/Sh WS/MS
Osmunda cinnamomea (cinnamon fern)	Fr, Lf, TH	Sh WS/MS
Osmunda claytoniana (interrupted fern)	Fr, Lf, UF, TH	Sh, MS
Osmunda regalis (royal fern)	Fr, Lf, UF, TH	Sh WS/MS
Polystichum acrostichoides (Christmas fern)	Lf, Ev, Gc	Sh MS/DS
Thelypteris hexagonoptera (broad beech fern)	Lf	Sh MS/DS
Thelypteris noveboracensis (New York fern)	Lf	S/Sh MS/DS
Woodsia obtusa (blunt-lobed cliff-fern)	Lf	Sh, Alk MS/DS
Woodwardia areolata (netted chain fern)	Lf	S/Sh WS/MS

Description, Culture, and Distribution

Adiantum pedatum (maidenhair fern).

Adiantum pedatum
Maidenhair Fern
[ay-dee-'an-tum peh-'day-tum]
Sinopteridaceae (Maidenhair Fern Family)

This fern offers a unique textural contrast with its finely cut fronds spreading horizontally in a fan shape on shiny, brownish black stems from 10 to 20 inches high. The main stem forks, and each rachis curls around, radiating outward a horizontal spray of 5 to 7 pinnae. The sori appear on the undersides of the pinnules. Lobed margins of the pinnules fold under to cover and protect these clustered spore capsules.

Despite its delicate appearance, maidenhair fern is an easy plant to grow, preferring moist but well-drained, humus-rich soil that is moderately acid to neutral in medium shade. Protect it from harsh winds. Propagate from rootstock cuttings. Statewide.

Asplenium platyneuron (ebony spleenwort).

Asplenium platyneuron
Ebony Spleenwort
[ass-'plee-nee-um plat-ee-'new-ron]
Aspleniaceae (Spleenwort Family)

Ebony spleenwort has two kinds of fronds. The 2- to 6-inch sterile fronds are pinnate with short, blunt, alternate pinnae. They are prostrate in habit and evergreen. Fertile fronds are narrow and erect, standing 10 to 20 inches tall on lustrous, dark brown stems. Short, alternate pinnae are toothed and eared on the top edge. On the undersides of the upper pinnae, hyphen-shaped sori angle away from the midvein in a herringbone pattern. Fertile fronds persist through winter, too, but do not hold up as well. This fern has short rootstocks and grows in more of a clump. It likes the rocky slopes, ledges, and crevices of well-drained uplands and the light shade of open deciduous woods. Humusy soil may be moist to dry and moderately acid to neutral. Statewide.

A. *rhizophyllum* [ry-zah-'fill-um] *(Camptosorus rhizophyllus)*, **walking fern,** has evergreen fronds 4 to 12 inches long and simple in form, meaning that they are not divided, lobed, or cut in any way and look like regular leaves. Each frond is narrowly triangular with 2 rounded lobes at the base and tapers to a long point. Wherever this leaf tip touches moist soil, it will root to form another plant. Elongated sori appear on the underside. Walking fern is an unusual fern with rather specialized needs that not everyone can meet. In the wild it is found clambering over moist limestone outcrops. With exposed rock, neutral to slightly alkaline soil, regular moisture, and medium shade, it is worth a try. It is also prone to slugs. Middle and East Tennessee.

Asplenium rhizophyllum (walking fern).

Athyrium filix-femina
Ladyfern
[uh-'theer-ee-um 'fy-liks-'feh-mih-nuh]
Woodsiaceae (Cliff-fern Family)

The southern variety (var. *asplenioides*) is Tennessee's best choice. Ladyfern has 1½- to 3-foot fronds that are bipinnate with toothed pinnules. Fronds are widest just above the base with lower pinnae more widely spaced. Petioles are greenish yellow, sometimes reddish in hue, with scales that soon fall off.

Athyrium filix-femina (ladyfern).

Both the petiole and rachis are grooved or flat in front. The sori are narrow and crescent shaped. Ladyfern is not evergreen, but is easy to grow in moist, humus-rich, moderately acid to neutral soil and makes a good ground-cover in light shade. It has a heavy, creeping rootstock and can become aggressive in favorable conditions. Statewide.

Cystopteris protrusa (lowland bladderfern).

Cystopteris protrusa (C. fragilis var. protrusa)
Lowland Bladderfern
[sih-'stop-teh-ris proh-'true-suh]
Woodsiaceae (Cliff-fern Family)

Growing in colonies, the fronds of lowland bladderfern are 8 to 15 inches tall, bipinnate, and usually widest just above the base. The rachis is smooth, and the pinnules on the lower pinnae are often stalked. All pinnules are lobed with irregularly spaced sori. During summer droughts the fronds can take on a russet hue, but since it sends up new fronds all season it bounces back quickly.

Slender, hairy rootstock creeps along ledges and rocky slopes in moist, neutral to slightly acid soil and light shade. Lowland bladderfern is often confused with the blunt-lobed cliff-fern, *Woodsia obtusa.* Compare their descriptions; surface similarities are over-come with close observation. Middle and East Tennessee.

Dennstaedtia punctilobula
Hay-scented Fern
[den-'steh-tee-uh punk-tih-'loh-byew-luh]
Dennstaedtiaceae (Bracken Family)

Hay-scented fern has narrow, lanceolate fronds 1½ to 2½ feet tall. They are yellow green and bipinnate with lobed pinnules. Cup-shaped sori are attached at the base of each lobe on the pinnules. Crushed fronds emit a sweet, hay fragrance. This fern performs best in moist, moderately to slightly acid, humus-rich soil and light shade to part sun, but it will also adapt to both wetter and drier soils. It has a weedy reputation, but apparently is not quite as bad in this (the southern) portion of its U.S. range. Hay-scented fern's spreading nature may be utilized effectively as a groundcover in large areas. East Tennessee.

Dennstaedtia punctilobula (hay-scented fern).

Deparia acrostichoides
(Athyrium thelypterioides)
Silvery Spleenwort, Silvery Glade Fern
[deh-'pay-ree-uh uh-kros-tih-koh-'eye-deez]
Woodsiaceae (Cliff-fern Family)

This fern is 2 to 3½ feet tall and light green with soft, arching fronds that are widest in the middle. Pinnate, the alternate pinnae are long, narrowly tapering, and pinnatifid with bluntly lobed and toothed margins. The rachis is hairy. Oblong sori are placed in a herringbone pattern and start off a lustrous, silvery green before turning brown at maturity. Fertile fronds are a bit longer than sterile ones. Silvery spleenwort likes humus-rich, well-drained, moist soil in light to medium shade. It is moderately creeping in growth habit. Statewide.

Deparia acrostichoides (silvery spleenwort).

Diplazium pycnocarpon
(Athyrium pycnocarpon)
Narrow-leaved Spleenwort, Glade Fern
[dih-'play-zee-um pik-noh-'kar-pon]
Woodsiaceae (Cliff-fern Family)

Narrow-leaved spleenwort is clumping in habit, 1½ to 3½ feet tall, and pinnate with light green, thin, tapering pinnae. Sterile

Diplazium pycnocarpon (narrow-leaved spleenwort).

Dryopteris marginalis (marginal woodfern).

fronds appear first and are followed later in the season by fertile fronds that are a bit taller and narrower with shorter pinnae. The leaf blade color darkens in the summer and becomes russet in the fall. Sori are oblong and arranged in a herringbone pattern. Give this fern rich, moist, neutral, well-drained soil in medium to light shade. It will produce new fronds until summer. Statewide, lightly in West Tennessee.

Dryopteris marginalis
Marginal Woodfern, Marginal Shield-fern
[dry-'op-teh-ris mar-jih-'nay-lis]
Dryopteridaceae (Shield-fern Family)

Marginal woodfern is an evergreen fern with broad, bipinnate fronds that are widest above the base and grow 12 to 24 inches tall in vase-like clumps. Large, round sori are on the outer margins of the blunt-toothed, rounded pinnules. There are light brown scales at the base of the petiole. A crown of tightly curled croziers covered in golden brown scales forms in the fall for next season's growth and sits partly above ground. It likes moist but well-drained uplands, loving moderately acid to neutral leaf mold in part sun to light shade. It makes a good groundcover. East Tennessee, lightly in Middle Tennessee.

D. intermedia [in-ter-'mee-dee-uh], common woodfern, is evergreen, 16 to 30 inches tall, and bipinnate with pinnules that are deeply lobed, toothed, and tipped with tiny hairlike bristles. The sori are kidney shaped and located near the leaflet margins. East Tennessee.

D. goldiana [goal-dee-'ay-nuh], **Goldie's** or **giant woodfern,** is semi-evergreen and 2 to 4 feet in height. The fronds are about 18 inches wide and pinnate with pinnatifid, toothed pinnae. It has pale brown scales, and sori are located in the center of the pinnae segments. Color varies from yellow to dark green, and it can become the focal point in the back of the shade garden. East Tennessee.

J. Paul Moore.

Dryopteris goldiana (Goldie's woodfern).

All the woodferns have a decided preference for the rocky soil of higher elevations, the cooler temperatures of a north facing slope, and moisture.

Equisetum hyemale
Scouring Rush
[eh-kwih-'see-tum hy-'may-lee]
Equisetaceae (Horsetail Family)

Scouring rush is an evergreen fern ally, a close relative to ferns with small scalelike leaves. In the case of scouring rush, this scalelike leaf is the gray brown sheath at each node along the green stem and is delineated by a black line above and below the sheath. Unbranched stems are 2 to 4 feet tall or more, and each is topped by a pointed cone-shaped structure that bears the spores. Stems are rough in texture outside, hollow inside, and spread via widely branching and creeping rhizomes. Wet to moist soil in light shade to full sun will give scouring rush all it needs to take over the entire area. While unique and interesting in form, this plant is notably aggressive and should be carefully contained and used with great caution. Once out of hand it is hard to regain control. Scattered statewide.

Equisetum hyemale (scouring rush).

Onoclea sensibilis
Sensitive or Bead Fern
[on-ah-'klee-uh sen-'sih-bih-lis]
Woodsiaceae (Cliff-fern Family)

Onoclea sensibilis (sensitive fern).

The height of the sensitive fern varies up to 3 feet, producing sterile fronds of light or mottled green. The upper portion of the frond is deeply lobed (pinnatifid), giving the rachis a winged appearance. The lower portion of the frond has widely spaced, paired pinnae that are tapered at both ends. Fertile fronds appear in summer and are bipinnate with the pinnules rolled into little beadlike forms around the sori. Turning from green to deep brown, the fertile fronds last through the winter, stiff and dried, to release spores in the spring. Sensitive fern will take moderately acid to neutral soil, full sun to light shade, and wet, muddy areas. With sufficient moisture this fern turns aggression into invasion, so beware. Drier soil will check the growth, but provide enough space or consider a less aggressive alternative. In drier soil give it more shade. The common name refers to its tendency to turn brown in early spring and late fall frosts or during a drought. New fronds appear with better weather. Statewide.

Osmunda cinnamomea
Cinnamon Fern
[oz-'mun-duh sih-nuh-'moh-mee-uh]
Osmundaceae (Royal Fern Family)

The fertile fronds responsible for this fern's name are the first to appear in a group of 2 to 4. These erect stems, 3 to 5 feet tall, feature specialized pinnae narrowly club shaped and loaded with clusters of round sporangia that turn from green to golden cinnamon brown. Sterile fronds of yellow green to dark green are pinnate with pinnatifid pinnae and grow up around the fertile fronds, bending outward in a vase shape. A tuft of cinnamon colored fuzz grows on the back base of each pinna at the main stem. Fertile fronds wither away quickly. When the young fronds or croziers first emerge, they are covered with a dense white fuzz that soon turns brown and drops off. Small birds use this fuzz in making their nests. Cinnamon fern needs moderately acid soil that is reliably moist to wet. In normal garden soils, it will be shorter. It prefers light shade, but can take some sun provided the soil moisture increases as well. Statewide.

Osmunda cinnamomea (cinnamon fern).

O. claytoniana [klay-toh-nee-'ay-nuh], **interrupted fern**, has an apt moniker. As the common name implies sterile pinnae are interrupted in the middle of the frond by 2 to 5 pairs of clustered brown sporangia. This fertile section soon withers leaving sterile pinnae above and below this gap. Shorter, completely sterile fronds come up around the partly fertile ones. Fronds are pinnate with pinnatifid pinnae. There is no tuft of fuzz at the pinna base, but croziers are covered with dense, brown fuzz. Interrupted fern is easy to grow, reaching 2 to 4 feet. It can take slightly drier sites in part sun and is not fussy about soil. East Tennessee.

Osmunda claytoniana (interrupted fern).

O. regalis [reh-'gay-lis], **royal fern**, is 3 to 5 feet tall with a less frilly texture than most ferns. The bipinnate fronds contain large leaflike pinnules in pairs quite unlike typical pinnae. Each pinna is about 6 inches long by 3 inches wide. Fertile portions are terminal, emerging erect from the top of the sterile fronds like a flower plume in spring. Leaflets in the sterile fronds are bright green, and the fertile portions mature from green to yellowish

Osmunda regalis (royal fern).

brown with the round sporangia clustered in bipinnate branches. Petioles are reddish at the base, and young croziers are woolly brown. Royal ferns are easy to grow in humusy, wet soil, moderately to slightly acid, in part sun to light shade. Statewide.

Polystichum acrostichoides (Christmas fern).

Polystichum acrostichoides
Christmas Fern
[pah-'lih-stih-kum uh-kros-tih-koh-'eye-deez]
Dryopteridaceae (Shield-fern Family)

This evergreen fern is quite common throughout our woods. The pinnate, sterile fronds are glossy dark green, leathery, and 12 to 30 inches tall with eared, toothed pinnae. Fine white scales on the stems of new fronds soon turn brown. The fertile fronds are taller with sori that expand to nearly cover the undersides of the short, narrow pinnae on the upper half of the frond. Stout roots creep slowly to produce clumps. Moist to dry, well-drained soil, rich in humus and moderately acid to neutral, in light to medium shade is best. Christmas fern grows well in city gardens, and the clumps can be divided. It makes a good groundcover. Statewide.

Thelypteris hexagonoptera (broad beech fern).

Thelypteris hexagonoptera
Broad or Southern Beech Fern
[theh-'lip-teh-ris heks-uh-gon-'op-teh-ruh]
Thelypteridaceae (Marsh Fern Family)

Perched atop a long petiole, the leaf blade of the beech fern is broadly triangular in shape and bipinnatifid. Fronds are not divided fully to the stem, which leaves a bit of green running the length of the stem and gives it a winged look. The bottom pair of segments slant downward. Each segment is also pin-natifid. There are brown scales on the stem; overall height is about 24 inches. Sori are small and round. Rootstock creeps through the leaf mold, but mostly the plant forms a clump or compact colony. Beech ferns like rich, moist to dry, moderately acid soil in light shade. Statewide.

T. noveboracensis [noh-veh-bore-uh-'sen-sis], **New York fern,** is chartreuse in color, about 1 to 2 feet high. The fronds are pinnate with pinnatifid pinnae and are widest in the middle tapering sharply on each end. It is known to spread quite rapidly, though allegedly not as badly in the southern United States as in the northern U.S. Give it moist to dry soil in part shade. Statewide.

Woodsia obtusa
Blunt-lobed Cliff-fern, Blunt-lobed Woodsia
['wood-zee-uh ob-'too-suh]
Woodsiaceae (Cliff-fern Family)

Blunt-lobed cliff-fern is bipinnate and 10 to 16 inches tall. The pinnules are sessile and deeply blunt-lobed with rounded teeth. It resembles the lowland bladderfern, *Cystop-teris protrusa*, described above, with these dif-ferences: pale yellow green stems have scales, minute hairs cover the rachis, and the sori appear star shaped. The fertile fronds die back in winter, but some sterile fronds may persist. Blunt-lobed cliff-fern prefers moist to dry, neutral to slightly alkaline, well-drained soil in the light to medium shade of sheltered, rocky cliffs and slopes. Statewide.

Woodsia obtusa (blunt-lobed cliff-fern).

Woodwardia areolata (netted chain fern).

Woodwardia areolata
Netted Chain Fern
[wood-'war-dee-uh air-ee-oh-'lay-tuh]
Blechnaceae (Deer Fern Family)

Chain fern has 2 types of fronds. Sterile fronds are up to 2 feet tall. The upper portion is pinnatifid with alternate, finely toothed, lanceolate segments; the lower portion is pinnate and more widely spaced. The fertile fronds have a similar design with longer and narrower segments and pinnae. A long chain of sori runs along the underside of segments/pinnae on the fertile fronds. This characteristic, plus the netlike veining pattern of the leaf, account for the common name. Reddish green when young, it matures to a deep, glossy green. Netted chain fern needs moist to boggy, strongly to moderately acid soil in part shade. Creeping in habit, it will spread. Statewide.

Grasses, Sedges, and Rushes
Ornamental Interest and Site Summary

This summary provides a quick reference to the distinctive horticultural characteristics and site preferences of the grasses, sedges, and rushes featured in this book. A complete description, cultural information, and state distribution for each plant follow the summary. The following abbreviations appear in the summary.

Distinctions:
    Fr—Fruit
    Lf—Leaf (shape or color)
    Gc—Groundcover
    Ev—Evergreen
    UF—Unique form
    TH—Tall herbaceous, over 4 feet

Site Preferences:

S—Full sun to part shade
Sh—Part sun to medium shade
Alk—Tolerates slight alkalinity
PS—Poor soil, low fertility
WS—Wet soil
MS—Moist soil
DS—Dry soil

Grasses	Distinctions	Site
Andropogon gerardii (big bluestem)	Lf, Fr, TH	S, MS
Andropogon glomeratus (bushy bluestem)	Lf, Fr	S WS/MS
Andropogon ternarius (splitbeard bluestem)	Lf, Fr	S, DS
Andropogon virginicus (broom sedge)	Lf	S, DS PS
Arundinaria gigantea (river cane)	Ev, TH	S/Sh WS/MS
Bouteloua curtipendula (side oats grama)	Fr	S, DS
Carex crinita & C. lupulina (drooping & hop sedge)	Fr, TH	S, WS
Carex frankii (Frank's sedge)	Fr	Sh, WS
Carex grayi (Gray's sedge)	Fr	S/Sh MS
Carex pensylvanica (Pennsylvania sedge)	Lf, Gc	Sh, DS
Carex picta (painted sedge)	Fr, Gc	Sh MS/DS
Carex plantaginea (seersucker sedge)	Lf, Gc	Sh, MS
Chasmanthium latifolium (river oats)	Lf, Fr	Sh, MS
Elymus hystrix (bottlebrush grass)	UF	S, MS

(Continued next page)

Grasses	Distinctions	Site
Eragrostis spectabilis (purple lovegrass)	Lf, Fr	S, DS
Erianthus alopecuroides & *E. contortus* (silver & bent-awn plumegrass)	Fr, TH	S, MS
Erianthus giganteus & *E. strictus* (sugarcane & narrow plumegrass)	Lf, Fr, TH	S WS/MS
Juncus effusus (common rush)	Fr, UF	S, WS
Luzula spp. (wood rush)	Lf, Fr	Sh, MS
Panicum virgatum (switch grass)	Lf, Fr	S, MS
Schizachyrium scoparium (little bluestem)	Lf, Fr	S, DS Alk
Scirpus atrovirens (black bullrush)	Fr, TH	S, WS
Sorghastrum nutans (Indian grass)	Fr, TH	S MS/DS
Tripsacum dactyloides (eastern gama grass)	Fr, TH	S, WS

Description, Culture, and Distribution

Andropogon gerardii
Big Bluestem, Turkey-foot
[an-drah-'poh-gon jeh-'rar-dee-eye]
Poaceae (Grass Family)

A perennial, clumping grass, upright to arching in habit, big bluestem is 4 to 8 feet tall with bluish green stems. The purplish seed head is a narrow cluster of linear racemes that resemble its other common name, turkey-foot.

Big bluestem turns a light reddish to purple brown in autumn and is one of the staple grasses of the tallgrass prairie. Big bluestem is a warm-season grass, needing full sun and moist, well-drained, fertile soil. It works well as a specimen plant in gardens, spaced 2 feet apart. In a meadow planting it benefits from either a late winter mowing or a controlled burn in early spring. It takes heat and drought well, though it may be shorter and more compact as a result. There are named cultivars for height and fall color. Statewide.

Andropogon gerardii (big bluestem).

A. glomeratus [glah-mer-'ay-tus], **bushy bluestem** or **bushy beardgrass**, forms a 2-foot clump of bright green foliage and 3- to 4-foot flower spikes. Dense, silky, silvery green flower heads become white to silver, feathery, plumy seed heads in the fall and turn a coppery coral color by winter. Leaves are reddish purple. It prefers full sun in moist to wet soils. Cumberland Plateau.

A. ternarius [ter-'nay-ree-us], **splitbeard bluestem**, is very similar to bushy bluestem, with a couple of exceptions. The silvery white bloom is in a **V** shape before turning plumy white in fall, and this species prefers dry, sandy soil in full sun to part shade and moderately acid soil. Cumberland Plateau and Western Highland Rim.

A. virginicus [vir-'jin-ih-kus], **broom sedge**, grows as a 2- to 4-foot clump. Flower and seed heads are relatively inconspicuous, but the leaves and stems turn a pleasing coppery brown and hold this color well throughout the winter. This grass is a good choice for meadows and areas needing erosion control with the added benefit of providing good cover for area wildlife. Broom sedge grows naturally in open fields or thinly scattered woods with poor, dry soil and responds well to periodic controlled burns. Propagate all *Andropogon* spp. by seed or division. Statewide.

Arundinaria gigantea
River Cane
[uh-run-dih-'nay-ree-uh jy-gan-'tee-uh]
Poaceae (Grass Family)

Arundinaria gigantea (river cane).

River cane is a running bamboo native to the south. It spreads by underground rhizomes and can reach heights approaching 30 feet. Lanceolate leaves alternate up the cane at nodes. It blooms rarely with loose panicles of flowers. In William Bartram's time huge cane-brakes were common along rivers and in swampy areas, but this grass has been hard hit by development. *A. gigantea* ssp. *tecta* ['tek-tuh] at 3 to 12 feet is a form that does not get so tall. In moist to wet soil river cane provides an evergreen screen and is a good native alternative to overly aggressive, exotic bamboo species. It grows well in shade. Scattered lightly statewide.

Bouteloua curtipendula
Side Oats Grama
[boo-teh-'lew-uh kur-tih-'pen-dyew-luh]
Poaceae (Grass Family)

Bouteloua curtipendula (side oats grama).

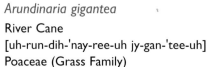

William Hall.

Here is a grass that could replace portions of a lawn, as it is a tough, low-water, low-maintenance plant. Side oats grama is a warm-season perennial grass that forms a sod by stolons. It is 1 to 2 feet tall, upright and narrow to arching in habit. Flower spikes have a series of short, purplish, flower clusters arranged along 1 side of the 10- to 15-inch stems, and the leaves are gray green and fine textured. Seed heads mature to a golden color and bleach out to straw in winter. It thrives in drier, well-drained soil and full sun and propagates easily from seed. Mow or burn in the spring. Central Basin, Valley and Ridge.

Carex spp.
Sedge
['kay-ricks]
Cyperaceae (Sedge Family)

Sedges are not true grasses. Their flowering stems are triangular in cross section—sedges have edges. They prefer rich soils, moderately acid to neutral, and can be propagated by division.

Carex crinita (drooping sedge).

    C. crinita [krih-'ny-tuh], drooping sedge, bears slim, pendulous spikes on 3- to 5-foot stems. Pistillate (female) spikes have loads of tiny flowers. Each blossom is tucked into a bristle-tipped scale, giving the 2- to 5-inch spike a fuzzy appearance. Male spikes are skinnier and not bristly. Grasslike leaves are present on the upper portion of the stem. Blooming in June this sedge needs wet swampy soil and part shade. Statewide.

Carex frankii (Frank's sedge).

    C. frankii ['frank-ee-eye], Frank's sedge, produces a clump of stems 1 to 2½ feet tall with linear, ½-inch-wide, ribbed leaves attached to the stem. A cluster of 1-inch, cylindrical spikes tops the stem. One spike has staminate (male) flowers, the others have female flowers. It likes wet soil in light shade or part sun. Statewide.

    C. grayi ['gray-eye], Gray's sedge, forms a grasslike clump with a round flower cluster in summer and light green leaves. Semi-evergreen with foliage ¼ to ½ inch wide, the plant grows about 2 feet tall. The fruits are clustered in a 1-inch, spiky-looking (but not sharp) ball that changes from greenish yellow

Carex grayi (Gray's sedge).

The Center for Field Biology, a Tennessee Center of Excellence at Austin Peay State University.

to brown. It needs consistently moist soil and full sun to light shade. Western half of the state.

C. lupulina [lew-puh-'ly-nuh], **hop sedge**, is 1 to 4 feet in height and has a cluster of flower spikes, 1 staminate, the rest pistillate. The female spikes are oblong cylinders that look like a large burr due to little pointy (but not sharp) sacs, each enclosing a pistil. Grasslike leaves are up to a ½-inch wide. It takes moist to wet soil in sun or part shade. Statewide, heavier in West Tennessee.

C. pensylvanica [pen-sil-'van-ih-kuh], **Pennsylvania** or **high meadow sedge**, produces low growing clumps of very fine, linear foliage and spreads by stolons. In early spring flower clusters appear on stems up to 12 inches tall with separate male and female brown to reddish purple flowers. Flower stalks are gone by summer with the lovely, soft foliage remaining year round and renewing in spring. Pennsylvania sedge grows naturally in dry oak woods and light shade. Middle and East Tennessee.

C. picta ['pik-tuh], **painted sedge**, is a woodland species that develops large populations and grows in dense low tufts of foliage 4 to 12 inches tall and ¼ inch wide. Dioecious, male and female flower spikes are on separate plants and are quite showy as a purple scale accompanies each flower in the spike in April and May and later the fruit (on female spikes). Painted sedge prefers light shade to part sun and moist to dry soil. Western Highland Rim.

C. plantaginea [plan-tuh-'jih-nee-uh], **seersucker** or **plantain-leaved sedge**, has bright green, 10-inch foliage that puckers between the veins. Leaves are a ½ to 1 inch wide and last through the winter. A spiky flower cluster rises 1 to 1½ feet in early spring above new

Carex pensylvanica (Pennsylvania sedge).

Carex picta (painted sedge).

Carex plantaginea (seersucker sedge).

The Center for Field Biology, a Tennessee Center of Excellence at Austin Peay State University.

foliage. Seersucker sedge needs consistently moist soil in light to medium shade and makes a good groundcover. Eastern half of the state.

Chasmanthium latifolium (Uniola latifolia)
River Oats, Upland Sea Oats, Spangle Grass
[kas-'man-thee-um lat-ih-'foh-lee-um]
Poaceae (Grass Family)

A perennial, clumping, warm-season grass, river oats is 2½ to 4 feet tall and upright to arching in habit. Narrowly lanceolate leaves alternate up a stem topped by loose clusters of flat seed heads 1 inch long that dangle on a gently curving stem in summer. The seed heads mature from green to copper and are often used in floral arrangements. The foliage turns a pale copper in autumn and brown in winter. River oats is right at home in any moist, well-drained soil with part to light shade. Clumps enlarge and self-sow generously in moist sites; propagate by seed or division. Statewide.

Chasmanthium latifolium (river oats).

Elymus hystrix (Hystrix patula)
Bottlebrush Grass
['el-ih-mus 'hih-striks]
Poaceae (Grass Family)

This clumping perennial is a cool-season grass with tufts of foliage 8 to 12 inches tall and flower spikes 2 to 3 feet high. Well-spaced flower clusters angle out horizontally from the stem. Each cluster is accompanied by 2 or 3 long bristles that give the flower spike the look of a bottlebrush. It blooms June through August and matures to brown in the fall. Bottlebrush grass likes moist, yet well-drained, fertile soil in part shade, and germinates slowly but easily from seed. Middle and East Tennessee.

Elymus hystrix (bottlebrush grass).

Eragrostis spectabilis (purple lovegrass).

Eragrostis spectabilis
Purple Lovegrass
[air-uh-'grahs-tis spek-'tab-ih-lis]
Poaceae (Grass Family)

In the summer open and airy panicles of reddish purple flower spikelets rise to a height of 1 to 2 feet above the low-growing foliage of this warm-season, clumping, perennial grass. In the fall the panicle turns a creamy tan and breaks off from the plant in winter to tumble around and spread its seeds. The leaves are a soft, light green and turn reddish in the fall. Purple lovegrass grows in sandy, well-drained, open fields in full sun, taking heat and some drought. Propagate by seed or division. Statewide.

Erianthus spp.
Plumegrass
[air-ee-'an-thus]
Poaceae (Grass Family)

Erianthus spp. are perennial, warm-season plants that tend to colonize around a clump and must be widely spaced, about 4 feet. Propagate by seed or division.

E. alopecuroides [al-ah-peh-kyew-roh-'eye-dees], silver plumegrass, is 5 to 6 feet or more in height with long leaves and a large, 7- to 15-inch, rosy copper plume in the fall that fades to a silvery peach. It needs the full sun of an open meadow with moist, moderately to slightly acid soil. Statewide.

E. contortus [kon-'tore-tus], bent-awn plumegrass, is narrowly upright with foliage 2 feet tall turning reddish purple in fall. The flower spikes are much taller (5 to 6 feet) with spikelets (flowers) that are silky purple then turn fluffy and cottony in seed. It needs moist, well-drained soil in full sun but will take a bit of shade and dryness.

E. giganteus [jy-gan-'tee-us], sugarcane **plumegrass,** has hairy leaves on stems 3 to 5 feet tall and large plumes rising as high as 9 feet. Plumes vary in color from reddish purple to silvery white August through the fall. Foliage turns orange red then bleaches to straw in winter. It prefers moist to boggy soil in full sun.

E. strictus ['strick-tus], **narrow plume-grass,** produces 4- to 6-foot stems with very narrow plumes in moist to wet soil. These last three *Erianthus* spp. are scattered lightly around the state.

Erianthus giganteus (sugarcane plumegrass).

Juncus effusus
Common Rush
['jun-kus eh-'fyew-sus]
Juncaceae (Rush Family)

Rush grows as a dense clump of slender green stems 2 to 4 feet tall. Flowers are small and packed into a many-branched panicle that appears to emanate from the middle of the stem. A long, erect bract extending above the flower cluster gives this impression. It blooms in midspring. Each flower produces a shiny, dark brown capsule containing many tiny seeds. Native to marshes and wet meadows, rush is a good bog or pond plant for full sun. Statewide.

Juncus effusus (common rush).

Luzula echinata
Wood Rush
['lew-zuh-luh eh-kin-'ay-tuh]
Juncaceae (Rush Family)

Wood rush is a clumping perennial with light green, narrow, grassy foliage. Clusters of chestnut brown flowers and seeds top wiry stems 8 to 20 inches tall. Foliage is about 6 to 10 inches high with long, soft hairs on the blade

Luzula multiflora (wood rush).

edges. It blooms in the spring in part sun to light shade in moist, well-drained, moderately acid soil. Statewide.

Other wood rush species to consider are *L. acuminata, L. bulbosa,* and *L. multiflora.* They may be hard to find commercially. Propagate by division or seed, from which wood rush germinates slowly but easily. Middle and East Tennessee.

Panicum virgatum
Switch Grass
['pan-ih-kum vir-'gay-tum]
Poaceae (Grass Family)

Panicum virgatum 'Heavy Metal' (switch grass).

At a height of 3 to 4 feet or more, switch grass bears broadly diffuse and lacy panicles of flowers and seed rising an additional 1 to 2 feet above leaves that become reddish gold in fall and tan in winter. Flowers can be purplish to silver gray. Its form is narrowly upright and lasts through the winter. This warm-season grass grows in a dense clump but continually spreads via rhizomes into colonies and must be well spaced. It is tolerant of poor, wet conditions and drought, but looks best in regular moist soil and full sun. A dark background sets off the billowy panicles. There are many species of *Panicum* throughout the state, some more common than *P. virgatum,* but this grass is widely grown as an ornamental and has several cultivars. Cut back in early spring and propagate by division or seed. Statewide.

Schizachyrium scoparium
(Andropogon scoparius)
Little Bluestem
[skits-uh-'keer-ee-um skah-'pay-ree-um]
Poaceae (Grass Family)

Schizachyrium scoparium (little bluestem).

Little bluestem is a 2- to 4-foot, warm-season, clump-forming perennial. It is upright and narrow to arching in form, with slender branching stems that, along with the leaves, turn a reddish to golden brown in fall and hold this color well into winter. In summer, as its name suggests, it has a bluish cast. In mid- to late summer, it produces from the upper leaf node a single raceme of spikelets (flowers) that become a fluffy plume of seeds. Little bluestem likes full sun and well-drained soil, is able to take drier sites than big bluestem, and grows well in clay soil or on limestone. Mow once a year; periodic burns keep it vigorous. Propagate by seed or division. Statewide.

Scirpus atrovirens
Black Bullrush
['skur-pus uh-'trah-vih-renz]
Cyperaceae (Sedge Family)

Leafy stems 2 to 5 feet tall end in a widely branched flower cluster of densely packed spikelets that are dark greenish brown in color. It blooms in midsummer. Black bull-rush prefers the wet soil of marshes and pond margins in full sun. Statewide.

Sorghastrum nutans (Indian grass).

Sorghastrum nutans
Indian Grass
[sor-'gas-trum 'new-tanz]
Poaceae (Grass Family)

Indian grass is a clumping, warm-season, perennial grass with blue green foliage about 18 to 24 inches high. Foliage takes on a reddish orange hue in the fall. Tall (up to 7 feet) bloom stalks are topped with narrow, bright golden clusters (4 to 12 inches long) of flowers mellowing to tawny amber and maroon seed plumes in late summer and fall. Very attractive for the garden, Indian grass likes full sun and moist to dry, well-drained soil but is not picky. It tolerates drought once established. There are cultivars. Space plants 3 to 5 feet apart and cut back or burn in late winter. It may be propagated by seed (slow but easy) or division. Statewide.

William Hall.

Tripsacum dactyloides (eastern gama grass).

Tripsacum dactyloides
Eastern Gama Grass
['trip-suh-kum dak-tih-loh-'eye-deez]
Poaceae (Grass Family)

Gama grass grows 4 to 8 feet tall with inch-wide leaves. Spikes have unisexual flowers with staminate flowers on the upper portion and pistillate flowers below. Male flowers produce orange stamens, and female flowers produce purple stigmas. It is a warm-season grass that likes wet soil and full sun. Statewide.

Fall paints the landscape with richly intense and quietly subtle colorations. The ripe red fruits of *Ilex decidua* 'Warren Red' (possumhaw) and *Cornus florida* (flowering dogwood) join the turning foliage of ash, maple, hickory, and oak trees.

Vines

Ornamental Interest and Site Summary

This summary provides a quick reference to the distinctive horticultural characteristics and site preferences of the vines featured in this book. A complete description, cultural information, and state distribution for each plant follow the summary. The following abbreviations appear in the summary.

Flower Season and Color:

    Sp—Spring
    Su—Summer
    Wh—White
    Y—Yellow
    O—Orange
    R—Red
    Pr—Purple
    Bl—Blue
    GBM—Green, brown, maroon

Distinctions:

Fr—Fruit
Lf—Leaf (shape or color)
Bk—Bark
Ar—Aromatic, fragrant
UF—Unique form

Site Preferences:

S—Full sun to part shade
Sh—Part sun to medium shade
Alk—Tolerates slight alkalinity
PS—Poor soil, low fertility
WS—Wet soil
MS—Moist soil
DS—Dry soil

Vines	Flower	Distinctions	Site
Aristolochia macrophylla & *A. tomentosa* (Dutchman's pipe & woolly pipevine)	Sp/Su GBM	UF	Sh, MS
Berchemia scandens (Alabama supplejack)	Sp GBM/Wh	Fr	S WS-DS
Bignonia capreolata (crossvine)	Sp R/Y		S, Alk WS-DS
Campsis radicans (trumpet creeper)	Su O		S WS-DS
Celastrus scandens (American bittersweet)	Sp Y	Fr	S, DS PS
Clematis crispa (marsh leather-flower)	Su Pr/Bl	Fr, Ar	S WS
Clematis versicolor & *C. viorna* (leather-flower)	Su Pr	Fr	Sh, MS
Clematis virginiana (virgin's bower)	Su Wh	Fr, Ar	S, MS
Cocculus carolinus (Carolina snailseed)	Su Wh	Fr	S/Sh, Alk MS/DS
Decumaria barbara (climbing hydrangea)	Sp Wh	Ar	Sh, MS
Gelsemium sempervirens (yellow jessamine)	Sp Y	Ar	S, MS

(Continued next page)

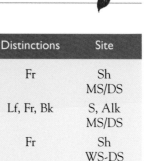

Vines	Flower	Distinctions	Site
Lonicera flava (yellow honeysuckle)	Sp Y	Fr	Sh MS/DS
Lonicera sempervirens (coral honeysuckle)	Sp/Su R	Lf, Fr, Bk	S, Alk MS/DS
Menispermum canadense (moonseed)	Su Wh/Y	Fr	Sh WS-DS
Parthenocissus quinquefolia (Virginia creeper)	Su Y/GBM	Lf, Fr	S/Sh WS-DS
Passiflora incarnata (passion-flower)	Sp/Su Bl/Pr	Fr	S, DS
Passiflora lutea (yellow passion-flower)	Su Y	Fr	Sh, MS
Vitis aestivalis, V. riparia, V. rotundifolia, V. vulpina (grapes)	Sp Y	Fr, Ar, Bk	S/Sh WS-DS
Wisteria frutescens (American wisteria)	Sp Pr	Ar	S WS/MS

Description, Culture, and Distribution

Aristolochia macrophylla (A. durior)
Dutchman's Pipe
[air-is-tah-'loh-kee-uh mak-roh-'fill-uh]
Aristolochiaceae (Birthwort Family)

The Dutchman's pipe vine has broad, heart-shaped leaves, each 6 to 15 inches across, in pairs. An inflated tubular flower veined with yellow green extends from the leaf axils. Each bloom is 3 inches long, flares at the end with purplish brown lobes, and is overall curved into a smoker's pipe shape. Blooms appear in late spring and summer and are replaced by oblong, cylindrical seed capsules. The vine twines with its smooth green stems

Aristolochia macrophylla (Dutchman's pipe).

and grows several feet per year to an ultimate height of 20 feet or more. Deciduous, it likes open shade and the organically rich, moist, well-drained soil of the woods, slightly acid to neutral. Pipevines are butterfly larval food. Eastern half of the state.

A. tomentosa [toh-men-'toh-suh], **woolly pipevine,** has downy, white hairs covering its young branches, flowers, and leaf undersides. The leaves (3 to 6 inches) and the flowers (1½ inches) are smaller. It blooms May to August in rich, moist soil and open shade. Scattered lightly across Tennessee.

Berchemia scandens
Alabama Supplejack, Rattanvine
[ber-'kee-mee-uh 'skan-denz]
Rhamnaceae (Buckthorn Family)

This twining woody climber grows to 20 feet or more and is long-lived. The alternate leaves are glossy, leathery, and elliptic in shape turning a golden yellow in autumn before falling. In May and June the vine produces loose terminal panicles of many-petaled, greenish white flowers, which by late summer and fall develop into oval, blue black drupes enjoyed by birds. Supplejack adapts to a wide variety of habitats and moisture situations, wet to dry, but looks best in moist, slightly acid to neutral soil in full sun to part shade. Mississippi River Valley and southern Middle and East Tennessee.

Bignonia capreolata (Anisostichus capreolata)
Crossvine
[big-'noh-nee-uh kap-ree-ah-'lay-tuh]
Bignoniaceae (Bignonia Family)

Bignonia capreolata (crossvine).

Crossvine is a high climbing (35 to 50 feet) woody vine. Leaves have paired, opposite leaflets and a branched tendril with suction disks to aid climbing. Clusters of 2 to 5 trumpet shaped flowers (2 inches long), red on the outside and yellow on the inside, hang from leaf axils and attract hummingbirds from April to June. In autumn flat, brown seedpods 4 to 7 inches long, split open to release winged seeds. Crossvine can be semi-evergreen, with leaves turning a purplish tone in winter. Training the vine horizontally will keep the flowers within view.

Cutting through a crossvine branch shows the center pith in the shape of a cross. It is a fast-growing and long-lived vine whose deep roots make transplanting very difficult. However, crossvine is a tough and adaptable plant that takes conditions wet to dry in full sun to part shade and soil pH to either side of neutral. Propagate from seed or cuttings. There are cultivars. Statewide.

Campsis radicans
Trumpet Creeper or Trumpet Vine
['kamp-sis rad-'eye-kanz]
Bignoniaceae (Bignonia Family)

"Keep your legs moving when in the vicinity of this plant," says horticulturist Michael Dirr. Trumpet creeper grows vigorously to 30 feet or more using aerial rootlets and requires sturdy support. Opposite leaves are compound with 7 to 11 coarsely toothed leaflets that come out late in the spring. From June

Campsis radicans (trumpet creeper).

to September large reddish to orange trumpets (2 to 3 inches) bloom in terminal clusters of 4 to 12 flowers and attract hummingbirds, butterflies, and bees. Later 3- to 5-inch seed-pods contain numerous seeds, each with 2 transparent wings.

Pruning is an important task in controlling this vine in smaller gardens. It can send up shoots from roots underground and is as likely to be considered a weedy pest as a desirable plant. Trumpet creeper is difficult to transplant, but like the crossvine is quite adaptable to a variety of moisture situations, even harsh conditions. It likes slightly acid to neutral soil in full sun to part shade. Site trumpet creeper in natural areas where it can do its thing without imposition. There are cultivars available for pure red or yellow flower color. Propagate trumpet creeper with stem or root cuttings and seed. Statewide.

Celastrus scandens
American Bittersweet
[seh-'las-trus 'skan-denz]
Celastraceae (Staff-tree Family)

American bittersweet is a twining woody vine that quickly grows 20 to 25 feet. Leaves are broadly oval, lustrous, and toothed, turning yellow in autumn. In late spring inconspicuous yellowish flowers bloom, but it is in the fall that this vine shows its stuff. Seed capsules, orange on the outside and yellow inside, split open to reveal bright scarlet seeds. Bittersweet is dioecious, so a plant with female flowers is necessary to get the handsome fruit. If there are not many plants in the wild nearby, purchase of a male plant may be necessary to ensure pollination for fruit development. Bittersweet will fruit well in lean, dry, slightly acid soil and full sun. Its rapid growth and lack of additional ornamental value would point to its use on fences or near wild areas. Please do not buy its Chinese cousin, C. *orbiculatus* (oriental bittersweet), a pesky exotic that threatens native plant communities. Birds will eat the fruit; all parts of the plant are poisonous to humans. Far West Tennessee, upper East Tennessee.

Clematis virginiana
Virgin's Bower, Traveller's Joy, Old Man's Beard
['klem-uh-tis vir-jih-nee-'ay-nuh]
Ranunculaceae (Buttercup Family)

Clematis virginiana (virgin's bower).

Known also by the name traveller's joy, virgin's bower is a comparatively low-growing vine at 12 to 15 feet with a loose and open form. Its toothed leaves are trifoliate and assist the plant in climbing by twining the leafstalks around anything they touch. In her 1900 classic, *Nature's Garden*, Neltje Blanchan poetically describes this trait: "[O]ur traveller's joy, that flings out the right hand of good fellowship to every twig within reach, winds about the sapling in brotherly embrace, drapes a festoon of flowers from shrub to shrub, hooks even its sensitive leafstalks over any available support as it clambers and riots on its lovely way." The foliage is a clean green, sporting numerous clusters of small, fragrant white flowers from the axils between July and September. A long, silvery, feathery plume attached to each seed gives the resulting seed heads a decorative appearance and inspired another common name, old man's beard. It is dioecious, so male plants will not produce seed. But often some flowers on a plant will have both pistils and stamens allowing pollination and seed set. In full sun to part shade,

Clematis viorna (leather-flower).

virgin's bower is adaptable to various moisture conditions, too. It grows quickly, preferring moist, slightly acid to neutral soil. It is also difficult to transplant. Prune to within a few feet of the ground every 2 to 3 years. Propagate from seed or cuttings. Statewide.

C. viorna [vee-'or-nuh], leather-flower, is another small vine (8 to 12 feet) with opposite, pinnately compound leaves of 3 to 7 elliptic leaflets that are thin and entire and 1-inch, bell-shaped flowers nodding at the ends of long stalks from the leaf axils. The flower is composed of 4 thick sepals, leathery in appearance and of a dull purple color. Sepal tips recurve slightly to give each blossom a dainty charm. The seed heads are graced with long plumes similar to virgin's bower. Leather-flower blooms in June and July in rich, moist soil and light shade to part sun. East Tennessee, lightly in Middle Tennessee.

C. versicolor [ver-'sih-kuh-ler], also called **leather-flower,** is very similar to *C. viorna* with the exceptions of slightly thicker leaves and greenish tips on the leathery, dull purple blossoms. Middle Tennessee.

C. crispa ['kris-puh], **marsh leather-flower** or **blue jasmine,** has compound leaves with 5 to 9 lance-shaped leaflets. Fragrant, blue purple, bell-shaped flowers nod on long stalks. The sepals have crinkled edges and recurved tips. The distinctive seed head has numerous flattened projections or spiky tails. This vine blooms in June in wet, swampy soil and part shade. West Tennessee.

Cocculus carolinus
Carolina Snailseed, Coralbeads
['kok-yew-lus kair-ah-'ly-nus]
Menispermaceae (Moonseed Family)

A slender, low-growing vine at 6 to 10 feet, Carolina snailseed twines but does not branch much. Hairy stems have alternate, triangular or broadly ovate leaves that can sometimes be slightly 3-lobed and have a woolly lower surface. In autumn the leaves may drop or may be persistent. Loose spikes of small, greenish white flowers protrude from leaf axils in July and August and produce glossy, pea-sized, bright red berries in September and October. Inside the berry the actual seed is flattened and resembles a snail shell. Birds and mammals eat the berries, which are poisonous to man. The vine is dioecious, so only the females will produce berries. The male flowers, however, are larger.

Carolina snailseed grows quickly during the year and dies back. It prefers sandy soil either side of neutral, but will tolerate a wide range of moisture conditions, flood to drought, in full sun to light shade. It can be considered pesky due to bird-sown seedlings and its suckering habit, but it scrambles easily among shrubs and small trees in a naturalized setting. New vines are slow to fruit. Statewide.

Cocculus carolinus (Carolina snailseed).

Decumaria barbara
Climbing Hydrangea
[dek-yew-'may-ree-uh 'bar-buh-ruh]
Saxifragaceae (Saxifrage Family)

Climbing hydrangea can reach 30 feet with the assistance of aerial rootlets. Horizontal branches extend outward 2 feet with terminal, flat-topped clusters of fragrant white flowers in May and June. A ribbed, urn-shaped seed

Decumaria barbara (climbing hydrangea).

capsule lasts through October. Opposite leaves are thick, ovate, glossy, and toothed near the tips. Climbing hydrangea likes slightly acid soil in a moist, rich woodland setting in part to light shade. Train it on a horizontal support to enjoy the blooms. It is hard to transplant unless pruned severely. Southern counties of West and Middle Tennessee, southern Unaka Mountains.

Gelsemium sempervirens (yellow jessamine).

Gelsemium sempervirens
Yellow or Carolina Jessamine (Jasmine)
[jel-'see-mee-um sem-'per-vih-renz]
Loganiaceae (Logania Family)

Yellow jessamine is a twining, semi-evergreen vine growing 10 to 20 feet, with thin, wiry stems and opposite, lance-shaped leaves. Very fragrant, funnel-shaped flowers bloom in April in small clusters of 1 to 3 blooms, each 1½ inches long. Fruit capsules contain winged seeds. Moist but well-drained soil with humus in full sun is best. It will take some shade and is not fussy about soil pH. Propagate by seed or cuttings. A coastal plain and piedmont native, yellow jessamine sneaks into Tennessee around Chattanooga and is a popular garden plant.

Lonicera sempervirens (coral honeysuckle).

Lonicera sempervirens
Coral or Trumpet Honeysuckle
[lah-'nih-ser-uh sem-'per-vih-renz]
Caprifoliaceae (Honeysuckle Family)

The botanical ornament of choice for mailboxes, coral honeysuckle can grow from 10 to 20 feet with semi-evergreen paired leaves, the upper pairs of which are united at the base around the stem. Whorled clusters of bright scarlet, slender tubular flowers, each about 1½ inches long, bloom at branch tips from April until September. They are pollinated

by hummingbirds and visited by bees and butterflies. The vine does not fruit reliably but
can produce clustered scarlet berries from late
summer to fall that are eaten by birds. Coral
honeysuckle is long-lived and has bark that
exfoliates in long, papery strips on older wood.

Our native honeysuckle is a delightful
and well-behaved alternative to the invasive,
exotic pest, Japanese honeysuckle (*Lonicera
japonica*), also called Hall's honeysuckle.
Coral honeysuckle likes rich, well-drained,
slightly acid to slightly alkaline soil, moist to
somewhat dry. Full sun is best, but it will take
some shade. Difficult to transplant, it is best
propagated through seed, layering, or cuttings.
There are several cultivars including 'Sul-
phurea', a pure yellow flower. Statewide.

There is also a yellow-flowered species,
L. flava ['flay-vuh], **yellow honeysuckle**, that
blooms in April and May. It produces yellow
to reddish orange berries and otherwise is
similar to the coral species. Lightly in southern counties.

Lonicera flava (yellow honeysuckle).

Menispermum canadense
Common or Canada Moonseed
[meh-nih-'sper-mum kan-uh-'den-see]
Menispermaceae (Moonseed Family)

Moonseed can sprawl on the ground or twine
to a height of 6 to 12 feet. Alternate leaves
are broadly heart shaped, often with gentle
palmate lobes, and turn yellow in autumn.
The leaf stem or petiole is attached to the leaf
underside. In June and July there are drooping panicles of small, greenish white to yellow
flowers. Dioecious, the female plants produce
blue black berries in loose clusters in the fall
that are eaten by birds and mammals but poisonous to man. Enclosed seeds are flat and
moon shaped.

This is another adaptable vine that can take wet or dry, rich soil, moderately acid to neutral, in part sun to medium shade. It grows fast and is short-lived. The slender stems need support. Statewide.

Parthenocissus quinquefolia
Virginia Creeper
[par-the-noh-'sih-sus kwin-kweh-'foh-lee-uh]
Vitaceae (Grape Family)

Parthenocissus quinquefolia (Virginia creeper)

Scott Woodbury, Shaw Arboretum.

Virginia creeper vigorously climbs 30 to 50 feet or more with the aid of aerial rootlets and branching tendrils that develop strong adhesive disks on the tips. This adhesive quality allows Virginia creeper to climb walls without any additional support, but it can be just as happy crawling along the ground. Alternate leaves are palmately compound with 5 toothed leaflets in a rich, dark green color. Clusters of tiny, yellow green flowers in June and July are inconspicuous when visible and usually hide beneath the foliage. In September and October globular blue black berries on red stalks are also often obscured by the foliage, but the rich crimson fall foliage, among the first to color in autumn, is Virginia creeper's greatest asset. In *How to Know the Wild Flowers*, Mrs. Dana describes "its blood-like sprays . . . outlined against the dark evergreens about which they delight to twine, showing that marvellous discrimination in background which so constantly excites our admiration in nature." Once the leaves have fallen, the berries become more visible provided the birds have left any behind.

Virginia creeper is very adaptable in culture growing in full sun or light shade in soil that is wet or dry and moderately acid to neutral. It is tough, fast growing, and long-lived. If a plant is nearby, bird-sown seedlings will crop up in the garden. Propagate by seed or cuttings. There are cultivars. Middle and East Tennessee, lightly in West Tennessee.

Passiflora incarnata
Passion-flower, Maypop
[pass-ih-'flor-uh in-kar-'nay-tuh]
Passifloraceae (Passion-flower Family)

Passiflora incarnata (passion-flower).

Passion-flower trails on the ground or clambers over shrubbery 10 to 25 feet with the aid of tendrils from the leaf axils. Alternate leaves are toothed and lobed, and in addition to the tendrils, 1 or 2 flowers are produced in the axils, too. The lavender flowers are large (2 to 3 inches across) and fringed, blooming from June through August. A yellowish, egg-shaped, edible fruit 2 inches long follows. The showy blossom, our state wildflower, is a complex arrangement of floral elements. Ten oblong, whitish blue petals and sepals underlie a wide corona of white and purple fringe over which a 3-lobed style and a 5-lobed anther tube spread horizontally across the flower face. Passion-flowers need well-drained, moderately to slightly acid soil on the dry side in full sun to part shade. Leaves are a butterfly larval food, bees like the flowers, and mammals eat the fruit. Be aware that underground runners shoot up clones around the parent plant, producing lush, heavy growth. Propagate by division or cuttings.

    P. lutea ['lew-tee-uh], **yellow** or **small passion-flower,** has quietly attractive, 1-inch, greenish yellow flowers and round (½-inch diameter), dark purple fruit on a dainty vine that tops out at 10 feet. It needs moist soil, can take more shade, and also spreads via underground runners though not as aggressively. Both are statewide.

Passiflora lutea (yellow passion-flower).

Vitis riparia
Riverbank Grape
['vy-tis rih-'pay-ree-uh]
Vitaceae (Grape Family)

Grapes are high-climbing vines that drape and loop over tall trees leaving long, leggy stems with shredding, loose bark. Alternate leaves are heart shaped, lobed, and toothed. They start out reddish in spring and turn yellow in autumn before dropping. Spikes of flowers, yellow green in color, are quite fragrant in May and June. In late summer loose clusters of blue black fruit are eaten with relish by songbirds, waterfowl, game birds, and mammals. Either a tendril or a flower cluster is opposite each leaf along the stem. Plants are considered dioecious, but there are usually a few flowers of the opposite sex present.

Grapes tolerate shade and a wide range of situations, wet to dry in slightly acid to neutral soil. They grow fast and live a long time. *V. vulpina* [vul-'py-nuh], **frost grape**, is very similar with the exception that its leaf is not lobed. As the common name implies the fruit, quite acid and sour, sweetens after frost. *V. rotundifolia* [roh-tun-dih-'foh-lee-uh], **muscadine grape**, has glossy leaves and tighter bark. The leaves of *V. aestivalis* [es-tih-'vay-lis], **summer grape**, are hairy below. These 3 species are more common in Tennessee than *V. riparia*, but are harder to find commercially.

Wisteria frutescens (W. macrostachya)
American Wisteria
[wis-'teer-ee-uh frue-'tes-enz]
Fabaceae (Pea Family)

American wisteria climbs to 30 feet and needs sturdy support. The vine has alternate, compound leaves with 9 to 15 elliptical leaflets. Fragrant flowers are clustered in a raceme 4 to 6 inches long and bloom in May and June on current growth. Each blossom is pale lilac purple with a yellow spot. Knobby linear seedpods are 2 to 4 inches long. The vine is a butterfly larval food. Our native wisteria is not as vigorous as the exotic species, *W. floribunda* and *W. sinensis*, which are considered pest plants. American wisteria needs slightly acid to neutral soil that is fertile and reliably moist to wet in full sun to part shade. It is fast growing, long-lived, and difficult to transplant. There are cultivars. Propagate from seed or cut tings. West Tennessee, lightly elsewhere.

Wisteria frutescens 'Amethyst Falls' (American wisteria).

Shrubs

Ornamental Interest and Site Summary

This summary provides a quick reference to the distinctive horticultural characteristics and site preferences of the shrubs featured in this book. A complete description, cultural information, and state distribution for each plant follow the summary. The following abbreviations appear in the summary.

Flower Season and Color:

Sp—Spring
Su—Summer
Wh—White
Y—Yellow
O—Orange
P—Pink

R—Red
Pr—Purple
GBM—Green, brown, maroon

Distinctions:

Fr—Fruit
Lf—Leaf (shape or color)
Bk—Bark
Ev—Evergreen
Ar—Aromatic, fragrant
UF—Unique form
LW—Low woody, under 6 feet

Site Preferences:

S—Full sun to part shade
Sh—Part sun to medium shade
Alk—Tolerates slight alkalinity
PS—Poor soil, low fertility
WS—Wet soil
MS—Moist soil
DS—Dry soil

Shrubs	Flower	Distinctions	Site
Alnus serrulata (tag alder)	Sp GBM	Fr	S, WS
Amorpha fruticosa (indigo bush)	Sp/Su Pr	Fr	S, PS WS-DS
Aronia arbutifolia (red chokeberry)	Sp Wh	Lf, Fr, Ar	S WS/MS
Aronia melanocarpa (black chokeberry)	Sp Wh	Lf, Fr, Ar, LW	S WS/MS
Callicarpa americana (beautyberry)	Su P	Fr, LW	S, MS
Calycanthus floridus (sweetshrub)	Sp GBM	Ar	Sh WS/MS
Ceanothus americanus (New Jersey tea)	Sp/Su Wh	LW	S/Sh DS, PS
Cephalanthus occidentalis (buttonbush)	Su Wh	Fr, Ar, UF	S, Alk WS/MS

(Continued next page)

Shrubs	Flower	Distinctions	Site
Clethra acuminata (cinnamon clethra)	Su Wh	Fr, Ar, Bk	S/Sh MS/DS
Clethra alnifolia (sweet pepperbush)	Su Wh	Fr, Ar, Bk	S WS/MS
Conradina verticillata (Cumberland rosemary)	Sp P	Ar, LW	S MS/DS
Cornus amomum (silky dogwood)	Sp/Su Wh	Lf, Fr	S WS/MS
Corylus americana (American filbert)	Sp GBM/R	Fr	S/Sh MS/DS
Diervilla lonicera & *D. sessilifolia* (northern & southern bush honeysuckle)	Su Y	LW	S, PS MS/DS
Dirca palustris (leatherwood)	Sp Y	Fr, LW	Sh, MS Alk
Euonymus americanus (strawberry bush)	Sp GBM	Fr, LW	Sh, MS
Fothergilla gardenii (dwarf fothergilla)	Sp Wh	Lf, Ar, LW	S WS/MS
Fothergilla major (large fothergilla)	Sp Wh	Lf, Ar	S WS/MS
Hydrangea arborescens (smooth hydrangea)	Sp/Su Wh	Fr, Bk, LW	Sh, MS Alk
Hydrangea quercifolia (oakleaf hydrangea)	Sp/Su Wh	Lf, Fr, Bk	Sh, MS Alk
Hypericum densiflorum (dense St. John's wort)	Su Y	Fr, Bk, LW	S WS-DS
Hypericum frondosum (golden St. John's-wort)	Su Y	Fr, Bk, LW	S, Alk MS/DS
Hypericum prolificum (shrubby St. John's-wort)	Su Y	Fr, Bk, LW	S, Alk WS-DS
Ilex decidua (possumhaw)	Sp Wh	Fr	S/Sh, Alk WS/MS
Ilex glabra (inkberry)	Sp Wh	Fr, Ev	S/Sh WS/MS
Ilex verticillata (winterberry)	Sp Wh	Fr	S WS/MS

(Continued next page)

Shrubs	Flower	Distinctions	Site
Itea virginica (Virginia sweetspire)	Sp Wh	Lf, Ar	Sh WS/MS
Kalmia latifolia (mountain laurel)	Sp Wh	Ev	Sh WS/MS
Leucothoe fontanesiana (doghobble)	Sp Wh	Ev, LW	Sh, MS
Lindera benzoin (spicebush)	Sp Y	Lf, Fr, Ar	Sh, MS
Philadelphus hirsutus, P. inodorus, & P. pubescens (hairy, common, & downy mock-orange)	Sp Wh	Bk	S/Sh MS/DS
Physocarpus opulifolius (ninebark)	Sp Wh	Fr, Bk	S, Alk WS-DS
Rhododendron alabamense (Alabama azalea)	Sp Wh	Ar, LW	Sh, DS
Rhododendron arborescens (sweet azalea)	Sp Wh	Ar	Sh WS/MS
Rhododendron calendulaceum & R. cumberlandense (flame & Cumberland azalea)	Sp Y/O/R		Sh, MS
Rhododendron canescens (piedmont azalea)	Sp Wh/P	Ar	Sh, MS
Rhododendron catawbiense (Catawba rhododendron)	Sp P/Pr	Ev	Sh MS/DS
Rhododendron minus (Carolina rhododendron)	Sp P	Ev, LW	Sh, MS
Rhododendron periclymenoides (pinxterbloom azalea)	Sp P	Ar, LW	Sh WS-DS
Rhododendron prinophyllum (roseshell azalea)	Sp P	Ar, LW	Sh, Alk MS/DS
Rhododendron vaseyi (pinkshell azalea)	Sp P		Sh WS/MS
Rhododendron viscosum (swamp azalea)	Su Wh	Ar	S, WS
Rhus aromatica (fragrant sumac)	Sp Y/GBM	Lf, Fr, Ar, LW	S, DS Alk
Rosa carolina (Carolina rose)	Sp/Su P	Lf, Fr, LW	S, Alk WS-DS

(Continued next page)

Shrubs	Flower	Distinctions	Site
Rosa palustris (swamp rose)	Sp/Su P	Lf, Fr	S/Sh WS/MS
Rosa setigera (prairie rose)	Su P	Lf, Fr, LW	S, Alk MS/DS
Rubus argutus & *R. occidentalis* (tall blackberry & blackcap raspberry)	Sp Wh	Fr, LW	S MS/DS
Rubus flagellaris (northern dewberry)	Sp Wh	Fr, LW	S, PS MS/DS
Sambucus canadensis (American elder)	Su Wh	Fr, Ar	S WS/MS
Spiraea tomentosa (hardhack)	Su P	Bk, LW	S WS/MS
Staphylea trifolia (American bladdernut)	Sp Wh	Lf, Fr, Bk	Sh WS/MS
Styrax americana (American snowbell)	Sp Wh	Fr	S WS/MS
Styrax grandifolia (bigleaf snowbell)	Sp Wh	Fr	Sh MS/DS
Symphoricarpos orbiculatus (coralberry)	Su Wh/P	Fr, LW	Sh, Alk MS/DS
Vaccinium arboreum (farkleberry)	Sp Wh	Lf, Fr, Bk	Sh, DS
Vaccinium corymbosum (highbush blueberry)	Sp Wh	Lf, Fr	S, MS
Vaccinium pallidum (late lowbush blueberry)	Sp Wh	Lf, Fr, LW	S/Sh DS
Vaccinium stamineum (deerberry)	Sp Wh	Lf, Fr	S/Sh DS
Viburnum acerifolium (mapleleaf viburnum)	Sp Wh	Lf, Fr, LW	Sh MS/DS
Viburnum cassinoides (northern witherod)	Sp/Su Wh	Lf, Fr	S/Sh WS-DS
Viburnum dentatum & *V. nudum* (arrowwood & possumhaw viburnum)	Sp/Su Wh	Lf, Fr	S/Sh WS/MS
Xanthorhiza simplicissima (yellowroot)	Sp GBM	Lf, Fr	Sh WS/MS

Description, Culture, and Distribution

Alnus serrulata (tag alder).

The Center for Field Biology, a Tennessee Center of Excellence at Austin Peay State University.

Alnus serrulata
Tag, Smooth, or Common Alder
['al-nus ser-ruh-'lay-tuh]
Betulaceae (Birch Family)

Alder is a large multi-stemmed shrub 10 to 20 feet high that branches out to a similar width. It suckers at the base to colonize. Leaves are obovate, finely toothed, dark green, and downy along the veins. In autumn alders color late, turning yellow tinged with red. Flowering in early spring before the leaves, they produce slender, drooping, male catkins and short, oval, female cones. The fruit is a woody, conelike structure that persists from midsummer through winter and is enjoyed by some birds. Deer and beaver like the tag alder, too. Tag alder grows in the wet, swampy soil of stream banks and bogs, moderately acid to neutral, in full sun, and can fix nitrogen in the soil like plants in the pea family. It transplants easily but may be hard to find in nurseries. Statewide.

Amorpha fruticosa
Indigo Bush, False Indigo
[uh-'more-fuh frue-tih-'koh-suh]
Fabaceae (Pea Family)

Amorpha fruticosa (indigo bush).

Scott C. Gunn, Division of Natural Heritage, Tennessee Department of Environment and Conservation.

A leggy shrub 6 to 12 feet tall, most of indigo bush's pinnately compound foliage is in the upper one-third of the plant. Each leaf has 9 to 25 leaflets. It bears narrow terminal spikes of purplish blue flowers with bright orange anthers in June. Flowers are followed by clusters of small brown pods that persist through winter and feed some birds and mammals. It is also a butterfly larval food. Indigo bush needs full sun and likes wet, swampy areas but is very adaptable to different moisture conditions, including drought. It is not particular about soil pH. This shrub self-sows and can be weedy, but it transplants well and is a good choice for poor areas. There are cultivars. Statewide.

Aronia arbutifolia (Pyrus arbutifolia)
Red Chokeberry
[uh-'roh-nee-uh ar-byew-tih-'foh-lee-uh]
Rosaceae (Rose Family)

Chokeberry has multiple, erect stems in a rounded crown 6 to 11 feet high with a spread of 3 to 5 feet. It will send out suckers to form colonies. Alternate leaves are elliptic and finely toothed, coloring a dark, glossy green in summer and a terrific red in autumn. New growth and leaf undersides are woolly. In April and May it blooms with flat-topped clusters of wonderfully fragrant white flowers sporting red anthers. Throughout the fall and winter, clusters of red berries load the shrub. Birds and small mammals will eventually eat them, and hoofed animals use the shrub for browse.

Red chokeberry is found naturally in wet to moist places, but it adapts quite well to regular garden moisture and even dryness. Full sun is best, though a little shade is acceptable in moderately to slightly acid soil. *A. melanocarpa (A. prunifolia, Pyrus melanocarpa)* [meh-lan-ah-'kar-puh], **black chokeberry**, is smaller than the red species, growing about 3 to 6 feet tall, and the berry is black to purplish black. Both species are found on the

Aronia arbutifolia (red chokeberry).

Aronia arbutifolia 'Brilliantissima'— fruit (red chokeberry).

Eastern Highland Rim, Cumberland Plateau, Unaka Mountains, and lightly in the West Tennessee Uplands.

Callicarpa americana
Beautyberry
[kal-ih-'kar-puh uh-mair-ih-'kay-nuh]
Verbenaceae (Vervain Family)

Callicarpa americana (beautyberry).

Beautyberry forms a loose, open shrub 3 to 6 feet tall with large, opposite, elliptic leaves that are toothed and hairy below. They turn yellowish in the fall. Cymes of lavender pink flowers appear in the leaf axils of new growth from June through September. Bright light purple berries in clusters that virtually encircle the twig put on quite a show in October. Birds eat the berries. Prune it as needed; it roots easily from cuttings during the summer. It will take some shade, but fruits best in full sun with reliably moist soil. Soil pH can vary. Statewide in the southern half.

Calycanthus floridus
Sweetshrub, Carolina Allspice,
**   Strawberry-shrub**
[kal-ih-'kan-thus 'flor-ih-dus]
Calycanthaceae (Strawberry-shrub Family)

Calycanthus floridus (sweetshrub).

Sweetshrub is a dense, rounded shrub 6 to 9 feet in height with an equal width. Leaves are opposite and elliptic. Its main asset is the flower, a 2-inch wide, solitary blossom with numerous narrow, straplike petals and sepals of maroon that curve up, overlap, and release a sweet, fruity fragrance in May and June. They appear at the tips of short branchlets. The twigs are aromatic, too. Narrow, pear-shaped, leathery, brown pods contain many seeds and persist through fall and winter.

Few plants are as amiable as sweetshrub. It is virtually trouble free and very adaptable to variations in light, moisture, and soil pH. In nature it chooses wet to moist forests with slightly acid to neutral soil and light shade. There is a yellow-flowered cultivar, 'Athens', that is very fragrant. Young suckering plants are easily transplanted in late winter or early spring. It prunes well and is easy to grow from seed. Flower fragrance may vary; buy with your nose. East Tennessee, lightly in Middle Tennessee.

Ceanothus americanus
New Jersey Tea
[see-uh-'noh-thus uh-mair-ih-'kay-nus]
Rhamnaceae (Buckthorn Family)

A small, dense shrub 3 feet high and wide, New Jersey tea has alternate, ovate, toothed leaves covered below in a rusty down when young. Short spikes of tiny white flowers bloom from the leaf axils of new growth in June. Three-lobed, dry capsules mature in September and October. Birds and small mammals eat the fruit; leaves and twigs feed browsers; and butterflies sip the flower nectar. New Jersey tea grows best in the part to light shade of upland woodland edges and tolerates poor, dry conditions. The soil must be very well drained and moderately to slightly acid. It is difficult to transplant. The common name comes from its use as a tea substitute during the Revolutionary War. Statewide.

Ceanothus americanus (New Jersey tea).

Cephalanthus occidentalis
(buttonbush).

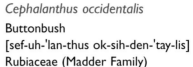

Cephalanthus occidentalis
Buttonbush
[sef-uh-'lan-thus ok-sih-den-'tay-lis]
Rubiaceae (Madder Family)

Boasting many attractive features, button-bush has a loose, open habit, branching at the ends to a height of 5 to 12 feet with a similar width. Oval glossy leaves in whorls of 3 or 4 set off long-stalked, spherical blossom heads. The 1-inch-diameter sphere is composed of numerous tiny, white, tubular flowers in July and August. These sweetly fragrant balls of flowers, studded with protruding styles, call to mind pin cushions and attract many bees and butterflies hungry for the nectar. Globular balls of nutlets change from reddish and greenish to bronzy brown with frost and per-sist through the winter. Water birds enjoy the seeds, and deer and beaver browse.

Buttonbush's native habitat is the wet soil of swamps and pond banks, and in a gar-den setting it needs reliably moist soil, slightly acid to slightly alkaline, and full sun. It transplants well. One source recommended periodic severe pruning to reinvigorate the plant and aid flower production. Statewide.

Clethra alnifolia
Sweet Pepperbush, Summersweet
['kleth-ruh al-nih-'foh-lee-uh]
Clethraceae (Clethra Family)

Sweet pepperbush has an erect, oval shape, growing 5 to 10 feet high and 4 to 6 feet wide. The alternate leaves are obovate, glossy, and sharply toothed. The deep green leaf color of summer becomes yellow orange to rich brown in autumn. Exfoliating bark adds an inter-esting winter texture. Small white flowers with long stamens and a protruding style are

Clethra alnifolia (sweet pepperbush).

clustered in terminal spikes in July and August on new growth and give off a satisfying spicy fragrance. Bees and butterflies love them. Dry brown fruit capsules, tipped with the long style, persist through winter and are eaten by birds and small mammals.

Swamps or damp thickets are the typical habitat. Moist soil is a preference but not a necessity as sweet pepperbush is adaptable. It can take full sun or part shade and a range of acid soils. It leafs out late in spring, should be pruned before leafing out, and does not transplant well. It will send out suckers and colonize. There are now several cultivars including 'Rosea' (pinkish in bud and flower) and 'Hummingbird' (dwarf). The natural range of the sweet pepperbush is coastal, but it was unexpectedly found growing in Coffee County (Arnold Engineering site) and is an established garden favorite here.

C. acuminata [uh-kyew-mih-'nay-tuh], **cinnamon clethra** or **mountain pepperbush**, differs from *C. alnifolia* in two respects. As the first common name suggests, its reddish brown, exfoliating bark adds a color dimension to its winter interest. As the second common name suggests, it is found naturally in the Cumberland and Unaka Mountains of East Tennessee on well-drained, rocky slopes. All other information is identical.

Conradina verticillata
Cumberland Rosemary
[kon-ruh-'dy-nuh ver-tih-sih-'lay-tuh]
Lamiaceae (Mint Family)

This densely branched little shrub resembles in look and aroma the rosemary of kitchen and herb gardens. It grows about a foot or so high, liberally producing opposite, linear

Conradina verticillata (Cumberland rosemary).

leaves that have smaller leaf pairs in each axil. Leaves are a smooth green on top and woolly gray below with the margins rolled under. Pinkish lavender flowers bloom in the upper leaf axils in May and June. Cumberland rosemary demands moist to dry, sandy, well-drained soil and full sun. It is listed as a threatened rare plant by both state and federal authorities; however, easy propagation (cuttings) makes it readily available in the nursery trade. Cumberland rosemary is found only along the sandy, rocky stream banks in the Cumberland Mountains in Tennessee and Kentucky.

Paul Somers, Division of Natural Heritage, Tennessee Department of Environment and Conservation.

Cornus amomum
Silky Dogwood
['kore-nus uh-'moh-mum]
Cornaceae (Dogwood Family)

Cornus amomum (silky dogwood).

Silky dogwood forms a mound nearly twice as wide as its 6- to 12-foot height and is quite twiggy with velvety hairs and woolly buds. Opposite, elliptic leaves appear reddish green in spring and purplish red in fall. Flat-topped clusters of yellowish white flowers in June are followed by blue berries with a whitish bloom in September. The berries do not last long as they are gathered with relish by birds and small mammals. The moist soil of low, wet areas in full sun to part shade provides an ideal habitat for silky dogwoods. Soil pH should be slightly acid to neutral. It transplants easily and looks good massed along the edges of a wood or thicket. It is good for erosion control and provides excellent wildlife cover. Statewide.

Corylus americana
American Filbert or Hazelnut
['kore-ih-lus uh-mair-ih-'kay-nuh]
Betulaceae (Birch Family)

Dense with widely spreading branches, American filbert is 6 to 12 feet high and nearly as wide. Alternate leaves are ovate, double toothed, and yellow tinged from spring to fall. Twigs and leaf stems are hairy. In early spring (March) drooping, yellow brown male catkins 1 to 3 inches long contrast with tiny, bright red female blossoms that attract early butterflies. Oval nuts wrapped in thin, hairy, ragged-edged husks are clustered in autumn. Birds and small mammals eat them and others browse the foliage. Place the hazelnut in an open natural area with well-drained soil, moist to dry and slightly acid to neutral, in full sun to light shade. It transplants well; prune to control suckering and maintain appearance. Statewide.

Corylus americana (American filbert).

Diervilla sessilifolia
Southern Bush Honeysuckle
[dy-er-'vih-luh seh-sih-lih-'foh-lee-uh]
Caprifoliaceae (Honeysuckle Family)

Our native bush honeysuckle grows 3 to 5 feet tall and wide, suckering at the base. The dark green leaves are opposite, sessile, ovate to lanceolate, and toothed. The flowers are yellow, tubular, ½ inch in length, and appear in axillary and terminal clusters in June and July. Each slender pointed fruit capsule has dried calyx lobes flaring out at the tip. This is one tough plant, growing vigorously even on dry, rocky soil in full sun. It is easy, adaptable to any well-drained situation, and tolerant of shade. *D. lonicera* [lah-'nih-ser-uh], northern

Diervilla sessilifolia (southern bush honeysuckle).

bush honeysuckle, is very similar except for smaller, stalked leaves. Please do not confuse these natives with the harmful, exotic pest bush honeysuckles (*Lonicera maackii*, *L. morrowii*). Both native bush honeysuckles should be pruned in early spring and are found in East Tennessee.

Dirca palustris
Leatherwood
['dir-kuh puh-'lus-tris]
Thymelaeaceae (Mezereum Family)

Dirca palustris (leatherwood).

Globular in shape, leatherwood grows up and out 3 to 6 feet. It is densely branched and often assumes a tree form even as a small shrub. Alternate obovate leaves turn yellow in autumn. In March and April short, pale yellow, tubular flowers hang in clusters and produce oval, red berries in June and July that drop early. Twigs are quite pliable and can be tied in knots. Leatherwood is hard to transplant and needs slightly acid to slightly alkaline, moist, well-drained soil in light to medium shade. It favors the cool ravines of rich woodlands. Middle and East Tennessee.

Euonymus americanus
Strawberry Bush, Heart's-a-bustin'
(Hearts-a-burstin')
[yew-'on-ih-mus uh-mair-ih-'kay-nus]
Celastraceae (Bittersweet Family)

Euonymus americanus (strawberry bush).

The branches of strawberry bush trace a loose, open growth habit 4 to 6 feet high and 3 to 4 feet wide with green, 4-sided twigs. Oblong leaves are opposite and finely toothed, turning a yellowish color in fall. Small pale green to purplish flowers appear singly or in clusters of 3 in the leaf axils in May. In September and October, strawberry bush/heart's-a-bustin' demonstrates why it has these names and just how apt they are. Lobed, warty-looking, rose red capsules quite reminiscent of strawberries split open to dangle shiny, bright orange seeds. Songbirds eat the scarlet seeds and deer browse the foliage. This native *Euonymus* needs deep, moist soil, rich in humus and slightly acid. It will take medium shade but fruits best in part sun to light shade. It transplants easily. Statewide.

Fothergilla gardenii
Dwarf Fothergilla, Dwarf Witch-alder
[fah-ther-'gih-luh 'gar-den-ee-eye]
Hamamelidaceae (Witch Hazel Family)

A small, rounded shrub, dwarf fothergilla is about 3 feet tall and wide, sometimes wider due to its suckering nature. Alternate oval leaves are pale and woolly below with a leathery, quilted appearance that reveals the plant's strong kinship with witch hazel. The leaves color beautifully in autumn with a swirl of yellows, oranges, and reds mixing about. In April and May 1- to 2-inch terminal spikes of white stamens and yellow anthers form little bottlebrushes delicately scented with a sweet honey fragrance before the leaves fully emerge. Fruit is a small beaked capsule in the summer. In the wilds of its coastal and southern Appalachian native habitat, dwarf fothergilla is endangered and rare, but it is readily available in the nursery trade. There are cultivars. It likes wet to moist soil with good drainage in full sun to part shade and a moderately acid soil pH. Flowering and autumn colors are best in sun. Sources claim it is hard to transplant, but mine has

Fothergilla gardenii (dwarf fothergilla).

Fothergilla gardenii—fall foliage (dwarf fothergilla).

been moved twice with no ill effects. Digging a large root ball might account for this success. It is not found naturally in Tennessee.

F. major [may'-jer], large fothergilla or mountain witch-alder, grows 6 to 12 feet in height and about as wide. Its cultural requirements are the same, and it is found sporadically in East Tennessee.

Hydrangea arborescens
Smooth or Wild Hydrangea
[hy-'dran-jee-uh ar-bor-'es-enz]
Saxifragaceae (Saxifrage Family)

Hydrangea arborescens (smooth hydrangea).

Smooth hydrangea is a dense, multi-stemmed small shrub 3 to 6 feet high that suckers to an equal or greater width. Older stems have exfoliating bark. Leaves are opposite, ovate to heart shaped, and toothed. In June and July flat-topped clusters of tiny greenish white fertile flowers are edged sporadically by large, white, sterile flowers. Dried brown seed heads with little urn-shaped seed capsules persist through winter. Smooth hydrangea is found in moist, cool forests with slightly acid to slightly alkaline, organically rich, well-drained soil in light shade. It blooms on new wood and transplants easily. Cultivars have more of the larger, sterile flowers producing a showier bloom than the species. Statewide.

H. quercifolia [kwer-sih-'foh-lee-uh], oakleaf hydrangea, is similar in form and shape to wild hydrangea and has the exfoliating bark on older stems. One additional feature is the velvety appearance of young twigs. The toothed leaves are also distinctive, having a broad oakleaf shape of 3 to 7 lobes. They are dark green in summer and variously reddish orange to purple and brown in autumn with downy felt beneath. Broadly conical clusters

Hydrangea quercifolia (oakleaf hydrangea).

of tiny fertile flowers are studded with larger sterile flowers that turn from greenish to white to pinkish to purple to brown in June and July and persist through the winter like a dried floral arrangement. Oakleaf hydrangea likes well-drained, moist, fertile soil, slightly acid to slightly alkaline, in part sun or light shade. It transplants well; there are cultivars. Southern tier of counties, Memphis to Chattanooga.

Hypericum frondosum
Golden St. John's-wort
[hy-'pair-ih-kum fron-'doh-sum]
Clusiaceae (Mangosteen Family)

Hypericum frondosum (golden St. John's-wort).

An upright shrub growing 3 to 4 feet in height and width, golden St. John's-wort has reddish brown, exfoliating bark and opposite, oblong, bluish green leaves. In July it is covered with large solitary or a few clustered, bright yellow flowers, 1 to 2 inches across, each with a broad ring of numerous stamens puffed out like a pompon. The red brown seed capsules that follow are narrowly conical; some birds eat the seeds. Golden St. John's-wort needs well-drained, dry, neutral to slightly alkaline soil and full sun to part shade. It grows easily from seed. Middle Tennessee.

H. prolificum [proh-'lih-fih-kum], shrubby St. John's-wort, is small and dense, 1 to 4 feet high with narrower leaves and exfoliating bark. Flowers are similar to *H. frondosum.* Shrubby St. John's-wort will take a site that is moist and swampy or dry and rocky in full sun or part shade. Soil can be slightly acid to slightly alkaline. Middle and East Tennessee.

H. densiflorum [den-sih-'flor-um], dense St. John's-wort, is 4 to 6 feet tall, upright, and densely twiggy with very narrow leaves, exfoliating bark, and terminal clusters of smaller yellow flowers arranged in a flat-topped corymb. It grows in full sun in low, swampy, slightly acid soils but is also drought tolerant. Valley and Ridge.

Ilex decidua

Possumhaw

['eye-leks deh-'sid-yew-uh]

Aquifoliaceae (Holly Family)

Possumhaw is a large shrub or small tree 12 to 20 feet high, sometimes taller in the wild. Its width is two-thirds to three-fourths the height, branching up and out. It will colonize. The leaves are a lustrous dark green, alternate, obovate, and toothed. Possumhaw is a deciduous holly. The leaves turn yellowish tan before dropping. It is also dioecious, producing small greenish to white flowers in May and June that are busily worked by bees. In autumn the female plants are loaded with glossy red berries, singly or in clusters, that persist through the winter and are eaten late in the season by song and game birds as tastier food options become scarce. Small mammals such as raccoons and opossums will eat the berries, too. Possumhaw is naturally found in moist to wet soil but adapts well to good garden soil in part shade. It prefers a moderately acid soil pH but can take variations up through slightly alkaline. It transplants well. Several cultivars are available, including 'Warren Red' and others with yellow or orange berries. A male pollinator is necessary; 'Red Escort' will take care of most any *I. decidua* cultivar. Southern and western parts of the state.

Ilex decidua (possumhaw).

I. verticillata [ver-tih-sih-'lay-tuh], **winter-berry**, is a suckering, deciduous shrub 6 to 12 feet tall with dark green leaves that are small, elliptic, and toothed. In June clusters of tiny, greenish white flowers produce an abundance of red berries along the twigs of female plants. These berries can persist all winter along the bare gray branches and feed the birds at season's end. Winterberry also likes wet to moist conditions, moderately acid soil, and full sun to part shade. It transplants well, though sources conflict on its ability to tolerate slightly alkaline soil. There are many cultivars including 'Winter Red' and 'Winter Gold', with a pinkish orange berry, both pollinated by 'Southern Gentleman'. A popular cross with an Asian species is 'Sparkleberry', pollinated by either 'Apollo' or 'Raritan Chief'. East and West Tennessee.

Ilex verticillata (winterberry).

I. glabra ['glay-bruh], **inkberry**, is a globular evergreen shrub 6 to 8 feet high and wide. It, too, will colonize via suckers. Leaves are oblong, alternate, and deep green. Small greenish white flowers in May and June attract bees, and the female plants produce black berries. Birds and small mammals love the berries. Inkberries like wet to moist soil that is strongly to moderately acid. They will grow fine in shade but do best in full sun with ample moisture. They transplant well. Several cultivars are available including dwarf forms and a white-fruited variety. Inkberry is not found naturally in Tennessee; its native range hugs the East Coast. However, it is a good North American native evergreen shrub that grows well here.

Ilex glabra (inkberry).

Itea virginica (Virginia sweetspire).

Itea virginica
Virginia Sweetspire, Virginia Willow
['eye-tee-uh vir-'jih-nih-kuh]
Saxifragaceae (Saxifrage Family)

Virginia sweetspire is an erect branching shrub 4 to 10 feet high and wide. It colonizes. Leaves are alternate, finely toothed, and elliptic. They turn a brilliant crimson to purplish red in autumn. In May and June very fragrant racemes of small, densely packed, white flowers droop from the ends of the branches and attract bees. Fruit capsules in August persist through winter. Sweetspire naturally loves wet to moist soils but can take some dryness reasonably well. Give it moderately acid to neutral soil in light shade or part sun. It transplants easily, and there are cultivars. Statewide.

Kalmia latifolia (mountain laurel).

Kalmia latifolia
Mountain Laurel
['kal-mee-uh lat-ih-'foh-lee-uh]
Ericaceae (Heath Family)

In its youth the evergreen mountain laurel is symmetrical in shape, but as it ages its height, variable from 7 to 15 feet or more, pulls the plant into an open, gnarled, and picturesque form. The leaves are leathery, elliptic, dark green, and glossy, appearing alternate or whorled along the stem. In May terminal clusters of pleated buds open into bowl-shaped, white or pale pink flowers. Each blossom resembles an upside-down umbrella. The ribs of this umbrella are arched stamens whose anthers are lodged in evenly spaced creases of the flower bell. The jar of an alighting bee springs them loose to dust his hairy body for cross pollination. Little spherical seed capsules persist through winter. Mountain laurel favors the light shade of cool ridges in wet, moist, or slightly dry soil that is strongly to moderately acid and well drained. It has shallow roots, so a thin layer of mulch will help keep the roots cool. It transplants well. Highland Rim and East Tennessee.

Leucothoe fontanesiana
(L. axillaris var. editorum)
Doghobble, Dog-laurel, Fetterbush
[lew-'koh-thoh-ee fon-tuh-nee-zee-'ay-nuh]
Ericaceae (Heath Family)

Leucothoe fontanesiana 'Girard's Rainbow' (doghobble).

Doghobble is an evergreen shrub, 2 to 6 feet in height, with reddish branches in a spreading and arching habit. The alternate leaves are a lustrous dark green in summer and take on a bronze or purplish cast in winter. They are oblong to lanceolate in shape, finely toothed, and spiny. In April or May 3-inch-long racemes of white to pinkish bell-shaped flowers droop from the leaf axils, followed by small brown fruit capsules. This plant loves cool mountain stream banks. Give it moist, well-drained, strongly to moderately acid soil in light to medium shade and protect it from drought and wind. It is susceptible to leaf spot, but gardeners have had good results with it. Propagate with cuttings. There are cultivars. Unaka Mountains, lightly elsewhere in East Tennessee.

Lindera benzoin
Spicebush
['lin-deh-ruh ben-'zoh-in]
Lauraceae (Laurel Family)

All parts of the spicebush are aromatic, and the stems can be boiled to make tea. At 6 to 12 feet in height and width, a cup can be enjoyed quite often. In mid- to late March

Lindera benzoin (spicebush).

Lindera benzoin—fruit (spicebush).

and early April, tiny yellow flowers bloom along the stems in clusters. Spicebush is dioecious. Female plants produce oval berries that turn a bright scarlet in September. These berries can be ground into a substitute for allspice. The leaves of the spicebush are alternate, oblong-obovate, and turn a clear yellow in autumn.

Plant spicebush in rich, moist, slightly acid to neutral soil in light shade to part sun. Humans are not alone in the tasty appreciation of the spicebush. A variety of wildlife derives delightful sustenance as well. Birds adore the high-fat berries that ripen at the peak of fall migration; browsers enjoy the twigs and leaves; the spicebush swallowtail butterfly lays her eggs on the leaves, a favorite larval food; and the flowers are a nectar source for early spring butterflies and bees. It germinates easily from seed but is difficult to transplant. Statewide.

Philadelphus spp.
Mock-orange
[fih-luh-'del-fus]
Saxifragaceae (Saxifrage Family)

P. inodorus [in-ah-'dore-us], common mock-orange, grows 6 to 9 feet tall with opposite, ovate, toothed leaves. The bark of year-old twigs exfoliates in thin strips. In May it produces 1 to 3 white, scentless flowers at the end of branchlets. Flowers are 1½ to 2 inches across with numerous yellow stamens. Lightly statewide.

P. hirsutus [hir-'sue-tus], hairy mock-orange, is similar with these exceptions: it is not as tall, has smaller flowers, and has hairy branchlets and leaf undersides. East Tennessee.

P. pubescens [pyew-'bes-ens], **downy mock-orange,** does not have exfoliating twig bark, grows as large as the common mock-orange, and has downy leaf undersides and 5 to 7 flowers in a raceme. Mock-orange fruits are small capsules; they are downy on *P. pubescens*. Middle Tennessee.

Downy and hairy mock-oranges are usually found in drier, neutral, rocky soil. Common mock-orange prefers richer, moister soil. All will grow best in good garden soil and full sun to light shade.

Philadelphus pubescens (downy mock-orange).

Physocarpus opulifolius
Ninebark
[fy-soh-'kar-pus ah-pyew-lih-'foh-lee-us]
Rosaceae (Rose Family)

Ninebark grows 5 to 10 feet tall and a bit wider, with a dense and rounded appearance. Branch bark exfoliates in long, papery strips for winter interest and is the inspiration for the common name. Leaves are alternate and broadly ovate with 3 or more toothed lobes. In autumn they turn yellow or bronzy. In May and June there are flat-topped clusters of numerous, small, white or pink-tinged flowers. In midsummer 3-parted, inflated fruit capsules are produced that start out red then turn brown and persist. Birds and small mammals eat them. Adaptable to moisture conditions ranging from wet to dry, ninebark does well in slightly acid to slightly alkaline soil with full sun or part shade. It transplants easily. Cultivars are available for leaf color and smaller form. Middle and East Tennessee.

Physocarpus opulifolius (ninebark).

Kurt Emmanuele.

Rhododendron arborescens (sweet azalea).

Rhododendron spp.
Azalea and Rhododendron
[roh-doh-'den-dron]
Ericaceae (Heath Family)

With such a beautiful legacy of native azaleas in the Southeast, it is hard to imagine why anyone would want or need to look further. Our azaleas are deciduous, but their subtle autumn colorings, floriferous habits, and ease of cultivation more than make up for bare winter branches. Butterflies enjoy the nectar and use azaleas for larval food. There are two native evergreen rhododendrons to consider as well.

R. alabamense [al-uh-bam-'en-see], Alabama azalea, grows 4 to 6 feet high and spreads by stolons to colonize. In late April or early May along with the new leaves it produces fragrant clusters of tubular, white flowers, often with a yellow blotch. Leaves are dark green and elliptical to obovate. It likes dry, rocky soil in light shade and often hybridizes with other azaleas. Middle Tennessee.

R. arborescens [ar-bor-'es-enz], sweet azalea, is a large, erect shrub 10 to 20 feet high with alternate, obovate, dark green foliage that is aromatic and takes on a reddish cast in the fall. In June it produces terminal clusters of fragrant, white funnel flowers with reddish or purplish styles and stamens. Sweet azalea is found in the well-drained but wet to moist, moderately acid soil of stream banks in light shade. There are cultivars and it transplants well. East Tennessee.

R. calendulaceum [kuh-len-dyew-'lay-see-um], flame azalea, is a bit loose and upright in its growth habit, getting 8 to 10 feet tall and wide. Young branches are hairy; alternate leaves are elliptic and hairy below and turn a dull yellow in fall. In June large terminal clusters of funnel-shaped flowers vary in color from yellow to orange to red and vary in intensity from brilliant to soft and subdued. This coloration could be attractive to hummingbirds. Soil should be moist, well drained, and moderately acid, though flame azalea will tolerate some dryness. It takes part sun to light shade (more light usually means better bloom) and transplants well. There are many cultivars that exploit the flame azalea's wide color range. Unaka Mountains. Similar in flower is *R. cumberlandense (R. bakeri)* [cumber-lan-'den-see], Cumberland azalea. It is smaller (3 to 8 feet) and blooms a couple of weeks later. East Tennessee.

Rhododendron calendulaceum (flame azalea).

R. *canescens* [kuh-'nes-enz], piedmont azalea, is 6 to 15 feet tall, erect and stoloniferous, spreading out to colonize. The leaves are hairy beneath, and the very fragrant flower clusters vary from white to rosy pink with very long stamens and styles. Filaments and style are pink. It blooms in March and April before the leaves emerge, and is known to hybridize readily with other species. Piedmont azalea is considered the most naturally abundant azalea in the Southeast. It likes moist yet well-drained, moderately acid soil in part sun to light shade. Statewide.

Rhododendron canescens (piedmont azalea).

R. *periclymenoides (R. nudiflorum)* [pair-ih-kly-men-oh-'eye-deez], pinxterbloom azalea, grows 4 to 6 or more feet tall and wide, tending to colonize. The alternate leaves are lanceolate-oblong, colored a rich green in summer and a dull yellow in autumn. In late April or May, before or just as the new leaves emerge, large clusters of pink to purplish funnel flowers charm the eye with very long stamens and styles and charm the nose with a

Rhododendron periclymenoides (pinxterbloom azalea).

George W. Hornal.

J. Paul Moore.

slight fragrance. Pinxterbloom naturalizes well in the light shade of moist to dry, well-drained, rocky woods with moderately acid soil, yet will also grow in wet, poorly drained areas. It transplants well. It occurs in East Tennessee, lightly on the Western Highland Rim and West Tennessee Uplands.

R. *prinophyllum* (*R. roseum*) [pry-nah-'fill-um], **roseshell azalea**, is 3 to 8 feet tall with alternate, lanceolate-oblong leaves that are woolly below. Large clusters of rosy pink funnel flowers with long stamens and longer styles bloom in May and June. The fragrance is a clove scent. Roseshell likes moist to dry, well-drained uplands and light shade in soil ranging from moderately acid to slightly alkaline. It is considered by some to be a superior choice to either pinxterbloom or piedmont azalea. Quite durable and hardy, it also transplants well. Middle Tennessee.

Rhododendron prinophyllum (roseshell azalea).

Kurt Emmanuele.

R. *vaseyi* ['vay-zee-eye], **pinkshell azalea**, produces glossy, alternate foliage in clusters at twig tips. Leaves turn a reddish purple in the fall. In May terminal clusters produce large rose flowers with orange spots. There is less of a funnel tube as with other azalea blooms, and the more flattened face of the blossom features 2 lower lobes that flare out, giving it the look of a butterfly. The shrub is 5 to 9 feet tall. Pinkshell likes wet to moist, moderately acid soil and light shade. The cooler it is kept, the happier it will be. It transplants well. It does not appear in the *Atlas of Tennessee Vascular Plants* with its range limited to the mountains of North Carolina.

R. *viscosum* [vis-'koh-sum], **swamp azalea**, is a loose, open shrub 4 to 8 feet tall and wide. Twigs and buds are velvety. Glossy leaves cluster at the ends of twigs and turn yellowish to red purple in the fall. Pink buds open to white funnel flowers in large clusters in July. It is one of the last to bloom and produces a spicy clove scent. Poor drainage is not a problem for the swamp azalea, which loves wet lowlands. It needs strongly to moderately acid soil in full sun to part shade and transplants well. East Tennessee.

    R. catawbiense [kuh-taw-bee-'en-see], **Catawba rhododendron,** and *R. minus (R. carolinianum)* ['my-nus], **Carolina rhododendron,** are evergreen rhododendrons. Catawba grows 6 to 12 feet tall and as wide with dark green, thick, leathery, elliptic leaves that alternate along the stem and cluster beneath the flowers. Gathered in terminal clusters in May and June, bell-shaped flowers are purplish rose and spotted. Catawba likes moist to somewhat dry, well-drained slopes with moderately acid soil and light shade. It transplants well, and there are many cultivars. Carolina rhododendron is more compact at 3 to 6 feet. The leaves are dotted underneath, and the blooms are rose pink. Both are in East Tennessee, especially the Unaka Mountains.

Rhododendron catawbiense (Catawba rhododendron).

Rhus aromatica
Fragrant Sumac
[roos air-ah-'mat-ih-kuh] (also pronounced russ)
Anacardiaceae (Cashew Family)

Growing 2 to 6 feet high, fragrant sumac will sucker and colonize to an equal or greater width. Leaves are trifoliate, toothed, and dark green. This deep summer coloring barely suppresses the bright scarlet, orange, and purple waiting to break through in the fall. Both leaves and twigs are aromatic. It is dioecious with small clusters of yellow female flowers on the branch ends of some plants and brownish

Rhus aromatica (fragrant sumac).

male catkins on others in March and April, attracting bees and butterflies. Small, dark red, densely hairy berries ripen in summer and are loved by birds and mammals; browsers go for the leaves and twigs. Fragrant sumac thrives in the dry, sunny areas that most plants scorn. Slightly acid to slightly alkaline, lightly textured soil is best. Middle and East Tennessee, lightly in the West Tennessee Uplands.

Rosa carolina
Carolina Rose, Pasture Rose
['roh-zuh kair-ah-'ly-nuh]
Rosaceae (Rose Family)

Carolina rose suckers to form dense thickets 3 to 4 feet high. Stems are armed with thin prickles. Alternate foliage is pinnately compound with 5 to 9 leaflets that are elliptic and toothed. They turn yellow, orange, and red in the fall. Large, solitary or 2-to-3-clustered, pink flowers with yellow stamens bloom from May to July. Red hips or berries, round to pear shaped, appear in August and persist through winter. Some birds eat them. Adaptable from dry woods and pastures to stream banks, Carolina rose does best in full sun and well-drained, slightly acid to slightly alkaline soil. Statewide.

Rosa palustris (swamp rose).

Rosa palustris—fruit (swamp rose).

    R. palustris [puh-'lus-tris], swamp rose, is taller (6 to 7 feet), spreads by rhizomes, and has stouter, recurved prickles. Foliage is similar except for a downy fuzz underneath. Blossoms and pea-sized fruit are similar, too. The main difference is habitat. Swamp rose is perfect for poorly drained areas as it can tolerate the standing water of low ground and swampy conditions. It is easy to grow in moist soil and will take full sun to light shade. Statewide, especially the Cumberland Plateau.

R. setigera [seh-'tih-jer-uh], **prairie rose,** has branches that grow as long as 12 feet, climbing or arching over in a 3- to 6-foot mound with stout yet sparse prickles. Compound foliage has 3 to 5 toothed leaflets of dark, glossy green in summer that take on a wide range of autumnal hues. The flowers, the last native roses to open in July, are deep to pale pink before fading to white and leaving behind a small, brownish green to red hip. Prairie rose is tolerant of a wide range of moisture conditions from moist to drought, and is a good choice for erosion control. It needs full sun and slightly acid to slightly alkaline soil. Statewide, especially the Central Basin and Valley and Ridge.

Rubus spp.
Raspberry and Blackberry
['rew-bus]
Rosaceae (Rose Family)

R. occidentalis [ok-sih-den-'tay-lis], **blackcap raspberry,** and *R. argutus* [ar-'gyew-tus], **tall blackberry,** are colonizing shrubs 3 to 6 feet tall with prickle-lined, arching canes. Both have compound leaves with 3 to 5 ovate, toothed leaflets and clusters of white flowers in May and June that are visited by bees. Spherical blackcap raspberry fruits start out red then turn black; tall blackberry fruits are black and oblong.

R. flagellaris [flaj-eh-'lay-ris], **northern dewberry,** is a prostrate plant with white flowers and oblong, black fruit.

Rubus species provide important sources of food for a diverse range of wildlife, including humans, and offer protective cover. All 3

Rubus sp. (blackberry/raspberry).

Rubus flagellaris (northern dewberry).

The Center for Field Biology, a Tennessee Center of Excellence at Austin Peay State University.

species tolerate drought well, growing in moderately to slightly acid soil that is moist to dry in full sun to part shade. Dewberry will prosper even in poor soil. They transplant well. All are statewide.

Sambucus canadensis

American or Common Elder, Elderberry
[sam-'boo-kus kan-uh-'den-sis]
Caprifoliaceae (Honeysuckle Family)

Sambucus canadensis (American elder).

The American elder is an open, suckering shrub from 6 to 8 feet high and nearly as wide with warty branches that reach upwards then spread out and arch over. Leaves are opposite and pinnately compound with 5 to 11 leaflets that are lanceolate and toothed; lower leaflets may be lobed. Many small, white, fragrant flowers are gathered in large, flat-topped clusters and bloom in June and July, attracting butterflies. Edible purplish black berries appear in August and September and are dearly loved by many birds as well as large and small mammals. Leaves and twigs are favored by browsers.

Tolerant of wet soil or drought in sun or shade, elderberry prefers full sun to part shade and slightly acid to neutral, moist soil. Because it can send out long underground runners, expect to prune this shrub to curb its spread or site it where natural tendencies will not be a problem. It transplants well. Statewide.

Spiraea tomentosa

Hardhack or Steeplebush
[spy-'ree-uh toh-men-'toh-suh]
Rosaceae (Rose Family)

Erect, woody stems rise 2 to 3 feet from the suckering roots. Reddish stem bark is rusty and woolly. Ovate, toothed leaves are whitish and woolly below. Dense pyramidal clusters of pink to rosy purple flowers appear from July to September and attract butterflies. Seed capsules persist through fall and are used by birds. It likes full sun and well-drained, wet to moist soil that is moderately acid and not too rich. Cumberland Plateau.

Staphylea trifolia
American Bladdernut
[staf-ih-'lee-uh try-'foh-lee-uh]
Staphyleaceae (Bladdernut Family)

Bladdernut has a vase shape, growing 8 to 14 feet tall and branching out two-thirds in width. The bark features white longitudinal stripes. It has trifoliate leaves; the leaflets are elliptic, finely toothed, hairy when young, and turn a pale yellow in autumn. The

Staphylea trifolia (American bladdernut).

blooms are drooping racemes of small greenish to creamy white bells in May. Seedpods are 3-lobed, inflated capsules that are 1½ to 3 inches long and pale green to light brown. They persist until December and are loved by woodland mice. Bladdernut prefers wet to moist soil that is well drained and slightly acid to neutral in part sun to light shade. It transplants well. Statewide, lightly in West Tennessee.

Styrax americana(us)
American Snowbell
['sty-raks uh-mair-ih-'kay-nuh(nus)]
Styracaceae (Storax Family)

Lovely white flowers in May are the main attraction of our snowbells. *S. americana* is a slender-stemmed, 6- to 10-foot shrub. Single or few-clustered, ¾-inch, bell-shaped flowers with reflexed petals hang from the leaf axils. Leaves are alternate, oval to obovate, and

Styrax grandifolia (bigleaf snowbell).

bright green. Small, round, dry berries develop in late summer. The American snowbell likes wet, swampy areas with moderately acid soil in part shade. West Tennessee.

S. grandifolia(us) [gran-dih-'foh-lee-uh(us)], **bigleaf snowbell,** is very similar with slightly larger leaves that are hairy below. It prefers moderately acid, moist to dry, forested slopes in part sun. Western Highland Rim and West Tennessee Uplands.

Symphoricarpos orbiculatus
Coralberry, Indian Currant
[sim-for-ih-'kar-pas or-bih-kyew-'lay-tus]
Caprifoliaceae (Honeysuckle Family)

Coralberry is a small suckering shrub 2 to 5 feet tall that grows erect into a spreading and arching habit. Its leaves are opposite and oval, and small, dense clusters of greenish white to pink bells bloom in the leaf axils in June and July. From October until late winter, coral red to purplish berries hang on waiting for birds to get hungry enough to need this food of last resort. Large and small mammals also eat the berries and browsers nibble the leaves and twigs.

Symphoricarpos orbiculatus (coralberry).

Coralberry is found in rocky woodlands with moist to dry soil in part to light shade. It is not fussy about soil pH, anything from moderately acid to slightly alkaline will do. Periodic pruning stimulates fruiting. It counters erosion, provides wildlife cover, and transplants easily. Middle and East Tennessee, West Tennessee Uplands.

Vaccinium arboreum
Farkleberry, Sparkleberry
[vak-'sin-ee-um ar-'bore-ee-um]
Ericaceae (Heath Family)

Vaccinium arboreum (farkleberry).

Farkleberry comes close to being a small tree at a height of about 20 feet. It has several decorative advantages: twisted, irregular branching; reddish, exfoliating bark; leathery, glossy, oval leaves that turn crimson red in autumn; leafy racemes of small, nodding, white bells in May and June; and black, lustrous berries persisting through fall and winter to feed wildlife late in the season. It likes dry uplands and strongly to slightly acid soil in part to light shade. This is the tallest of the blueberry tribe, and though its fruit is not palatable to humans, wildlife are not as picky. *Vaccinium* species attract bees and butterflies and are a larval food source. Statewide, except Central Basin.

V. corymbosum (V. constablaei) [kore-im-'boh-sum], highbush blueberry, is a dense upright shrub 6 to 12 feet tall and wide. Leaves are alternate, elliptic, and dark green in summer, with an excellent range of autumn colors from yellow to orange to red. It is very floriferous, producing numerous small, white to pinkish, urn-shaped bells drooping in clusters in May. A battle in July and August between enterprising wildlife of all types and human beings determines who will enjoy the dark blue berries. Found from the wet lowlands to the dry uplands, blueberries grow best in consistently moist, well-drained, strongly to moderately acid soil with lots of organic matter in full sun or part shade. Highbush blueberry transplants well. Recommended cultivars for fruit are 'Berkeley', 'Bluecrop', 'Blueray', 'Herbert',

Vaccinium pallidum (late lowbush blueberry).

Vaccinium stamineum (deerberry).

and 'Jersey'. East Tennessee, Highland Rim, West Tennessee Uplands. *V. ashei* ['ash-ee-eye], **rabbiteye blueberry,** is reportedly easier for home gardeners to grow. It is described by Michael Dirr in his *Manual of Woody Landscape Plants* as "the southern equivalent of *V. corymbosum*." There are several cultivars, but this species is not documented in the *Atlas of Tennessee Vascular Plants*.

V. pallidum (V. vacillans) ['pal-ih-dum], **late lowbush blueberry,** is slender and erect, 1 to 3 feet tall, featuring toothed leaves, dense clusters of flowers in May, and midsummer fruit. It likes the strongly to moderately acid soil of dry, upland woods in full to part sun and may be hard to find commercially. Middle (except Central Basin) and East Tennessee.

V. stamineum [stuh-'men-ee-um], **deerberry,** grows upright 6 to 12 feet and becomes twiggy with an equal spread. Oval alternate leaves are whitish and woolly below. Fall color is red. Little greenish white to pinkish flaring bells hang in clusters from the leaf axils in May and June. Round to pear-shaped berries turn from greenish yellow to bluish with a white bloom in September and October. They fall quickly and are devoured by birds and mammals. Well-drained, dry soil of varying acidity and part shade suits deerberry. It transplants well. Middle (except Central Basin) and East Tennessee, West Tennessee Uplands.

Viburnum acerifolium
Mapleleaf Viburnum
[vy-'bur-num uh-seh-rih-'foh-lee-um]
Caprifoliaceae (Honeysuckle Family)

Mapleleaf viburnum is a narrow, upright shrub 3 to 6 feet tall that spreads by stolons to form loose, open colonies. Leaves are opposite, palmately divided into 3 lobes similar to a maple, and toothed. The undersides of the leaves are woolly with small black dots. In autumn they can take on gorgeous shades of yellow, pink, rose, red, and purple. In May and June creamy white flowers appear in terminal flat-topped clusters. By late summer (August and September) oval berries, red to bluish black, adorn the shrub and persist through winter if not eaten by birds or mammals. Browsers chew on the leaves and twigs. Given moist to dry, moderately acid soil and light shade, mapleleaf viburnum is a beautiful plant. It transplants well. Viburnum species are a larval food source for butterflies. Eastern half of the state.

Viburnum acerifolium (mapleleaf viburnum).

V. nudum ['new-dum], possumhaw viburnum, **southern** or **smooth witherod,** is an upright shrub 6 to 15 feet tall and 4 to 10 feet wide, with glossy, opposite, ovate, toothed leaves that take on red purple coloring in autumn. Terminal, flat-topped clusters of creamy white flowers in June are rather foul smelling. In late summer to early fall, oval berries run through several colors from green to pink to blue and finally black. Birds and mammals love them. Adaptable to a range of soil moisture from wet to somewhat moist, possumhaw viburnum prefers moist, moderately acid soil in part shade to part sun. It transplants well and is good for hedges or planted in masses. A popular cultivar is 'Winterthur'. Cumberland Plateau, Eastern Highland Rim, and West Tennessee Uplands.

Viburnum acerifolium—fruit (mapleleaf viburnum).

V. cassinoides [kas-in-oh-'eye-deez], northern witherod, is a bit smaller than *V. nudum* with velvety twigs and can tolerate drier soil. East Tennessee, especially the Unaka Mountains.

Viburnum nudum 'Winterthur' (possumhaw viburnum).

V. dentatum [den-'tay-tum], **arrowwood viburnum,** grows upright, spreading at the top and eventually arching over to a height and width of 6 to 12 feet. The leaves are similar to *V. nudum* except they are coarsely toothed. Similar flowering in May and June produces small blue to blackish berries in early fall, eaten by birds and small mammals. Wet to moist, well-drained soil in part shade to part sun is best. Soil should be moderately acid. Eastern half of the state.

Xanthorhiza simplicissima
Yellowroot
[zan-thah-'ry-zuh sim-pli-'sih-sih-muh]
Ranunculaceae (Buttercup Family)

Xanthorhiza simplicissima (yellowroot).

Yellowroot is a small mat-forming shrub that spreads into wide colonies of erect stems no higher than 3 feet. Alternate, pinnately compound leaves have 5 leaflets that are ovate and toothed. Bright green in summer, they turn yellow and red in autumn and often hang onto the plant rather than drop off. In April its tiny, starry flowers are dark purple to brown and arranged on drooping racemes that hang in clusters. A small cluster of little fruit pods, which are eaten by birds and small mammals, replaces each flower. A good choice as a groundcover or for erosion control, yellowroot spreads well in wet to moist soil of any acidity (4–6 pH) and in light shade to part sun. In drier soil its growth will be slower. It transplants well. Bright yellow roots and inner bark account for the common name. East Tennessee.

Trees

Ornamental Interest and Site Summary

This summary provides a quick reference to the distinctive horticultural characteristics and site preferences of the trees featured in this book. A complete description, cultural information, and state distribution for each plant follow the summary. The following abbreviations appear in the summary.

Flower Season and Color:

Sp—Spring
Su—Summer
A—Autumn
Wh—White
Y—Yellow
P—Pink
R—Red
Pr—Purple
GBM—Green, brown, maroon

Distinctions:

Fr—Fruit
Lf—Leaf (shape or color)
Bk—Bark
Ev—Evergreen
Ar—Aromatic, fragrant
UF—Unique form

Site Preferences:

S—Full sun to part shade
Sh—Part sun to medium shade
Alk—Tolerates slight alkalinity
PS—Poor soil, low fertility
WS—Wet soil
MS—Moist soil
DS—Dry soil

Trees	Flower	Distinctions	Site
Acer pensylvanicum (striped maple)		Lf, Fr, Bk	Sh, MS
Acer rubrum (red maple)		Lf, Fr	S WS-DS
Acer saccharum ssp. *floridanum* (Florida maple)		Lf, Fr	S/Sh WS/MS
Acer saccharum ssp. *leucoderme* (chalk maple)		Lf, Fr	S/Sh DS
Acer saccharum ssp. *nigrum* (black sugar maple)		Lf, Fr	S/Sh MS
Acer saccharum ssp. *saccharum* (sugar maple)		Lf, Fr	S/Sh MS
Aesculus flava (yellow buckeye)	Sp Y	Lf, Fr	S/Sh MS
Aesculus glabra (Ohio buckeye)	Sp Y	Lf, Fr	S WS/MS
Aesculus pavia (red buckeye)	Sp R	Lf, Fr	S, MS
Aesculus sylvatica (painted buckeye)	Sp R/Y	Lf, Fr	S, MS
Amelanchier arborea & *A. laevis* (downy & Allegheny serviceberry)	Sp Wh	Lf, Fr	S MS/DS
Amelanchier canadensis (serviceberry)	Sp Wh	Lf, Fr	S/Sh WS
Aralia spinosa (devils-walkingstick)	Su Wh	Lf, Fr	S MS/DS
Asimina triloba (pawpaw)	Sp GBM	Lf, Fr	Sh, MS
Betula lenta (sweet birch)		Lf, Bk, Ar	S, MS
Betula nigra (river birch)		Lf, Bk	S WS/MS
Carpinus caroliniana (American hornbeam)		Lf, Fr, Bk	Sh, MS
Carya cordiformis (bitternut hickory)		Lf, Fr	S, MS Alk

(Continued next page)

Trees	Flower	Distinctions	Site
Carya glabra (pignut hickory)		Lf, Fr	S MS/DS
Carya ovata (shagbark hickory)		Lf, Fr, Bk	S MS/DS
Carya tomentosa (mockernut hickory)		Lf, Fr, Ar	S, DS
Castanea dentata (American chestnut)		Fr	S MS/DS
Celtis laevigata & C. occidentalis (sugarberry & hackberry)		Fr, Bk	S, Alk WS-DS
Cercis canadensis (redbud)	Sp Pr	Lf, Fr	S, Alk MS/DS
Chionanthus virginicus (fringe tree)	Sp Wh	Lf, Fr, Ar	S/Sh MS
Cladrastis kentukea (yellowwood)	Sp Wh	Lf, Fr, Ar	S, MS Alk
Cornus alternifolia (pagoda dogwood)	Sp Wh	Lf, Fr, UF	S/Sh MS
Cornus florida (flowering dogwood)	Sp Wh/P	Lf, Fr, Bk	S/Sh MS/DS
Crataegus crus-galli, C. phaenopyrum, & C. viridis (cockspur, Washington, & green hawthorn)	Sp Wh	Lf, Fr	S, MS Alk
Crataegus marshallii (parsley hawthorn)	Sp Wh	Lf, Fr	S WS/MS
Diospyros virginiana (persimmon)	Sp Y/Wh	Lf, Fr, Ar, Bk	S MS/DS
Euonymus atropurpureus (eastern wahoo)	Su R	Lf, Fr	S, MS
Fagus grandifolia (American beech)		Lf, Fr, Bk	S/Sh MS
Fraxinus americana (white ash)		Lf, Fr	S, MS
Fraxinus pennsylvanica (green ash)		Lf, Fr	S WS/MS
Fraxinus quadrangulata (blue ash)		Lf, Fr	S, DS Alk

(Continued next page)

Trees	Flower	Distinctions	Site
Gymnocladus dioicus (Kentucky coffeetree)	Sp Wh	Lf, Fr	S, MS Alk
Halesia tetraptera (silverbell)	Sp Wh	Lf, Fr	Sh, MS
Hamamelis virginiana (witch hazel)	A Y	Lf, Fr, Ar	Sh, MS
Ilex opaca (American holly)	Sp Wh	Fr, Ev	S/Sh MS/DS
Juglans nigra (black walnut)		Fr, Ar	S, PS, Alk MS/DS
Juniperus virginiana (eastern red cedar)		Lf, Fr, Ar, Bk, Ev	S, Alk MS/DS
Liquidambar styraciflua (sweetgum)		Lf, Fr	S WS/MS
Liriodendron tulipifera (tulip tree)	Sp Y	Lf, Fr	S, MS
Magnolia acuminata (cucumber tree)	Sp Y	Fr, Ar	S, MS
Magnolia grandiflora (southern magnolia)	Sp Wh	Lf, Fr, Ar, Ev	S, MS
Magnolia macrophylla (bigleaf magnolia)	Sp/Su Wh	Lf, Fr, Ar	S, MS
Magnolia tripetala (umbrella tree)	Sp Wh	Lf, Fr	S, MS
Malus angustifolia (southern crabapple)	Sp Wh	Fr, Ar	S, MS
Morus rubra (red mulberry)	Sp Y	Lf, Fr	S, Alk MS/DS
Nyssa aquatica (water tupelo)		Fr	S, WS
Nyssa sylvatica (blackgum)		Lf, Fr	S MS/DS
Ostrya virginiana (American hophornbeam)		Lf, Fr	S, MS
Oxydendrum arboreum (sourwood)	Su Wh	Lf, Fr	S, MS
Pinus echinata & P. rigida (shortleaf & pitch pine)		Ev, Fr	S, DS

(Continued next page)

Trees	Flower	Distinctions	Site
Pinus strobus (eastern white pine)		Ev, Fr	S, MS
Pinus taeda (loblolly pine)		Ev, Fr	S, PS MS/DS
Pinus virginiana (Virginia pine)		Ev, Fr	S, DS PS
Platanus occidentalis (sycamore)		Fr, Bk	S, Alk WS/MS
Prunus americana & *P. angustifolia* (American & chickasaw plum)	Sp Wh	Fr	S MS/DS
Prunus serotina (black cherry)	Sp Wh	Lf, Fr, Ar	S, MS
Ptelea trifoliata (hoptree)	Sp Y	Lf, Fr, Ar	S/Sh MS/DS
Quercus alba (white oak)		Fr	S MS/DS
Quercus coccinea & *Q. stellata* (scarlet & post oak)		Fr	S, DS
Quercus falcata (southern red oak)		Fr	S, DS PS
Quercus imbricaria, Q. phellos, Q. rubra & *Q. shumardii* (shingle, willow, northern red, & Shumard oak)		Fr	S, MS
Quercus lyrata & *Q. pagoda* (overcup & cherrybark oak)		Fr	S, WS
Quercus macrocarpa & *Q. muhlenbergii* (bur & chinkapin oak)		Fr	S, Alk MS/DS
Quercus michauxii & *Q. palustris* (swamp chestnut & pin oak)		Fr	S WS/MS
Quercus montana (chestnut oak)		Fr	S, PS MS/DS
Quercus velutina (black oak)		Fr	S, PS MS/DS

(Continued next page)

Trees	Flower	Distinctions	Site
Rhamnus caroliniana (Carolina buckthorn)	Sp Y	Lf, Fr	Sh MS/DS
Rhododendron maximum (rosebay rhododendron)	Sp/Su Wh/P	Ev	Sh, MS
Rhus copallina, R. glabra, & *R. typhina* (shining, smooth & staghorn sumac)	Su Y	Lf, Fr	S, DS
Robinia pseudoacacia (black locust)	Sp Wh	Lf, Fr, Ar	S, Alk, PS MS/DS
Sassafras albidum (sassafras)	Sp Y	Lf, Fr, Ar	S, PS MS/DS
Taxodium distichum (bald cypress)		Lf, Fr, Bk, UF	S WS/MS
Tilia heterophylla (white basswood)	Sp/Su Y	Fr, Ar	S, MS
Tsuga canadensis (eastern hemlock)		Fr, Ev	Sh, MS
Ulmus americana (American elm)		Lf	S, MS Alk
Viburnum prunifolium & *V. rufidulum* (blackhaw viburnum)	Sp Wh	Lf, Fr	S/Sh, Alk MS/DS

Kurt Emmanuele.

Acer rubrum (red maple).

Description, Culture, and Distribution

Acer rubrum
Red Maple
['ay-ser 'rue-brum]
Aceraceae (Maple Family)

Red maple is a large canopy tree, 50 to 75 feet tall with a three-quarters to equal spread. Strong ascending branches form an ovoid to globular shape at maturity. The buds, young twigs, and flowers are reddish to bright red. These traits are best visible in winter and early spring when color is most welcome. Leaves are opposite and palmate with 3 main lobes that are irregularly toothed. Fall color varies from yellow green to crimson. Most of the cultivars available focus on superior autumn color, including 'Autumn Blaze', 'October Glory', and 'Red Sunset'. Male and female flowers appear in clusters along twig ends and bloom in March and April before the leaves. Red maples are mostly dioecious, though trees may have a few flowers of the opposite sex. Paired, winged seeds, which can also be red to reddish brown, mature between April and June. Birds and small mammals eat these seeds and browsers munch the twigs. Found on a wide range of sites, red maples are nonetheless associated with low, wet to moist areas. Soil should be moderately acid in full sun to part shade. They can be easily transplanted when small. Besides fall coloring other cultivars, such as 'Columnare', are based on shape, this one being narrower. Maples in general are shallow rooted, making it more difficult to grow other plants under them. Statewide.

A. pensylvanicum [pen-sil-'van-ih-kum], **striped maple,** is a small understory tree 20 to 30 feet tall. The bark of young trees is green with longitudinal white stripes. Leaves are 3-lobed and toothed and turn yellow in the fall. Striped maple needs part to light shade and moist, moderately acid soil that is cool and well drained in a protected location. Cumberland Plateau and Unaka Mountains.

A. saccharum ssp. *saccharum (A. saccharum)* ['sak-kuh-rum], **sugar, rock,** or **hard maple,** is another large canopy tree, 70 to 100 feet tall with a two-thirds to equal spread, and is very dense. The leaves are 5-lobed and

Acer saccharum ssp. saccharum
(sugar maple).

Bill Davit, Shaw Arboretum.

slightly toothed and in the fall turn shades of yellow, orange, and red. Clusters of greenish yellow flowers, each on a long, thin, drooping stalk, appear in April before the leaves. Green, paired seeds mature to brown in September and October and are eaten by birds and small mammals; browsers eat the twigs and leaves. Male and female flowers can appear on the same or separate trees and attract bees. Sugar maple is shade tolerant and appreciates cool sites, needing well-drained, moist soil that is slightly acid. Tennessee is the southernmost edge of the sugar maple's range, so its needs should be met. Stressful sites, such as droughty areas, high urban pollution, salt, or restricted growth areas will adversely affect it. There are many cultivars. Statewide.

A. saccharum ssp. *leucoderme (A. leucoderme)* [lew-kah-'der-mee], **chalk maple**, is more of an understory tree at 25 to 30 feet. Leaves are smaller and a tad broader than long. They color well in autumn, ranging from yellow to orange to deep red. The bark is whitish in color and the fruits are widely forking, paired seeds, reddish to tan, that mature in midsummer. Unlike sugar maple, chalk maple shows good dry soil tolerance, preferring drier, upland woods. Documented only around Chattanooga.

A. saccharum ssp. *floridanum (A. barbatum, A. floridanum)* [flor-ih-'day-num], **Florida maple** or **southern sugar maple**, is very similar to the subspecies above and grows in wet to moist areas. It is very tolerant of southern summers with fall foliage in the yellow to rusty range. Lightly in the western half of the state.

A. saccharum ssp. *nigrum (A. nigrum)* ['ny-grum], **black sugar maple**, is similar in appearance to the sugar maple. It, too, likes moist, cool sites. Lightly statewide, heavier in Middle Tennessee.

Aesculus glabra
Ohio or Fetid Buckeye
['es-kyew-lus 'glay-bruh]
Hippocastanaceae (Horse-chestnut Family)

Ohio buckeye is a large understory tree, 30 to 50 feet tall and ovoid in shape, with branches often bending downwards. Opposite leaves are palmately compound with 5 finely toothed, elliptic leaflets. The leaves emerge (among the earliest in March and April) a bright light green, turn yellow or orange in the fall, and drop early. Erect terminal spikes of yellow green, tubular flowers bloom and blend with the new leaves in May, attracting butterflies. Through the summer the tree bears glossy nuts hidden in a prickly husk. These nuts are poisonous, but squirrels will eat them.

Give the buckeye deep, well-drained, wet to moist soil that is slightly acid in part shade. This tree is considered better in natural areas than urban backyards. It is difficult to transplant. It also has the common name of fetid buckeye, which refers to the foul smell produced by the flowers and the stems when crushed. Middle Tennessee and Valley and Ridge.

A. flava (A. octandra) ['flay-vuh], **yellow buckeye,** has brighter yellow flowers and smooth nut husks. It prefers the cool, moist, slightly acid soil of the protected mixed mesophytic forests in part shade to part sun. Eastern half of the state.

Aesculus pavia (red buckeye).

A. pavia ['pay-vee-uh], red buckeye, is a large shrub or small, rounded tree that grows over 12 feet. Palmately compound leaves of 5 large, toothed leaflets are a dark lustrous green, appear early, and drop early after turning yellow. In April and May showy upright spikes of bright red flowers 6 to 8 inches long bloom on the tips of branches. Shiny nuts in light brown, smooth husks are poisonous and ripen in September. Red buckeye needs a moist, fertile, well-drained soil that is slightly acid in full sun to part shade. Cultivars, such as 'Splendens', showcase flower color and form. West Tennessee and the southern tier of counties in Middle Tennessee.

A. sylvatica [sil-'vat-ih-kuh], painted buckeye, is similar with flowers that are often bicolored red and yellow. It needs some shade. East Tennessee.

Amelanchier arborea
Downy Serviceberry, Juneberry, Shadblow, Service or Sarvis Tree
[am-eh-'lan-kee-er ar-'bore-ee-uh]
Rosaceae (Rose Family)

Amelanchier arborea (downy serviceberry).

The downy serviceberry is a multi-stemmed large shrub or small tree 15 to 25 feet high with a rounded crown. The smooth, gray bark has whitish vertical streaks. Leaves are alternate, obovate, and toothed. They have long white hairs on them as young buds and on their undersides as young leaves. Fall coloring is yellow to orange to reddish. In April racemes of narrow-petaled, white flowers, 2 to 4 inches long, put on a lovely show and attract bees. In June edible red to purplish black, globular berries ripen and are immediately devoured by birds and squirrels and are also a favorite treat of bears. Serviceberries

Amelanchier arborea—fruit (downy serviceberry).

like moist to dry, well-drained uplands with slightly acid soil in full sun to part shade. Middle and East Tennessee, West Tennessee Uplands.

A. *arborea* has been crossed with A. *laevis* ['lee-vis], **Allegheny serviceberry,** to produce the popular cultivar A. *x grandiflora* 'Autumn Brilliance'. A. *canadensis* [kan-uh-'den-sis] is a smaller serviceberry. More shrublike in growth, it colonizes in wet woods and swamps. Service-berries transplant fairly well. A. *laevis* and A. *canadensis* are mostly in East Tennessee.

Aralia spinosa
Devils-walkingstick, Hercules Club
[uh-'ray-lee-uh spih-'noh-suh]
Araliaceae (Ginseng Family)

Aralia spinosa (devils-walkingstick).

At 10 to 20 feet, *Aralia spinosa* can either be a large shrub or small tree with leggy, multiple trunks and stout, coarse branches armed with scattered orange prickles. It suckers into colonies and can be aggressive. The foliage is immense—alternate, bipinnately compound leaves, 3 or 4 feet in length, with numerous dark green leaflets, each 2 to 4 inches and toothed. Fall coloring varies from yellow to soft pinkish orange to purplish. In July and August small, round clumps of white flowers are clustered into large panicles at the ends of branches. By October this panicle has become a great, colorful haze of purplish black berries on reddish stems. The berries are eaten by birds and small mammals. Devils-walkingstick is adaptable to moist or dry soils, but prefers moist, fertile soil that is slightly acid and well drained in full sun to part shade. It grows well in urban settings and transplants easily. Statewide.

Asimina triloba (pawpaw).

Asimina triloba
Pawpaw
[uh-'sih-mih-nuh 'trih-lah-buh]
Annonaceae (Custard Apple Family)

Pawpaw is a small, upright, multi-trunked understory tree. It grows 15 to 20 feet or more tall with an equal spread and can sucker into a loose colony. Leaves are alternate, obovate, and oblong (6 to 12 inches) with a drooping pendant look. They turn a pale yellow in fall. Maroon flowers have 3 reflexed petals and are borne singly in April and May with the new leaves. The round to oblong fruit starts off yellowish then turns dark in August and September when people and animals alike enjoy the fragrant custard taste similar to bananas. The nutritious fruit is attractive to birds, raccoons, squirrels, and opossums.

Pawpaws like a deep, fertile, moist soil that is slightly acid and well drained in part shade to light shade and are a great choice for naturalizing along streams. Young plants especially appreciate shade. If fruit is important, two trees will ensure greater cross pollination and fruit set. Since the fruit can be messy, site accordingly. *A. triloba* is the northernmost species of this tropical family. It is difficult to transplant. Statewide.

Betula nigra
River Birch
['beh-tyew-luh 'ny-gruh]
Betulaceae (Birch Family)

River birch is a small canopy tree with a single or multiple trunks 40 to 70 feet tall. Ascending branches arch outward and are pendulous at the ends. Reddish brown to pinkish tan bark exfoliates in papery, horizontal chunks. Leaves are alternate and ovate

Betula nigra (river birch).

with a wedge-shaped base and double-toothed edge. They turn yellow in fall. In April male catkins are long and drooping. Female flower clusters are shorter and upright and become oblong to elliptic pods in summer with winged nutlets. Butterflies, birds, small mammals, and browsers feed on the river birch.

As the name would imply, river birch prefers the wet to moist soil of the floodplain, but is able to tolerate drier sites once established, particularly if the dryness is seasonal in nature during summer and fall. It likes moderately acid soil, and true to its pioneering spirit (helping to settle recently disturbed sites) it needs full sun. The cultivar 'Heritage', featuring creamy tan bark, is considered superior to the species. River birch takes the heat of southern summers without complaint, unlike its northern relatives. It transplants well when young. Statewide, except the Central Basin.

B. lenta ['lin-tuh], **sweet, cherry,** or **black birch,** has shining reddish brown bark when young and a wintergreen odor in the twigs. The leaves do not have a wedge-shaped base. It will tolerate drier sites but grows best in moist, rich, moderately acid soil and full sun to part shade. Soil must be well drained. East Tennessee.

Carpinus caroliniana
American Hornbeam, Musclewood, Blue Beech
[kar-'py-nus kair-ah-lih-nee-'ay-nuh]
Betulaceae (Birch Family)

American hornbeam is a large understory tree 25 to 40 feet tall with an equal spread. It can be multi-trunked in form with wide-spreading, low branches. The smooth, gray bark shows off the undulating nature of the wood below, resembling flexed, rippling

Carpinus caroliniana (American hornbeam).

muscles. The alternate, ovate leaves are double toothed and turn variations of yellow, orange, and red in autumn. Male and female catkins are produced on the same tree in April and May. Three-lobed bracts, each with a seed at the base, hang in drooping clusters from June to October. Some game birds eat them and deer browse the foliage, which is also a butterfly larval food. American hornbeam is very shade tolerant and requires consistently moist, deep soil that is slightly acid to neutral. It is difficult to transplant and temperamental. Statewide.

Carya spp.
Hickory
['kay-ree-uh]
Juglandaceae (Walnut Family)

All the hickories are large canopy trees growing between 50 to 80 feet in the garden and higher in the wild. They spread about half their height with ascending branches in the top of the tree and drooping branches at the base. Hickory foliage is alternate and pinnately compound, turning a rich golden color in autumn. Male catkins droop in clusters of 3, and female flowers are in terminal spikes in late April or May. Brown round nuts in 4-sectioned husks appear from August to October. Birds and mammals love them. Several large and wonderful species of moths, including the luna moth, feed on hickory leaves. Hickories are slow growers, display sensitivity to root disturbance, and are hard to transplant. Now for some of the differences among the species.

　　C. cordiformis [kore-dih-'fore-mis], **bitternut hickory,** has bright sulfur yellow buds in spring, foliage with 7 lanceolate leaflets, and a broader crown. Adaptable to a wide range of moisture levels, bitternut is best in moist soils in full sun with the soil pH variable from moderately acid to slightly alkaline. It is a bit faster growing. Statewide.

C. glabra ['glay-bruh], **pignut hickory,** has 5 to 7 leaflets; the terminal leaflet is larger than the others. The nut is pear shaped. Pignut is drought tolerant and occupies well-drained upland ridges and hillsides with slightly acid to neutral soil in full sun to part shade. Statewide.

Carya glabra (pignut hickory).

C. ovata [oh-'vay-tuh], **shagbark hickory,** has exfoliating bark that pops loose in long vertical plates curling out at the ends. Leaves have 5 leaflets that unfold from the midst of large reddish bud scales. It, too, is adaptable to moisture, taking well-drained, moist to dry, slightly acid soil. This nut is palatable to humans, too. Statewide.

C. tomentosa [toh-mon 'toh-suh], **mocker- nut hickory,** has woolly, silvery buds, 7 leaflets that are hairy underneath, and a nut eaten by humans. Leaves and nuts are aromatic. Mockernut is drought tolerant, needing well- drained, somewhat moist to dry soil that is slightly acid in full sun. It prefers upland areas. Statewide.

Carya ovata (shagbark hickory).

Castanea dentata
American Chestnut
[kas-'tay-nee-uh den-tay'-tuh]
Fagaceae (Beech Family)

Massive and spreading at a height of 100 feet, this majestic tree once characterized Ameri- can forests but is now reduced to stump sprouts that rarely reach fruiting age before succumbing to the imported chestnut blight. The leaves are alternate, oblong, leathery, and coarsely toothed. Catkins in June produce

Castanea dentata (American chestnut).

spiny husked nuts enjoyed by humans and other animals.

The American chestnut grows in moderately acid, moist to dry soil and can take some shade. Decades of work on the chestnut are about to pay off. A combination of advances in attacking the blight itself as well as the development of resistant hybrids that are nearly 98 percent *C. dentata* may produce landscape plants in the not-too-distant future. Statewide.

Celtis occidentalis
Common Hackberry
['sel-tis ok-sih-den-'tay-lis]
Ulmaceae (Elm Family)

Celtis occidentalis (hackberry).

Hackberries are large canopy trees growing to a height of 60 to 80 feet or more with a similar spread. Bark is light gray and features narrow, corky ridges or wartlike projections. Alternate leaves are toothed and turn yellow in the fall. April flowers are small and inconspicuous, but the little reddish to dark purple berries that develop in September and October are greatly loved by lots of birds and small mammals. Moths and butterflies also use the ubiquitous hackberry.

This is one tough tree, taking to most any site—wet or dry, acid or alkaline, urban or rural. It does require lots of sun, but it grows quickly and transplants readily. The tree can be a picturesque beauty in a suitable site with rich, moist soil. In fact the Central Basin is considered the center for prime growth and development of this tree. On the downside, hackberries are a bit weedy, the berries are messy, and the wood is rather brittle. *C. occidentalis* is found throughout the state and moves north in its range. *C. laevigata* [lee-vih-'gay-tuh], sugarberry, inhabits lower, moister areas, and its bark is usually smoother. It is found throughout Tennessee and ranges south.

Cercis canadensis
Redbud
['ser-sis kan-uh-'den-sis]
Fabaceae (Pea Family)

Cercis canadensis (redbud).

Redbuds are small understory trees 20 to 30 feet high. The trunk is usually divided low and the wide-branching crown arches over like an umbrella. Leaves are large, heart shaped, alternate, and yellow in autumn. In April, before the leaves emerge, clusters of red purple to rosy pink flowers outline the branches and even the trunk. Flat, oblong seedpods develop in midsummer and persist until winter. Early butterflies enjoy the flower nectar; redbud is also a larval food.

Redbuds grow in well-drained, moist to dry soils, slightly acid to slightly alkaline, and full sun to part shade. They are short-lived trees, averaging less than 50 years. There are cultivars based on flower color or leaves including 'Silver Cloud' (variegated leaf) and 'Forest Pansy' (reddish purple leaf). The flowers are reputed to be a tasty as well as colorful addition to salads. It transplants well when young. Self-sown seeds produce robust trees. Statewide.

Chionanthus virginicus
Fringe Tree, Old Man's Beard, Graybeard
[ky-oh-'nan-thus vir-'jin-ih-kus]
Oleaceae (Olive Family)

In the garden fringe trees will probably resemble shrubs at 12 to 20 feet in height with a spreading, open habit, but in the wild they can grow higher. They leaf out late with opposite, oblong leaves, lustrous and dark

Chionanthus virginicus (fringe tree).

green, turning yellow in the fall. In April and May the blooms are drooping, feathery panicles of clustered flowers with fringelike, creamy white petals perfumed with a slight but sweet honey fragrance—it is a true multisensory delight to rub your nose in them. Fringe tree is dioecious. The male tree is a bit more effective in flower, but the female produces oval blue black berries in August and September that birds love. It blooms on the previous season's wood and begins blooming when quite young. Fringe tree needs well-drained, moist soil, moderately to slightly acid, in full sun to open shade. It adapts well to urban environments and can be somewhat hard to transplant. The genus name means snowflower. East Tennessee, lightly on the Highland Rim.

Cladrastis kentukea (C. lutea)
Yellowwood
[kluh-'dras-tis ken-'tuk-ee-uh]
Fabaceae (Pea Family)

Cladrastis kentukea (yellowwood).

Cladrastis kentukea—flower (yellowwood).

Yellowwood, designated as Tennessee's Bicentennial Tree, is a small canopy tree. It is upright and low branching in habit, growing 40 to 60 feet in height with a near equal spread. The bark is smooth and gray. Foliage is alternate and pinnately compound with 7 to 9 elliptic leaflets that turn yellow in the fall. Large clusters of fragrant, white, pea-shaped flowers bloom in May on 8- to 12-inch, drooping racemes. Yellowwood is not a consistent bloomer, beginning only after 12 to 18 years and then producing a good show about every 2 to 3 years. Seedpods are flat and oblong (3 to 4 inches) ripening in late summer and persisting through winter.

Give the yellowwood well-drained, rich, moist, neutral to slightly alkaline soil in full sun to part shade. Pruning establishes strong branching to overcome the brittle nature of the wood and should be done in the fall. The common name comes from the clear yellow color of newly exposed heartwood. It transplants well when small. Its natural range is limited, scattered lightly throughout Tennessee, central Kentucky, and parts of Arkansas, but it can be cultivated over a broader area.

Cornus florida
Flowering Dogwood
['kore-nus 'flor-ih-duh]
Cornaceae (Dogwood Family)

Arguably the most popular ornamental tree in the nursery trade, dogwood is a staple in the landscape. An understory tree with a height and spread of 20 to 30 feet, it is low branching and horizontal in habit with bark in checkered squares. Oval, opposite leaves turn red to purplish in autumn. The small greenish yellow flowers are surrounded by 4 large, white or pink notched bracts (or involucre) in April and May. Clusters of egg-shaped, red berries grace the tree in autumn and feed a diverse group of wildlife, including birds, squirrels, other small mammals, large mammals, and browsers. Butterflies, too, use the dogwood. Buds holding next year's bloom are visible all winter.

Dogwoods need well-drained soil, moist to dry and moderately to slightly acid. They grow best in part shade. In their native rocky, woodland settings they are sparse, open trees; given the additional room and sunlight of

Cornus florida (flowering dogwood).

Cornus florida—fruit (flowering dogwood).

the typical home landscape, they assume a more rounded and compact form. Site dogwoods for good air circulation, which helps prevent anthracnose disease, a fungus that affects leaves and twigs, often causing dieback. There are many cultivars based on flower, leaf, fruit, and form. Statewide.

C. alternifolia [all-ter-nih-'foh-lee-uh], **pagoda dogwood,** is another small understory tree 15 to 25 feet tall. Its distinctive horizontal branching habit and upturned branchlets give it a tiered appearance. The leaves resemble C. *florida,* but the flowers do not. Fragrant, small, creamy flowers are gathered in a flat-topped cluster in May. In autumn red stems support blue purple fruit. Moist, slightly acid soil in part to light shade is best. Keep the roots cool. Eastern half of the state.

Cornus alternifolia (pagoda dogwood).

William Hall.

Crataegus phaenopyrum
Washington Hawthorn
[kruh-'tee-gus fee-noh-'py-rum]
Rosaceae (Rose Family)

Small understory trees, 20 to 30 feet high and 13 to 20 feet wide with horizontal branching, hawthorns are best characterized by their long slender thorns, which can be quite intimidating. Alternate leaves are broadly ovate (nearly triangular), lobed, and toothed. A lustrous dark green in summer, they turn orange to scarlet and purplish in fall. In May and June flat clusters of white flowers with red anthers put on a show and are followed in September by glossy red berries that persist if not eaten by birds, mammals, or humans. Browsers also nibble the hawthorn, and birds love it for nesting amid the security of armed branches. Several butterflies also use the hawthorn for nectar and larval food.

Plant hawthorns in well-drained, slightly acid to slightly alkaline soil in full sun. They are drought tolerant but prefer moist conditions. Some species of hawthorn are susceptible to rust, a fungus-derived spotting and disfiguring of the leaves. Washington hawthorn is less prone to this disease, works well in the landscape, and has several cultivars. Hawthorns can be difficult to transplant. Northern half of Middle Tennessee.

C. crus-galli [kruse-'gah-lee], cockspur hawthorn, has narrow, elliptic leaves that are thick, leathery, and shiny. It has long, fierce spines (though there is a thornless variety) and the fruit is a dull, dark red. Scattered statewide.

C. marshallii [mar-'shall-ee-eye], parsley hawthorn, has distinctive, deeply divided foliage that turns yellow in fall, exfoliating bark, earlier bloom, and small, oblong, bright red fruit. It takes wetter soils and has a more southerly distribution. Southern tier of West Tennessee counties.

C. viridis ['vir-ih-dis], green hawthorn, has bright red fruit and ovate leaves lobed near the tip. Cultivar 'Winter King' is popular. West Tennessee, lightly elsewhere.

Scott Woodbury, Shaw Arboretum.

Crataegus viridis (green hawthorn).

Diospyros virginiana (persimmon).

Diospyros virginiana—fruit (persimmon).

Diospyros virginiana
Common Persimmon
[dy-ah-'spy-ros vir-jih-nee-'ay-nuh]
Ebenaceae (Ebony Family)

The persimmon tree is a small canopy tree 35 to 60 feet tall and, with a 25- to 40-foot spread, develops an oval shape. The bark is checkered and blocky, and a single plant can colonize into a thicket. Foliage is alternate, elliptic, and glossy dark green, becoming yellowish or reddish purple in autumn. Dioecious, the solitary female flowers are yellow to greenish white, bell shaped, and fragrant. Males are in clusters of 3, and sometimes both flowers appear on the same plant in May and June. In September and October the 1- to 1½-inch yellow to orange fruit is quite tart until it ripens after frost. Then raccoons, opossums, skunks, and foxes all vie to enjoy a ripe persimmon. Humans, birds, and other small mammals do, too, as well as deer. Bees delight in the flowers, and several moths, including the luna, utilize the persimmon tree.

Persimmons are probably best naturalized in an area with full sun and well-drained, slightly acid soil that is either moist or dry. They tolerate drought fairly well, yet with good soil and moisture become picturesque trees. There are cultivars, and transplanting is difficult. Statewide.

Euonymus atropurpureus
Eastern Wahoo
[yew-'on-ih-mus at-troh-per-'pure-ee-us]
Celastraceae (Bittersweet Family)

Varying in height from 12 to 30 feet, eastern wahoo can be a large shrub or a small understory tree. It often has multiple trunks in an upright to arching form. Twigs are green and often ridged with wings running lengthwise. Opposite, elliptic leaves are finely toothed and turn a pleasing pinkish red in fall. It flowers in early summer (June and July) with loose clusters of small, dark red to purple blossoms. A 3- or 4-lobed, reddish capsule opens in September and October to reveal bright scarlet fruit inside, similar to its kin, *E. americanus*, strawberry bush. The fruit is long lasting, and birds do eat it, though it is not high on their list.

Euonymus atropurpureus (eastern wahoo).

A resident of the lowlands, eastern wahoo likes moist, rich, neutral soil in full sun to part shade. It is very shade tolerant but is more attractive with sun. Consider pairing it with *Hamamelis virginiana*, witch hazel, for a colorful fall display. It transplants easily. Two interesting notes: sculptors like working with this wood, and charcoal made from the wood is a favorite of artists. Middle and East Tennessee, Mississippi River Valley.

Fagus grandifolia
American Beech
['fay-gus gran-dih-'foh-lee-uh]
Fagaceae (Beech Family)

Beeches are large canopy trees growing to 85 feet or more, with horizontal branches spreading at least two-thirds that height. In winter the beech is easily recognizable with long, spiky leaf buds and smooth, silvery to slate gray bark. Alternate, elliptic, and coarsely toothed leaves turn yellow in fall then a fine, papery tan and often persist on the tree through the winter. Flowers in April and May are small globular clusters of male blossoms and small spikes of female blossoms. A winged pyramidal nut in a prickly husk develops and in the fall attracts a broad range of song and

Fagus grandifolia (American beech).

game birds, large and small mammals, and humans. Browsers enjoy the beech, too.

Moist soil is a must for beech trees; it should be well drained and moderately to slightly acid. Part shade is fine, as this tree has quite a tolerance for shade; in fact, young beeches benefit from some shade. It transplants easily, but due to its shallow roots and very dense crown, it is difficult to grow anything underneath a beech tree. The tree can sucker into groves, is very sensitive to disturbance and soil compaction, and is not very tolerant of urban settings. Statewide.

Fraxinus americana (white ash).

Fraxinus americana
White Ash
['fraks-ih-nus uh-mair-ih-'kay-nuh]
Oleaceae (Olive Family)

A large canopy tree, white ash grows to 85 feet and forms a conical to rounded, dense crown with a spread up to 60 feet. Pinnately compound, opposite leaves are 12 inches long with about 7 ovate leaflets. Autumn foliage can be red purple or yellow. White ash is dioecious with tiny, inconspicuous flowers in April. In August female trees produce dense clusters of tan winged seeds, that are used by a few birds and small mammals. Ashes are also butterfly larval food. Well-drained, moist soil, slightly acid to neutral, in full sun is best. It tolerates a wide range of moderate conditions, but not extremes. Pests and diseases can be a problem, but it stands up to urban smog and is a relatively fast growing shade tree. There are cultivars and it transplants easily. Statewide.

F. pennsylvanica [pen-sil-'van-ih-kuh], **green ash,** is smaller (to 60 feet tall, 30 feet wide) and fast growing. Native to wetter soils,

Scott Woodbury, Shaw Arboretum.

it needs moisture in the beginning, but once established can be drought tolerant. Female trees seed prolifically each year. Fall foliage is bright yellow. Since it can grow quickly in a good site, proper pruning for stronger branching patterns is important. Statewide.

F. quadrangulata [kwah-drang-yew-'lay-tuh], **blue ash**, is also quite drought tolerant and takes neutral to slightly alkaline soil. Its twigs are square shaped in cross-section due to 4 corky ridges running lengthwise. Fall foliage is golden yellow, and male and female flowers appear on the same tree. Middle and East Tennessee.

Gymnocladus dioicus(a)
Kentucky Coffeetree
[jim-'nah-kluh-dus dy-oh-'eye-kus (-kuh)]
Fabaceae (Pea Family)

Kentucky coffeetree is a large canopy tree from 60 to 85 feet tall with an equal spread. The alternate leaves are large and bipinnately compound, up to 3 feet in length, with numerous ovate leaflets. It is among the last to leaf out in spring. Leaf color evolves from red tinged in spring to dark blue green in summer and yellow in fall. Greenish white flowers are in terminal, pyramidal clusters in June. Dioecious, the female trees produce purple brown, leathery pods 5 to 10 inches long that ripen in October and persist through winter.

Gymnocladus dioicus (Kentucky coffeetree).

Kentucky coffeetree prefers deep, moist, well-drained soil that is neutral to slightly alkaline and in full sun. It can adapt to drier conditions and once established shows good resistance to disturbance, which makes it a good candidate for cities. Slow growing but strong, it casts light, filtered shade allowing healthy plants to grow beneath. It is difficult to transplant. Its native range is very patchy, and it is not abundant anywhere. Lightly in Middle Tennessee and the Mississippi River Valley.

Halesia tetraptera (H. carolina)
Silverbell
[huh-'lee-zee-uh teh-'trap-ter-uh]
Styracaceae (Storax Family)

Halesia tetraptera (silverbell).

A small understory tree at about 30 feet or so, the silverbell is low branching and often multi-trunked with a widely spreading, open crown. Leaves are alternate, elliptic, toothed, and hairy when young. Autumn color is yellow. The silverbell's most charming feature is the clusters of 2 to 5 white bells that dangle from the undersides of year-old branches in April and May. These are soon replaced by dangling, oblong seedpods with 4 wings. The pods change from light green to light brown by autumn and each contains 2 to 3 seeds. Squirrels will eat them. It grows in well-drained, humus-rich, moist soil that is moderately acid in part to light shade. Keep the roots cool and moist with mulch. It transplants well. East Tennessee and the western valley of the Tennessee River.

Hamamelis virginiana
Witch Hazel
[ham-uh-'mee-lis vir-jih-nee-'ay-nuh]
Hamamelidaceae (Witch Hazel Family)

A 20- to 30-foot understory tree, witch hazels have crooked, spreading branches that produce an open, rounded crown. Leaves are alternate, oval, and wavy toothed. In the midst of the yellow fall foliage in October

J. Paul Moore.

Hamamelis virginiana (witch hazel).

and November, fragrant flowers open with narrow, twisting, strap or fringelike petals of bright yellow. Woody seed capsules develop through the following year, and when the new flowers unfurl in autumn, these mature, dry capsules pop open to send seeds flying a great distance. Some birds enjoy the seeds. Witch hazels are found in moist woods. They can take drier soils but are sensitive to drought extremes and need a moderately to slightly acid soil in part sun to light shade. East Tennessee and the Highland Rim.

Ilex opaca
American Holly
['eye-leks oh-'pay-kuh]
Aquifoliaceae (Holly Family)

Ilex opaca (American holly).

The American holly is a dense 20- to 40-foot evergreen tree that is pyramidal in youth and attractively open and irregular in shape at maturity. Leaves are alternate, thick, leathery, and spine tipped. It is dioecious. Plants produce bee-friendly, greenish white flowers in May and June, and females bear red berries in October. These persist through winter to feed birds late in the season.

This holly is slow growing and needs well-drained, sandy, moderately acid soil that is moist to dry and in part shade. It benefits from wind protection. There are cultivars based on habit, fruit, and leaf characteristics. To ensure fruit, 1 male plant is needed for every 2 or 3 females. North of Tennessee American holly is more coastal in its distribution, but it spreads westward as its range moves farther south. It is found more in East and West Tennessee than in the middle of the state.

Juglans nigra (black walnut).

Juglans nigra
Black Walnut
['joo-glans 'ny-gruh]
Juglandaceae (Walnut Family)

Black walnuts are large canopy trees rising to 85 feet with an equal spread. Foliage is alternate and pinnately compound, 12 inches or more in length, with 14 to 22 lanceolate, toothed leaflets that turn yellow in the fall. The leaves emerge late in spring, are aromatic, and drop early in autumn. In May and June it flowers with male catkins and female spikes producing nuts enclosed in tough, 2-inch, round, black, ridged shells with soft outer coverings of light green flesh that rots away. In September and October, humans and squirrels alike gather them to enjoy the tasty nutmeat. Birds will go after cracked nuts. Black walnuts play host to several large and showy moth species, including the luna, and butterflies.

Deep, rich, moist, well-drained soils, neutral to slightly alkaline, are preferred by black walnuts, but they will grow neglected in poor, dry soil and resist disturbances. They do need full sun. Black walnuts are well known for their allelopathic quality, producing a chemical called juglone that serves to prevent the growth of other plants nearby. This is a protective mechanism to reduce competition. Plants particularly sensitive to black walnuts are tomatoes and other garden vegetables, blackberries, apples, rhododendrons, birches, and pines. Other plants are not affected, and some even show improvement near black walnuts, such as pasture grasses, mints, black raspberries, and other fruit trees besides apples. The large nuts can cause damage and stains when they drop. Black walnuts are difficult to transplant. Middle and East Tennessee.

Juniperus virginiana
Eastern Red Cedar
[joo-'nih-peh-rus vir-jih-nee-'ay-nuh]
Cupressaceae (Cypress Family)

Juniperus virginiana (eastern red cedar).

Eastern red cedar is a 40- to 50-foot evergreen conifer, conical to columnar in shape and rounding with age. It features shredding bark and scalelike, blue green to olive green foliage. Male and female cones are on separate trees in the spring. Berrylike cones develop on female trees through the remainder of the year. They are grayish to bluish green with a waxy, frosty bloom, and birds and small mammals love them. The red cedar also offers nesting and cover so important to birds and lends part of its name to the cedar waxwing. The wood is aromatic. Seedlings have prickly needles to deter browsers, but once big enough they develop the mature foliage, which is a butterfly larval food.

This native evergreen takes moist to dry, slightly acid to alkaline soil. Full sun is important; eastern red cedar does not tolerate shade except when very young. It is susceptible to cedar apple rust, which does not harm the tree. There are many good cultivars for form and winter color (foliage can take on an amber, purple, or silver cast), and it works well for hedges and windbreaks. The eastern red cedar is not really a cedar at all but a juniper. Its role is pioneering in nature, taking advantage of disturbed open areas as well as laying claim to unique habitats such as the cedar glades. Eastern red cedar is perfectly adapted to the demanding conditions of thin soil over flat limestone rock that characterize the glades and is the only true conifer native to the Central Basin. Statewide.

Liquidambar styraciflua
Sweetgum
[lih-kwid-'am-bar sty-ruh-'sih-flew-uh]
Hamamelidaceae (Witch Hazel Family)

Liquidambar styraciflua (sweetgum).

Sweetgums are large canopy trees in the garden, 60 to 85 feet, growing higher in the wild. The shape is strongly pyramidal when young and becomes oblong to rounded with age. Twigs are often lined with corky ridges. The leaves are alternate and palmately lobed in a star shape. Toothed and lustrous, dark green in summer, they become a brilliant scarlet red to red purple in autumn. In April and May male flowers bloom in racemes and female flowers are gathered in a small, round, pendant cluster. The female flowers coalesce into a globular, woody and spiny, brown seed-ball that ripens in late summer and persists through winter. Sweetgums are larval food for luna moths, and birds eat the seeds.

Found in wet soils of the floodplain as well as the drier uplands, the sweetgum is adaptable, but prefers deep, moist, moderately to slightly acid soil in full sun. There are cultivars based on leaf shape and color. It is difficult to transplant. The spiky gumballs have been suggested as a good mulch additive to deter felines from using the garden as a large catbox. Statewide.

Liriodendron tulipifera
Tulip Tree, Tulip Poplar
[lih-ree-oh-'den-dron too-lih-'pih-fer-uh]
Magnoliaceae (Magnolia Family)

Liriodendron tulipifera (tulip tree).

Tennessee's state tree is huge, rising 70 to 90 feet (often much higher in the wild) to a high crown atop a straight, branchless trunk. The leaves are alternate and rather square in overall shape with shallow lobes that are not unlike a child's drawing of a tulip. Foliage turns a clear yellow in autumn. Large solitary flowers bloom in May and June. Also tuliplike in appearance, they are cup shaped and yellow green with a bright orange splotch at the base. Erect pyramidal clusters of winged seeds develop in fall that persist through winter and are used by songbirds and small mammals. Wildlife as diverse as bees, hummingbirds, butterflies, and bears use the tulip tree.

Tulip trees need a deep, well-drained, moist soil that is slightly acid. Full sun is another requirement. They grow rather fast, need plenty of room, and are sensitive to drought, pollution, and soil compaction. There are cultivars. Statewide.

Magnolia acuminata
Cucumber Tree
[mag-'noh-lee-uh uh-kyew-mih-'nay-tuh]
Magnoliaceae (Magnolia Family)

Pyramidal and slender in youth, the cucumber tree becomes a 50- to 80-foot deciduous canopy tree with an equal spread at maturity. Its leaves are alternate and elliptic, 4 to 10 inches long. Flowers in May and June are large, solitary and yellow green, appearing high in the tree with a slight fragrance. A reddish brown, oblong aggregate of fruits splits open to reveal orange red seeds hanging on slender threads. Before it matures this conelike aggregate is green, the basis for its common name. Birds and small mammals eat the seeds. Moisture extremes of wet and dry do not suit the cucumber tree. It likes well-drained, moist, deep soil, moderately acid to neutral in full sun or part shade. There are cultivars including a 30-foot dwarf. It is difficult to transplant and benefits from protection against wind and heat. Eastern half of the state and the Mississippi River Valley.

M. grandiflora [gran-dih-'flor-uh], **southern** or **bull-bay magnolia,** is a low-branching, broadleaf evergreen, pyramidal or columnar in shape. It grows 60 to 80 feet tall and about half as wide. The large leaves are alternate, glossy, leathery, dark green, and 5 to 10 inches long with rusty wool beneath and edges that turn under. In May and June it is dotted with large, solitary, creamy white, waxy flowers that are very fragrant. It produces a velvety, red brown, conelike aggregate of fruits with bright red seeds dangling on threads. The cones fall off in late autumn; leaves are replaced approximately every 2 years. Rich, well-drained, moist, moderately acid soil in full sun to part shade is best for southern magnolia. Locate it in a spot where it receives protection from winter winds. Because of its low-branching habit, it needs lots of room. There are many cultivars, and it is difficult to transplant. Believe it or not, southern magnolia is not native to any part of Tennessee, though it is a horticultural favorite that grows very well here.

Magnolia grandiflora (southern magnolia).

Magnolia grandiflora—fruit (southern magnolia).

M. macrophylla [mak-roh-'fill-uh], **bigleaf magnolia,** has a moderate height of 30 to 40 feet. This is the only aspect of this tree that is not large. Twigs are stout, buds are big, fragrant white flowers in June are about a foot across, and the leaves are huge—1 to 2½ feet long and nearly a foot wide with whitish hairs below and an eared base. Culture is similar to other magnolias. The rather coarse nature of this tree should be considered in its placement. East Tennessee and the southern counties of Middle Tennessee.

Magnolia macrophylla (bigleaf magnolia).

M. tripetala [try-'peh-tuh-luh], **umbrella tree,** is a smaller version of M. *acuminata* at 30 feet, yet has larger obovate leaves, larger creamy flowers with an unpleasant fragrance, and reddish cones with seeds. It also needs moist soil and protection from wind. Eastern half of the state.

Magnolia tripetala (umbrella tree).

Malus angustifolia (Pyrus angustifolia)
Southern Crabapple
['may-lus an-gus-tih-'foh-lee-uh]
Rosaceae (Rose Family)

Crabapple is a small tree, 20 to 35 feet tall, with a short trunk and spreading, open branches. Leaves are elliptic and toothed with blunt tips. Clusters of April flowers are pink in bud and open white with a sweet fragrance. Lots of birds and numerous small mammals love the ¾-inch yellow green fruit.

Plant crabapples in moist soil that is well drained and moderately acid. Full sun provides best flower and fruit production. Cedar apple rust can be a problem, spotting the leaves in May and June and causing early leaf drop. A natural control is to keep a distance of at least 500 feet between eastern red

Malus sp. (crabapple).

cedars (*Juniperus virginiana*) and crabapples. There are many, many named cultivars derived from the approximately 25 *Malus* species known around the world. Statewide.

Morus rubra (red mulberry).

Morus rubra
Red Mulberry
['more-us 'rue-bruh]
Moraceae (Mulberry Family)

At 40 to 50 feet in height, red mulberry is a tall understory tree. Its leaves are broadly ovate, hairy, and toothed. They turn yellow in the fall. Dioecious, the clusters of yellow green flowers in May are larger on male plants than female, but in June the females produce dark red, cylindrical fruits resembling blackberries that are eaten with relish by many birds, large and small mammals, and humans. The messy aftermath of this wildlife feast might cause dismay, so site the tree where such gastrointestinal abandon will not be a problem. Red mulberry can tolerate a drier soil but prefers it rich, moist, and slightly acid to slightly alkaline in full sun to part shade. It transplants well and grows from seed or cuttings. Statewide.

Nyssa sylvatica (blackgum).

Nyssa sylvatica
Blackgum, Black Tupelo
['niss-uh sil-'vat-ih-kuh]
Nyssaceae (Tupelo Family)

A small canopy tree 30 to 60 feet high, blackgum starts out pyramidal in shape and matures to a 20- to 40-foot spread with dense, horizontal branches. The bark of older trees turns black. Alternate leaves are elliptic and oblong. The deep, glossy green foliage of summer turns brilliant scarlet red in autumn.

Dioecious, blackgum's tiny male and female flowers are usually on separate trees. Fruit is an oblong, blue black berry in September and October eaten by many birds and small mammals.

Blackgum is adaptable, tolerating drier sites but preferring reliably moist, deep soil that is moderately acid in full sun. Once established it will resist both droughts and flooding. It makes an excellent ornamental shade tree growing slowly on strong wood. It is very difficult to transplant. Statewide.

N. aquatica [uh-'kwah-tih-kuh], **water tupelo,** is a taller tree with larger leaves and a flaring trunk base. It is a swamp tree of the floodplain. West Tennessee.

Ostrya virginiana
American Hophornbeam
['ahs-tree-uh vir-jih-nee-'ay-nuh]
Betulaceae (Birch Family)

Ostrya virginiana (American hophornbeam).

American hophornbeam is a large understory tree, 25 to 40 feet tall with a two-thirds spread. It is conical to rounded in shape with horizontal branches that often droop. Leaves are alternate, elliptic, double toothed, and fuzzy below. Fall foliage is pale yellow. Male catkins, drooping in clusters of 3, form in the fall and are visible through winter. Female flowers bloom in small clusters in April on the same tree. Seeds are contained in thin, inflated oval sacks in 2-inch clusters from July through October and are consumed by game birds and small mammals.

Very similar to moist bottomland resident *Carpinus caroliniana* (American hornbeam), the hophornbeam prefers the moist, well-drained, slightly acid soil of the uplands in full sun or part shade but can tolerate a drier soil and more shade. It grows well in the city and is a good choice for small lawns, as it is both slow growing and strong. It is difficult to transplant. Statewide.

Oxydendrum arboreum
Sourwood
[oks-ih-'den-drum ar-'bore-ee-um]
Ericaceae (Heath Family)

Oxydendrum arboreum (sourwood).

A straight and narrow tree of the upper understory, sourwood grows 25 to 45 feet tall and half as wide. Alternate leaves are elliptically oblong, sometimes finely toothed, and a lustrous dark green. In autumn they are often brilliantly colored red to red purple. In early summer (June and July) drooping, 1-sided racemes of small, white, urn-shaped flowers drape the tree from the branch tips. These become small, dried capsules in the fall and are eaten by birds and small mammals. Bees make a highly prized honey from the flowers.

Sourwood likes the well-drained, moderately acid soil of the uplands. It prefers moist soil but can take a bit of dryness. Give it full sun to part shade. Flowering and autumn coloring are best in full sun. It can be somewhat difficult to transplant, is slow growing, and shows sensitivity to soil compaction. Statewide, lightly in West Tennessee.

Pinus spp.
Pine
['py-nus]
Pinaceae (Pine Family)

P. echinata [eh-kih-'nay-tuh], **shortleaf** or **yellow pine**, is a large evergreen conifer, 50 to 75 feet tall (much larger in the wild). Pyramidal in form, it develops an open crown with age.

Dark bluish green needles, 3 to 5 inches long, are in bundles of 2 (sometimes 3), and the bark is in large plates. The ovoid cone is 2 inches long and 1 inch wide. It adapts from dry upland soil (tolerating drought) to the floodplain and needs full sun. It is hard to transplant. Birds eat the seeds and nest in the trees. Middle Tennessee, heavier in East Tennessee.

P. rigida ['ridge-ih-duh], pitch pine, is 45 to 65 feet tall and develops an irregular shape as it ages. On harsh, exposed sites it can be dwarfed and quite gnarled. Needles are twisted, 3 to 5 inches long, and in groups of 3. Cones are ovoid, 3 inches long, and in clusters. It grows in strongly to slightly acid, well-drained, dry soil and tolerates drought. Give it full sun. Northeastern Tennessee.

P. strobus ['stroh-bus], eastern white pine, grows best in New England where it reaches a height topping 100 feet in the wild. In Tennessee expect a height of 50 to 85 feet and a width of 40 to 55 feet with horizontal, tiered branching. The soft blue green needles are 2 to 4 inches long in groups of 5 that change every 2 years. It blooms at an early age, producing 6- to 8-inch cylindrical cones, often curved, in late summer or early fall. Birds, small mammals, and browsers love the seeds. It is easy to transplant, but is sensitive to urban pollutants and needs full sun in moist, moderately to slightly acid soil. Its natural range extends down through the Appalachians into East Tennessee. While it has been a popular horticultural choice elsewhere in the state, gardeners in these areas would be best advised to consider other conifers, as white pine can easily succumb to the stresses of heat, drought, and pollution.

Pinus taeda (loblolly pine).

Pinus virginiana (Virginia pine).

P. taeda ['tee-duh], **loblolly pine**, is a southern pine of the coastal plain. Smaller in the home landscape (50 to 60 feet), it can reach over 100 feet in the wild. Needles are long, 6 to 9 inches, and in groups of 3. They are dark yellow green and fragrant. The cone is narrowly conical, 3 to 6 inches long. Loblolly pine can take a wide range of conditions including poor, moderately acid, sandy soil, either moist or dry in full sun. It occurs most often in counties along Tennessee's southern border and is considered an exotic pest plant (lesser threat) in counties to the north of its natural range.

P. virginiana [vir-jih-nee-'ay-nuh], **Virginia** or **scrub pine**, is a pioneer plant. It is broad and open in habit, 15 to 40 feet tall and 10 to 30 feet wide, and creates a picturesque silhouette. The slightly flattened, twisted needles are yellowish to dark green and 1½ to 3 inches long in groups of 2. Female cones are solitary or in clusters, each 1 to 3 inches long, often remaining on the tree for years. Yellow male cones appear in April and May. It will grow in any poor, dry soil in full sun as long as it is not too shallow and drains well. Virginia pine transplants well and is utilized by birds for food and nesting. Middle Tennessee, heavier in East Tennessee.

Platanus occidentalis
Sycamore, American Planetree
['plat-uh-nus ok-sih-den-'tay-lis]
Platanaceae (Sycamore Family)

To call sycamore a large canopy tree is an understatement. Reaching 75 to 100 feet in the air, and sometimes much more in the wild, its massive trunk supports a crown of equal or greater spread. A distinctive feature is the flaking bark of the upper trunk and branches that exposes the creamy inner bark and gives the tree a mottled appearance. The large leaves are alternate and palmate with 3 to 5 shallow lobes and coarse teeth. They turn a tannish color in fall. Male and female flowers appear on separate twigs and both form dense, ball-like clusters in May. Female clusters become a small globe of ripe seed in September and persist through the winter dangling from the branches.

Platanus occidentalis (sycamore).

Sycamores grow quickly in the deep, rich, moist soil of the lowlands and floodplain, preferring neutral to slightly alkaline soil in full sun to part shade. Given its size and frequent problems with anthracnose, a fungus-derived disease that spots the leaves, the sycamore is better suited for naturalized areas. The tree is easily transplanted, and its large leaves operate as air cleaners by gathering dust from the air. Statewide.

Prunus americana
American or Wild Plum
['prew-nus uh-mair-ih-'kay-nuh]
Rosaceae (Rose Family)

A large shrub or small understory tree, American plum grows 15 to 25 feet tall and can colonize into a thicket or be trained as a single-trunked tree. Its branching is horizontal, and its spread often exceeds its height. Leaves are alternate, elliptic, and toothed, changing from dark green in summer to pale yellow in autumn. Clusters of 2 to 5 unpleasantly scented, white flowers bloom in April with the unfolding leaves. In midsummer 1-inch, yellowish to red, round fruits attract small

Prunus americana (American plum).

mammals, birds, and humans. It is also a good cover and nesting plant for wildlife and supports several butterfly species. American plum will thrive with little attention. Give it well-drained, neutral soil, moist or dry, and full sun. It tolerates drought and transplants well. Leaves are susceptible to various fungal diseases that can disfigure or cause early leaf drop. Site American plum where its late season appearance and fruit drop will not be a problem. Statewide.

P. angustifolia [an-gus-tih-'foh-lee-uh], **chickasaw plum,** is a shrub 5 to 15 feet tall, which has smaller fruit and smaller, narrower, shiny leaves. Statewide.

P. serotina [seh-'rah-tih-nuh], **black** or **wild cherry,** is more of a small canopy tree at 50 to 75 feet with half the spread. Leaves are alternate, elliptically oblong, and toothed. Summer color is a lustrous dark green, becoming yellow, orange, or red in autumn. Pendulous racemes (4 to 6 inches) of small white, fragrant flowers bloom in May. Birds and small mammals love the red to glossy black berries in August and September. Black cherries like moist yet well-drained, slightly acid to neutral soil in full sun. They can tolerate drier conditions and are disease resistant. Eastern tent caterpillars, along with nearly 200 other species of butterflies and moths, love black cherry foliage, but a diverse, organic yard attracts enough insect-eating birds to keep them in line. Black cherry is a pioneer plant, settling disturbed sites. It is difficult to transplant. Statewide.

Prunus serotina (black cherry).

Ptelea trifoliata
Common Hoptree, Wafer-ash
['tee-lee-uh try-foh-lee-'ay-tuh]
Rutaceae (Rue Family)

Ptelea trifoliata (hoptree).

Low branched and bushy, the hoptree is a small understory tree growing 15 to 25 feet tall. The alternate leaves are trifoliate with ovate leaflets. A lustrous dark green in summer, foliage turns yellow in the fall. Fragrant, greenish white to yellow flowers bloom in terminal clusters in May and June. Each seed is situated in the middle of a 1-inch, circular and flat, papery disk or wafer that changes from light green to tan and hangs in dense clusters in late summer. Twigs and leaves stink when bruised. Butterflies, birds, small mammals, and browsers find sustenance in the hoptree.

The hoptree is very adaptable. Well-drained, neutral soil can be moist or dry and in all light conditions from full sun to medium shade. There are cultivars based on leaf color, and it works well in a shrub border. It transplants readily. Middle Tennessee, lightly in East Tennessee.

Quercus spp.
Oak
['kwer-kus]
Fagaceae (Beech Family)

The mighty, sturdy oak tree plays a symbolic and near mythic role in our culture as effectively as it provides summer shade in our yards. These slow-growing, stately trees are very long-lived, some surviving multiple centuries. Generally they are pyramidal in youth and become spreading and rounded with age. In mid-spring male flowers hang in loose, droop-ing catkins clustered together. Female flowers are singular to few clustered in the leaf axils. Acorns vary in appearance and are used in species identification. Oaks like full sun, and most prefer a moderately to slightly acid soil. Humans, birds, small mammals, and browsers enjoy the bounty of all oaks, as do numerous insects, butterflies, and moths. Many oaks are sensitive to soil compaction, an important consideration in areas of construction.

Oaks are divided into two categories: white and red. Those in the white group have no bristles on the leaves, often edible acorns that mature the first year, and light gray, scaly bark. These include *Q. alba, Q. lyrata, Q. macrocarpa, Q. michauxii, Q. montana, Q. muhlenbergii,* and *Q. stellata.* Oaks in the red group share the characteristics of bristle tips on the leaves, bitter acorns that require two years to mature, and dark, furrowed bark. They include *Q. coccinea, Q. falcata, Q. imbri-caria, Q. pagoda, Q. palustris, Q. phellos, Q. rubra, Q. shumardii,* and *Q. velutina.*

Q. alba ['al-buh], **white oak,** is wider than its 60- to 85-foot height and can get taller in the wild. It is pyramidal when young and becomes wide spreading with horizontal branches at maturity. Leaves have 5 to 9 deep, rounded, pinnate lobes and turn brown to wine red in fall. The acorn is about ¾ of an inch long with a bumpy cup that covers over 25 percent of the nut; they occur singly or in pairs and are highly valued by animals. White oak takes well to the moist, warm, western and southern slopes. Well-drained, moist soil, slightly acid to neutral in full sun is best. It will tolerate drier soil and germi-

Quercus alba (white oak).

Scott Woodbury, Shaw Arboretum.

nates quickly but is difficult to transplant. The white oak is a magnificent shade tree that can live for centuries. Statewide.

Q. lyrata [ly-'ray-tuh], **overcup oak,** has a variable crown shape at 35 to 60 feet tall. The dark green leaves are woolly on the undersides and obovate in overall shape with 5 to 9 lobes. The base of each leaf is narrow, including the lower pairs of lobes. A 1-inch acorn is virtually enclosed by a roughly scaled cup. Overcup oak is found in low, wet soil and is very tolerant of flooding. Western half of the state, lightly in the east.

Q. macrocarpa [mak-roh-'kar-puh], **bur** or **mossycup oak,** becomes a massively trunked 70- to 85-foot tree with stout branches that often spread wider than the height. Leaves are a dark glossy green, obovate, and pinnately lobed. They turn yellow brown in fall. Solitary acorns are fat, ¾ to 1½ inches long, and more than half enclosed by a deep, fringed cup. It is a very adaptable tree: occurring in plain or forest, in wet or dry soil that can be acid or alkaline, and proving itself tolerant of city conditions. It is best in moist soil, often sharing sites with white oaks. Give it full sun. It is difficult to transplant. Central Basin, lightly western half of the state.

Quercus macrocarpa (bur oak).

Q. montana (Q. prinus) [mahn-'tay-nuh], **chestnut oak,** gets 55 to 70 feet tall with an equal spread. Lustrous leaves are entire, round toothed, and obovate-oblong. They turn yellow brown in the fall. Acorns are 1 to 1½ inches long and half enclosed in the cup. Chestnut oaks grow best in well-drained, moist, slightly acid soil but are also found on the poor, dry, rocky soil of the uplands in full sun to part shade. They are difficult to transplant. Middle and East Tennessee. *Q. michauxii* [mih-'shaw-ee-eye], **swamp chestnut oak,** is taller and grows in moist, coastal plain bottomlands. Statewide, especially West Tennessee.

Quercus muhlenbergii (chinkapin oak).

Q. muhlenbergii (Q. muehlenbergii) [myew-len-'ber-jee-eye], **chinkapin oak,** gets 40 to 50 feet tall, larger in the wild, with an equal spread assuming an open, rounded habit. Its leaves are oblong and obovate in shape, coarsely toothed, entire, and slightly hairy below. Autumn color is yellow brown. The small acorn is ½ to 1 inch long and half enclosed by the cup. Chinkapin needs a well-drained soil, moist to dry, and demonstrates drought tolerance. Best growth is in moist, rich, neutral soil. It tolerates alkalinity, often growing on limestone outcrops and ridges. It germinates quickly and under favorable conditions grows at a faster rate. Statewide.

Q. stellata [steh-'lay-tuh], **post oak,** is considered a large understory tree at 40 to 50 feet tall. It takes on a rounded shape with spreading branches in the open. The leaves have 3 to 5 large, round to square lobes and are very dark green and glossy in summer, yellow brown in the fall. Acorns are solitary or in pairs, and the ¾-inch length is one-third to one-half enclosed by the cup. Dry, moderately acid soil on rocky ridges and southern slopes in full sun suit the post oak. It is hard to transplant. Post oaks are very slow growing and drought tolerant. Statewide.

Q. coccinea [kok-'sih-nee-uh], **scarlet oak,** is a small canopy tree up to 70 feet tall and nearly as wide, with dark green, glossy foliage. Leaves have 5 to 7 bristle-tipped lobes, are whitish below, and turn red in the fall. The acorn, ½ to 1 inch long, has a deep, bowl-shaped cup enclosing about half the nut. Scarlet oak does best in well-drained, slightly acid soil on the dry side in full sun. Statewide.

Q. falcata [fal-'kay-tuh], **southern red oak** or **Spanish oak,** grows 70 to 80 feet tall with a rounded crown. Leaves are highly variable in appearance with 3 or more lobes and gray-ish, fuzzy undersides. The striped, ½-inch nut has a shallow cup. Southern red oak grows well on dry, poor, upland soil that is moderately acid in full sun. Statewide. *Q. pagoda (Q. falcata* var. *pagodifolia)* [puh-'goh-duh], **cherrybark oak** or **swamp Spanish oak,** has leaves more uniformly 5-lobed and inhabits wetter soil in the coastal plain. West Tennessee.

Q. imbricaria [im-brih-'kay-ree-uh], **shingle** or **laurel oak,** is a large understory tree at 35 to 55 feet tall with a near equal spread, grow-ing larger in the wild. Leaves are glossy, dark green, entire, and lance shaped with a bris-tle tip. In fall they turn a rich brown and often persist on the tree into winter. The acorn is small, about ½ inch in length, and one-third to half enclosed by the cup. Shin-gle oaks like the well-drained uplands and prefer moist, rich, deep, moderately acid soil in full sun. They are tolerant of drier soil and city conditions. Middle Tennessee, lightly elsewhere.

Q. palustris [puh-'lus-tris], **pin** or **swamp oak,** is a small canopy tree, 50 to 75 feet in height and pyramidal to oval in shape. The lower branches are pendulous and drop off with age. Leaves have 5 to 7 deeply cut, pin-nate lobes with bristly tips. Summer color is glossy, dark green and turns reddish brown in fall. The acorn is a globular, ½-inch nut with

Quercus imbricaria (shingle oak).

a thin, flat cup. Pin oak likes wet soil and can tolerate some seasonal flooding. Soil needs to be moderately acid; this oak does not like neutral or alkaline soil. Give it full sun. It will also tolerate city conditions, growing fairly fast. It transplants readily. Lightly in West and Middle Tennessee.

Q. phellos ['feh-los], willow oak, is another small canopy tree at a height of 50 to 70 feet and near equal spread, transforming in shape from a youthful pyramid to a mature rounded oval. The entire leaves are narrowly lance shaped with a bristle tip and turn yellow brown in fall. The ½-inch acorn is solitary or in pairs with a thin, flat cup. Willow oaks are adaptable but prefer moist, well-drained soil in full sun. They are good choices for urban areas and transplant readily. Due to their rapid growth, willow oaks can form weak crotches and require pruning for a stronger branching pattern. Statewide.

Q. rubra (Q. borealis) ['rue-bruh], northern red oak, seems an ideal choice for the home landscape. It is a large canopy tree 60 to 85 feet high (more in the wild) with a near equal spread and rounded shape. Glossy foliage is alternate and pinnate with 7 to 11 bristle-tipped lobes. Newly emerging foliage is pinkish to red and autumn foliage is yellow brown, sometimes reddish. The brown acorn is ¾ to 1 inch long with a shallow cup. Suited to city life, northern red oak is one of the faster-growing oaks and does best in well-drained, moderately acid, moist soil in full sun to part shade. In fact, northern red oak tolerates shade better than the other oaks. It transplants readily. Statewide.

Q. shumardii [shue-'mar-dee-eye], Shumard oak, is similar to the red and scarlet oaks. It is pyramidal in youth, rounding out at maturity to a width equal its height of 50 to 80 feet. Glossy leaves have wider, deeper lobes and bristle tips. They turn reddish in autumn. Acorns are ¾ to 1 inch long with a shallow cup. It likes rich, moist, well-drained soil in full sun, but shows good tolerance of both drought and wet soil. It grows quickly, transplants well, and makes a good shade tree. Statewide.

Quercus shumardii (Shumard oak).

Q. velutina [veh-'lew-tih-nuh], black oak, is a narrow to rounded canopy tree, 50 to 75 feet tall and 35 to 50 feet wide. Foliage is a glossy dark green in summer and yellow, orange, or reddish brown in fall. Seven to nine pinnate lobes can be deep or shallow and are bristle tipped. The acorn is striped, ¾ inch long, and half enclosed by a slightly fringed cup. Black oaks can tolerate the poor, dry soil of gravelly uplands but prefer well-drained, moist soil that is slightly acid in full sun to part shade. They are difficult to transplant. Statewide.

Rhamnus caroliniana
Carolina Buckthorn
['ram-nus kair-ah-lih-nee-'ay-nuh]
Rhamnaceae (Buckthorn Family)

A large shrub or a small tree, Carolina buckthorn only exceeds 20 feet in height in the wild and has a spreading crown. Contrary to its name it has no thorns, but the twigs and leaves give off a stink when crushed. Leaves are alternate, elliptic, and sometimes finely toothed. They are glossy dark green in summer and yellow in autumn. In May clusters of creamy yellow green flowers bloom in the leaf axils and attract bees. The ½-inch berries are lovely in late summer as they slowly turn

Rhamnus caroliniana (Carolina buckthorn).

a rich red and finally a shiny black in October. Songbirds eat them.

Carolina buckthorn is drought tolerant, adapting to moist or dry soil, slightly acid to neutral, in part to light shade. It transplants well. Middle and East Tennessee, lightly in West Tennessee.

Rhododendron maximum
Rosebay or Great Laurel Rhododendron
[roh-doh-'den-dron 'maks-ih-mum]
Ericaceae (Heath Family)

Rhododendron maximum (rosebay rhododendron).

Rosebay rhododendron is a tall evergreen shrub or small tree to 20 feet or more. It is loose and open in habit and often narrow, spreading half the height. The large leathery leaves are dark, glossy, oblong, and downy below. They droop in winter. In June it dresses up with terminal clusters of 2-inch, bell-shaped, white to pale pink or rose flowers with greenish to yellow orange spotted throats. Oblong fruit capsules are downy.

Rosebay seeks a cool, consistently moist but well-drained, strongly to moderately acid soil. Medium shade is best, but a little sun does promote good bloom. East Tennessee.

Rhus copallina
Shining, Flameleaf, or Winged Sumac
[roos koh-puh-'ly-nuh] (also pronounced russ)
Anacardiaceae (Cashew Family)

Shining sumac grows 20 to 30 feet tall with an equal spread. Dense when young, it becomes more open with age. Foliage is alternate and pinnately compound with 9 to 21 oblong, glossy, dark green leaflets. A winglike ridge of tissue runs up either side of the leaf stalk between each pair of leaflets. Fall color is a stunningly rich, crimson red. Statewide.

R. glabra ['glay-bruh], smooth sumac, is smaller, 9 to 15 feet tall, with smooth young branches and no wings on the leaf stalks. Foliage is smooth and whitish below and bright green above. In the fall leaves turn orange red. It is a good choice for droughty, poor areas in full sun. Statewide.

R. typhina [ty-'fy-nuh], staghorn sumac, is a bit more treelike in form (to 25 feet) and has a velvety, reddish brown fuzz on younger branches. Its natural range is well to the north, yet it lightly dips down into East Tennessee and occurs sporadically in Middle Tennessee.

Rhus glabra (smooth sumac).

Sumacs are dioecious. The dense pyramidal spikes of yellow green flowers in late spring and early summer on the female plants become dense pyramidal spikes of very hairy, small, red berries by late summer, which persist through the fall to provide welcome food to migrating birds and other animals. In compensation for the lack of berries, flowers on male plants are more noticeable. Bees and butterflies like the nectar. Sumacs are definitely for naturalizing. They can colonize rapidly and overrun a garden. In the right spot, however, with well-drained, dry soil that is slightly acid to neutral and in full sun, they are attractive and wildlife friendly. Sumacs transplant readily, but the bark is easily damaged.

Robinia pseudoacacia
Black Locust
[rah-'bin-ee-uh 'sue-doh-uh-'kay-see-uh]
Fabaceae (Pea Family)

Black locust grows rapidly to a height of 40 to 70 feet. The foliage is pinnately compound with 7 to 10 leaflets and takes on a yellowish cast in autumn. In late April or

Robinia pseudoacacia (black locust).

May showy racemes of fragrant, white flowers droop in clusters. Short, flat seedpods persist through winter.

This tree has some rather undesirable baggage, too. As a pioneer plant, it has a tendency to send out suckers profusely in an effort to colonize the immediate area. The suckers and the branches are lined with sharp, stout, paired prickles. Compared with many trees, it is relatively short-lived. Yet it will take just about any environment except flooding and has a wide soil pH range including slightly alkaline. It is good for poor, wild areas and erosion control. It needs full sun. There are cultivars—some without prickles and with different flower colors. Bees make a tasty honey from black locust flowers. Statewide.

Sassafras albidum

Sassafras
['sass-uh-frass 'al-bih-dum]
Lauraceae (Laurel Family)

Sassafras is an irregularly shaped tree, 30 to 60 feet tall with a 20- to 40-foot spread. Its stems, leaves, and roots are aromatic. The alternate, ovate leaves can be entire (spoons), 2-lobed (mittens), or 3-lobed (forks). Summer color is yellow green, and in the fall it displays a rainbow of delicious yellows, oranges, reds, and purples. Sassafras is dioecious, producing terminal clusters of yellow flowers in April and, on the females, dark blue berries on bright red stems in September that are eaten by the birds. Sassafras plays host to many moths and butterflies.

Drought tolerant, sassafras takes a well-drained, moist to dry, slightly acid soil. As a pioneer species it likes full sun and can take poor sites as well. It does sucker to form

Sassafras albidum (sassafras).

Bill Davit, Shaw Arboretum.

colonies; prune to control. It is difficult to transplant. Statewide.

Taxodium distichum
Bald Cypress
[tax-'oh-dee-um 'dis-tih-kum]
Taxodiaceae (Bald Cypress Family)

Taxodium distichum (bald cypress).

Bald cypress is a deciduous conifer with small, linear leaves spiraling around branchlets. The green leaves emerge with a yellow tint in spring, develop a blue or gray tint in summer, and turn dark brown in autumn. The tree grows 70 to 100 feet tall and is pyramidal with a strong central trunk buttressed at the base. The bark is fibrous and shredding; the cone is a 1-inch globe changing from green to purple in the fall.

Associated with swamps, where it produces the characteristic knees—upright growths that help supply oxygen to the roots—bald cypress will also grow in reliably moist, slightly acid soil in full sun. It is long-lived and has few problems beyond sensitivity to drought. It does not like alkaline soil. West Tennessee.

Tilia heterophylla
White Basswood, Linden
['tih-lee-uh heh-teh-rah-'fill-uh]
Tiliaceae (Linden Family)

Tilia americana (American linden).

Tilia heterophylla is a southern variation of *T. americana*, American linden. It grows 60 to 80 feet high obtaining an oblong shape with a spread of 40 to 50 feet. Alternate leaves are ovate to heart shaped, toothed, dark green above, and woolly, whitish below. They turn yellow in the fall. Fragrant yellow flowers hang in pendulous clusters from a leaflike bract in June and attract bees, which make a prized honey from the nectar. Small, round seeds follow. *Tilia* spp. are a butterfly larval food. White basswood needs space to grow in a deep, well-drained, moist, and neutral soil with full sun or part shade. It transplants readily, but may be hard to find in nurseries. Middle and East Tennessee, lightly in West Tennessee.

Tsuga canadensis
Eastern or Canada Hemlock
['tsoo-guh kan-uh-'den-sis]
Pinaceae (Pine Family)

The eastern hemlock is broadly conical, spreading half its height of 40 to 70 feet. The dark green, round-tipped needles have 2 parallel white bands beneath. Small ½ to 1-inch cones are a light to medium brown and provide food for songbirds and mammals. It is best suited to cool, moist, moderately acid, northern and eastern slopes and is quite shade tolerant. Sensitive to disturbance, drought, and pollution, it is not an appropriate choice for the demands of city life. Eastern hemlock is slow growing, needs protection from wind, and casts dense shade. It is difficult to transplant. East Tennessee.

Tsuga canadensis (eastern hemlock).

Ulmus americana
American or White Elm
['ul-mus uh-mair-ih-'kay-nuh]
Ulmaceae (Elm Family)

A large, graceful tree that obtains a beautiful vase shape, American elm grows 80 feet tall or more with double-toothed, ovate leaves that turn a lovely yellow in the fall. Flat, winged seeds are produced in spring. It is adaptable to a wide range of environments,

Ulmus americana (American elm).

Scott Woodbury, Shaw Arboretum.

preferring moist soil in full sun to part shade, and tolerates alkaline soil. Statewide.

At one time a traditional street tree planted by cities and towns, American elm has fallen victim to the imported Dutch elm disease. Uncontrollable and fatal, this disease has devastated the species. It also suffers from a laundry list of additional diseases and pests. Other elm species are susceptible to Dutch elm disease as well, and some are considered rather weedy due to their high germination rate. Reports assert that healthy American elms can be maintained with fungicide injections every 3 years. Anyone fortunate enough to have such a tree should try to follow this simple regimen. Individuals showing resistance are being selectively bred in hopes of genetically improving the tree's ability to fight off the disease.

Viburnum rufidulum

Rusty Blackhaw Viburnum
[vy-'ber-num rue-'fih-dyew-lum]
Caprifoliaceae (Honeysuckle Family)

Viburnum rufidulum (rusty blackhaw viburnum).

Growing as either a small understory tree or a large shrub (20 to 25 feet or more), rusty blackhaw viburnums can be single or multi-trunked. Glossy leaves are opposite, broadly elliptic, toothed, and dark green. In autumn the foliage turns purplish red. A rusty, woolly fuzz coats the buds and leaf petioles. Creamy white, terminal clusters of flowers appear in May followed by clusters of berries on red stems in the fall. The berries range in color from pinkish rose to blue black with a whitish bloom and feed birds and small mammals. Rusty blackhaw viburnum is adaptable to well-drained, moist or dry soil, neutral to slightly alkaline, and develops an open form in shade, a denser one in sun. Fruiting is best with a few hours of sun. It is a good choice for xeric (dry) sites and transplants well. Statewide.

V. prunifolium **[prew-nih-'foh-lee-um]**, **blackhaw viburnum**, is similar in most respects to its rusty brother above. The differences include a lack of woolly fuzz, less purple color in the fall leaves, and greater cold hardiness, which reflects the blackhaw viburnum's northern range. Northeast corner of Tennessee, lightly elsewhere.

Sources for Further Reading

(Full citation information can be found in the bibliography.)

The Standard Cyclopedia of Horticulture, L. H. Bailey

Hortus Third: A Concise Dictionary of Plants Cultivated in the United States and Canada, Liberty Hyde Bailey and Ethel Zoe Bailey

Growing and Propagating Showy Native Woody Plants, Richard E. Bir

Nature's Garden, Neltje Blanchan

Grasses: An Identification Guide, Lauren Brown

Great Smoky Mountains Wildflowers, Carlos C. Campbell, William F. Hutson, and Aaron J. Sharp

Wildflowers of the Land Between the Lakes Region, Kentucky and Tennessee, Edward W. Chester and William H. Ellis

Atlas of Tennessee Vascular Plants, Edward W. Chester, et al.

A Field Guide to Ferns and Their Related Families of Northeastern and Central North America, Boughton Cobb

The New England Wildflower Society Guide to Growing and Propagating Wildflowers of the United States and Canada, William Cullina

How to Know the Wild Flowers, Mrs. William Starr Dana

Manual of Woody Landscape Plants, Michael A. Dirr

Wildflowers of the Eastern United States, Wilbur H. Duncan and Marion B. Duncan

The Book of Forest and Thicket: Trees, Shrubs, and Wildflowers of Eastern North America, and *The Book of Swamp and Bog: Trees, Shrubs, and Wildflowers of Eastern Freshwater Wetlands*, John Eastman

"How Do You Say That?" *Horticulture*, Thomas Fischer

Native Shrubs and Woody Vines of the Southeast, Leonard E. Foote and Samuel B. Jones Jr.

The Gardener's Fern Book, F. Gordon Foster

Manual of Vascular Plants of Northeastern United States and Adjacent Canada, Henry A. Gleason and Arthur Cronquist

Gray's Manual of Botany, Asa Gray and Merritt L. Fernald

The Encyclopedia of Ornamental Grasses, John Greenlee

The Illustrated Book of Wildflowers and Shrubs, William Carey Grimm

Wildflowers of the Central South, Thomas E. Hemmerly

Native Trees, Shrubs, and Vines for Urban and Rural America, Gary L. Hightshoe

Trilliums in Woodland and Garden: American Treasures, Don L. Jacobs and Rob L. Jacobs

Gardening with Native Wild Flowers, Samuel B. Jones Jr. and Leonard E. Foote

Trees of the Central Hardwood Forests of North America, Donald J. Leopold, William C. McComb, and Robert N. Muller

The Audubon Society Field Guide to North American Trees, Eastern Region, Elbert L. Little

Southeastern Wildflowers, Jan W. Midgley

Wildflower Perennials for Your Garden, Bebe Miles

The Audubon Society Field Guide to North American Wildflowers Eastern Region, William A. Niering and Nancy C. Olmstead

Identification, Selection and Use of Southern Plants for Landscape Design, Neil Odenwald and James Turner

A Field Guide to Wildflowers of Northeastern and Northcentral North America, Roger Tory Peterson and Margaret McKenny

Growing and Propagating Wild Flowers, Harry R. Phillips

Wild Flowers of the United States, Vol. 2: The Southeastern States, Harold William Rickett

Ferns of Tennessee, Jesse M. Shaver

A Guide to Wildflowers of the Mid-South, Arlo I. Smith

Botanical Latin, William T. Stearn

Landscaping with Native Trees, Guy Sternberg and Jim Wilson

Gardening with Wild Flowers, Frances Tenenbaum

Gardening with Native Plants of the South, Sally Wasowski and Andy Wasowski

A Guide to the Wildflowers and Ferns of Kentucky, Mary E. Wharton and Roger W. Barbour

"Checklist of the Vascular Plants of Tennessee," B. Eugene Wofford and Robert Kral

Wyman's Gardening Encyclopedia, Donald Wyman

Collecting, Processing and Germinating Seeds of Wildland Plants, James A. Young and Cheryl G. Young

Mail-Order Nurseries

The following mail-order nurseries carry a wide variety of plants native to North America and most of the plants listed in this book. Nurseries that have stated they only sell nursery-propagated plants are marked with an asterisk (*).

Be sure to shop local nurseries. Many local nurseries carry some native plants, and evidence of customer interest might prompt them to carry more in the future. Encourage them to order from wholesalers providing nursery-propagated stock.

Eco-Gardens
P.O. Box 1227
Decatur, GA 30031
Phone: (404) 294-6468
Fax: (404) 294-8173
E-mail: eco-gardens@mindspring.com
Catalog: $2.00

Enchanter's Garden*
HC77, Box 108
Hinton, WV 25951
Phone/fax: (304) 466-3154
Catalog: Free

Goodness Grows*
P.O. Box 311
Lexington, GA 30648
Phone: (706) 743-5055
Catalog: Free

Kurt Bluemel, Inc.
2740 Green Lane
Baldwin, MD 21013-9523

Native Gardens*
5737 Fisher Lane
Greenback, TN 37742-2744
Phone/fax: (865) 856-0220
Website: www.native-gardens.com
Catalog: Free

Niche Gardens*
1111 Dawson Rd.
Chapel Hill, NC 27516-8576
Phone: (919) 967-0078
Fax: (919) 967-4026
Website catalog: www.nichegdn.com
Catalog: $3.00

Nurseries Caroliniana, Inc.*
100 East Hugh Street
North Augusta, SC 29841
Phone: (803) 278-2336
Fax: (803) 278-5574
E-mail: nurcar1@nurcar.com
Website: www.nurcar.com
Catalog: Free

Pine Ridge Gardens*
832 Sycamore Road
London, AR 72847
Phone: (501) 293-4359
E-mail: office@pineridgegardens.com
Website: www.pineridgegardens.com
Catalog: $5.00, two-year subscription

Plant Delights*
9241 Sauls Rd.
Raleigh, NC 27603
Phone: (919) 772-4794
Fax: (919) 662-0370
E-mail: office@plantdel.com
Website: www.plantdelights.com
Catalog: Free

Prairie Moon Nursery*
Rt. 3 Box 163
Winona, MN 55987-9515
Phone: (507) 452-1362
Fax: (507) 454-5238
E-mail: pmnrsy@luminet.net
Website:
　　www.prairiemoonnursery.com
Catalog: Free

Prairie Nursery*
P.O. Box 306
Westfield, WI 53964
Phone: (800) 476-9453
Fax: (608) 296-2741
E-mail: cs@prairienursery.com
Website: www.prairienursery.com
Catalog: Free

Prairie Ridge Nursery
9738 Overland Rd.
Mt. Horeb, WI 53572-2832
Phone: (608) 437-5245
E-mail: crmeco@chorus.net
Catalog: Free
Habitat Restoration Guide: $5.00

The Primrose Path*
921 Scottdale-Dawson Rd.
Scottdale, PA 15683
Phone: (724) 887-6756
Fax: (724) 887-3077
E-mail: primrose@a1usa.net
Website: www.theprimrosepath.com
Catalog: $2.00

Roslyn Nursery*
211 Burrs Lane
Dix Hills, NY 11746
Phone: (631) 643-9347
Fax: (631) 427-0894
E-mail: roslyn@roslynnursery.com
Website: www.roslynnursery.com
Catalog: $3.00 (refunded with
　　purchase)

Shady Oaks Nursery*
1101 S. State St.
P.O. Box 708
Waseca, MN 56093
Phone: (507) 835-5033
　　(800) 504-8006
Fax: toll-free (888) 735-4531
E-mail: shadyoaks@shadyoaks.com
Website: www.shadyoaks.com
Catalog: Free

Sunlight Gardens*
174 Golden Lane
Andersonville, TN 37705
Phone: (865) 494-8237
Fax: (865) 494-7086
E-mail: sungardens@aol.com
Catalog: Free

WE-DU Nurseries
2055 Polly Spout Rd.
Marion, NC 28752-7349
Phone: (828) 738-8300
Fax: (828) 738-8131
E-mail: wedu@wnclink.com
Website: www.we-du.com/
Catalog: Free

Woodlanders*
1128 Colleton Ave.
Aiken, SC 29801
Phone/fax: (803) 648-7522
E-mail: Woodlander@triplet.net
Catalog: $2.00 (for two years)

Appendix B

Agencies and Organizations

These are a few of the area agencies and organizations dedicated to preserving and improving Tennessee's natural environment. Educational programs, newsletters, field trips, and informational materials are offered by many of them.

Great Smoky Mountains Institute
9275 Tremont Rd.
Townsend, TN 37882
Phone: (865) 448-6709
E-mail: gsmit@smokiesnha.org
Website:
www.nps.gov/grsm/tremont.htm

Great Smoky Mountains Natural History Association
115 Park Headquarters Road
Gatlinburg, TN 37738
Phone: (865) 436-0120
Website: www.smokiesstore.org

Ijams Nature Center
2915 Island Home Avenue
Knoxville, TN 37901
Phone: (865) 577-4717
Website: www.ijams.org

Land Between the Lakes National Recreation Area
100 Van Morgan Drive
Golden Pond, KY 42211
Phone: (270) 924-2000
         (800) 455-5897
Website: www.lbl.org

Lichterman Nature Center
Pink Palace Family of Museums
5992 Quince Road
Memphis, TN 38119
Phone: (901) 767-7322
Website: www.memphismuseums.org

National Audubon Society
(Chattanooga, Clarksville, Memphis, Nashville,)
Website: www.audubon.org
(click "States," "Chapters")

The Nature Conservancy of Tennessee
2021 21st Avenue South, Suite C400
Nashville, TN 37212
Phone: (615) 383-9909
Website: www.tnc.org
(click "What We Do,"
"United States," "Tennessee")

Sierra Club
(Chattanooga, Cookeville, Knoxville,
Memphis, Nashville, Tri-Cities)
Website:
www.sierraclub.org/chapters/tn

Tennessee Citizens for Wilderness Planning
130 Tabor Rd.
Oak Ridge, TN 37830
Phone: (865) 481-0286
E-mail: marcyrreed@aol.com
Website: www.korrnet.org/tcwp

Tennessee Conservation League
300 Orlando Ave.
Nashville, TN 37209
Phone: (615) 353-1133

Tennessee Department of Environment and Conservation
Division of Natural Heritage
401 Church St. (14th Floor,
L&C Tower)
Nashville, TN 37243-0447
Phone: (615) 532-0431
Website:
www.state.tn.us/environment/nh

Tennessee Environmental Council
One Vantage Way, Suite D-105
Nashville, TN 37228
Phone: (615) 248-6500
E-mail: tec@tectn.org
Website: www.tectn.org

Tennessee Environmental Education Association
c/o Great Smoky Mountains Institute
(see address above)
Website:
www.utm.edu/departments/ed/
cece/TEEA.html

Tennessee Exotic Pest Plant Council
State Chapter of Southeast Exotic
Pest Plant Council
Call Tennessee Dept. of Environment
& Conservation
Website: www.se-eppc.org

Tennessee Native Plant Society
P.O. Box 159274
Nashville, TN 37215

Tennessee Ornithological Society
Website: www.tnbirds.org

Tennessee State Parks and Recreation
(Tennessee Department of
Environment and Conservation)
401 Church St. (7th Floor, L&C
Tower)
Nashville, TN 37243-0446
Phone: (615) 532-0001
Website: www.tnstateparks.com

Tennessee Wildflower Society
c/o Jennie Rogers
938 Ridgeway Ave.
Signal Mountain, TN 37377
Phone: (423) 886-1267

Tennessee Wildlife Center (Chattanooga Nature Center)
400 Garden Rd.
Chattanooga, TN 37419
Phone: (423) 821-1160
Website: www.tnwildlifecenter.org

Tennessee Wildlife Resources Agency
Ellington Agricultural Center
P.O. Box 40747
Nashville,TN 37204
Phone: (615) 781-6500
Website: www.state.tn.us/twra

Warner Park Nature Center
7311 Highway 100
Nashville, TN 37221
Phone: (615) 352-6299
E-mail: wpnc@metro.nashville.org
Website:
    www.nashville.org/parks/wpnc

Native Plant Societies of Surrounding States

Alabama Wildflower Society
www.gardenweb.com/directory/aws

Arkansas Native Plant Society
www.anps.org

Georgia Native Plant Society
www.gnps.org

Indiana Native Plant and
Wildflower Society
www.inpaws.org

Kentucky Native Plant Society
http://sac.uky.edu/~mthomO/KNPS/
    knps.htm

Mississippi Native Plant Society
c/o Ronald Wieland
Mississippi Museum of
    Natural Science
2148 Riverside Drive
Jackson, MS 39202

Missouri Native Plant Society
www.missouri.edu/~umo_herb/monps

North American Native Plant Society
www.nanps.org

North Carolina Wildflower
Preservation Society
www.ncwfps.org

South Carolina Native Plant Society
www.clemson.edu/scnative plants

Virginia Native Plant Society
www.vnps.org

Appendix C

Botanical Gardens

The following botanical gardens and arboretums feature at least one natural or cultivated area devoted to the display of native plants. Many, if not most, of the plants featured will be native to Tennessee. The only exception is the Lady Bird Johnson Wildflower Center in Texas. It is a national clearinghouse on native plant information and research for all regions of the United States, though its display gardens emphasize plants native to Texas.

Atlanta Botanical Garden
1345 Piedmont Avenue NE
Atlanta, GA 30309
Phone: (404) 876-5859
Fax: (404) 876-7472
Website:
    www.atlantabotanicalgarden.org
(Southern U.S. native plants,
    emphasis on woodland plants and
    the conservation of carnivorous
    and bog plants)

Atlanta History Center
130 West Paces Ferry Road NW
Atlanta, GA 30305-1366
Phone: (404) 814-4000
Fax: (404) 814-4186
Website:
    www.AtlantaHistoryCenter.com

(Southeastern U.S. native plants,
emphasis on piedmont and Georgia)

Birmingham Botanical Gardens
2612 Lane Park Road
Birmingham, AL 35223
Phone: (205) 414-3900
Website: www.bbgardens.org
(Southeastern U.S. native plants,
    emphasis on central Alabama
    woodland)

Botanical Garden at Asheville
151 W. T. Weaver Blvd.
Asheville, NC 28804
Phone: (828) 252-5190
(Southeastern U.S. native plants,
    emphasis on southern
    Appalachian Mountains)

Bowman's Hill Wildflower Preserve
Washington Crossing Historic Park
P.O. Box 685
New Hope, PA 18938-0685
Phone: (215) 862-2924
Fax: (215) 862-1846
Website: www.bhwp.org
    (Native plants of Pennsylvania)

Callaway Gardens
Highway 27, P.O. Box 2000
Pine Mountain, GA 31822-2000
Phone: (800) 225-5292
Fax: (706) 663-5068
Website: www.callawaygardens.com
(Southeastern U.S. native plants,
    native azaleas, and hollies)

Cheekwood Botanical Garden
1200 Forrest Park Drive
Nashville, TN 37205
Phone: (615) 353-2148
Fax: (615) 353-2731
Website: www.cheekwood.org/garden
    (Southeastern U.S. native plants)

Crosby Arboretum
Mississippi State University
P.O. Box 1639
Picayune, MS 39466
Phone: (601) 799-2311
Fax: (601) 799-2372
Website:
    http://msstate.edu/dept/crec/
    camain.html
(Gulf Coast native plants, by plant
    communities: savanna, woodland,
    water)

Dixon Gallery & Gardens
4339 Park Ave.
Memphis, TN 38117
Phone: (901) 761-5253
Fax: (901) 682-0943
Website: www.dixon.org
(Southeastern U.S. woodland native
    plants)

Garden in the Woods
New England Wild Flower Society
180 Hemenway Road
Framingham, MA 01701-2699
Phone: (508) 877-7630
Fax: (508) 877-3658
Website: www.newfs.org
(North American native plants)

Huntsville–Madison County Botanical Garden
4747 Bob Wallace Ave.
Huntsville, AL 35805
Phone: (256) 830-4447
Fax: (256) 830-5314
Website: www.hsvbg.org
(Southeastern U.S. native plants)

Lady Bird Johnson Wildflower Center
4801 LaCrosse Ave.
Austin, TX 78739-1702
Phone: (512) 292-4200
Fax: (512) 292-4627
Website: www.wildflower.org
(Information on North American
    native plants)

Memphis Botanic Garden
750 Cherry Road
Memphis, TN 38117-4699
Phone: (901) 685-1566
Fax: (901) 682-1561
(Southeastern U.S. native plants)

North Carolina Arboretum
100 Frederick Law Olmsted Way
Asheville, NC 28806-9315
Phone: (828) 665-2492
Fax: (828) 665-2371
Website: www.ncarboretum.org
(Southeastern U.S. native plants and
    native azaleas)

North Carolina Botanical Garden
University of North Carolina at
Chapel Hill
CB 3375, Totten Center
Chapel Hill, NC 27599-3375
Phone: (919) 962-0522
Fax: (919) 962-3531
Website: www.unc.edu/depts/ncbg
(Southeastern U.S. native plants in
  habitats)

Reflection Riding Arboretum and Botanical Garden
400 Garden Road
Chattanooga, TN 37419
Phone: (423) 821-9582
Fax: (423) 822-2300
Website: www.reflectionriding.org
(Southeastern U.S. native plants,
  emphasis on southern
  Appalachian Mountains)

Shaw Arboretum of Missouri Botanical Garden
P.O. Box 38
Gray Summit, MO 63039
Phone: (636) 451-3512
Website: www.mobot.org
  (click on Arboretum)
(Tallgrass prairie, Missouri and
  eastern U.S. native plants)

State Arboretum of Virginia
Blandy Experimental Farm
400 Blandy Farm Lane
Boyce, VA 22620
Phone: (540) 837-1758
Website: www.virginia.edu/~blandy
(Southeastern U.S. native plants)

State Botanical Garden of Georgia
University of Georgia
2450 Milledge Ave.
Athens, GA 30605
Phone: (706) 542-1244
Fax: (706) 542-3091
Website: www.uga.edu/~botgarden
(Southeastern U.S. native plants,
  native azaleas)

Tennessee Aquarium
1 Broad Street
P.O. Box 11048
Chattanooga, TN 37401
Phone: (423) 265-0695
Fax: (423) 267-3561
Website: www.tnaqua.org
(Tennessee native plants: mountain
  cove forest and Mississippi delta)

University of Alabama Arboretum
15th St. & Loop Road
Tuscaloosa, AL 35487
Phone/fax: (205) 553-3278
(Southeastern U.S. native plants,
  emphasis on ecological zones of
  Alabama)

University of Tennessee Arboretum
901 Kerr Hollow Road
Oak Ridge, TN 37830
Phone: (865) 483-3571
Fax: (865) 483-3572
E-mail: utforest@utk.edu
(Woody plants of Tennessee)

Native Plant Conferences

Attending one of the annual native plant conferences in the region is another good way to learn more about native plants, their role in natural environments, and their uses in the home landscape. Plant sales, book sales, and field trips enhance seminar-styled presentations and discussions. Most run about three days. Contact the universities or organizations listed below for more information.

Central South Native Plant Conference

Birmingham Botanical Society &
Birmingham Botanical Gardens
2612 Lane Park Road
Birmingham, AL 35223
Phone: (205) 414-3900
Rotates every three years with Gulf Coast and Mid-South conferences, usually in October

Gulf Coast Native Plant Conference

Louisiana Native Plant Society
c/o Carolyn Dormon Nature Preserve
216 Carolyn Dormon Road
Saline, LA 71070
Phone: (318) 576-3379
Rotates every three years with
    Central South and Mid-South
    conferences, location and time
    of year varies

Landscaping with Native Plants

Western Carolina University
Continuing Education Dept.,
Attn: Sue Deitz
138 University Outreach Center
Culowhee, NC 28723
Phone: (828) 227-7397
Yearly, late July

Mid-South Native Plant Conference

Memphis Horticultural Society
P.O. Box 11665
Memphis, TN 38111-0665
Rotates every three years with
Central South and Gulf Coast
conferences, late October

Native Plants in the Landscape Conference & Plant Sale
Millersville University
Department of Continuing Education
P.O. Box 1002
Millersville, PA 17551
Phone: (717) 872-3030
Yearly, early June

Shaw Arboretum Native Plant Conference
Shaw Arboretum
P.O. Box 38
Gray Summit, MO 63039
Phone: (636) 451-3512
Every two years in September,
    alternating with Prairie Day

Bibliography

Bailey, L. H. *The Standard Cyclopedia of Horticulture*, Vol. 1–3. New York: Macmillan, 1942.

Bailey, Liberty Hyde, and Ethel Zoe Bailey. *Hortus Third: A Concise Dictionary of Plants Cultivated in the United States and Canada*. New York: Macmillan, 1976.

Bartram, William. *Travels*. 1791. Reprint, New York: Penguin Books, 1988.

Baskin, Jerry M., Elsie Quarterman, and Carole Caudle. "Preliminary Checklist of the Herbaceous Vascular Plants of Cedar Glades." *Journal of the Tennessee Academy of Science* 43 (3) (July 1968): 65–71.

Bir, Richard E. *Growing and Propagating Showy Native Woody Plants*. Chapel Hill: Univ. of North Carolina Press, 1992.

Birdseye, Clarence, and Eleanor G. Birdseye. *Growing Woodland Plants*. 1951. Reprint. New York: Dover, 1972.

Blanchan, Neltje. *Nature's Garden*. Garden City, N.Y.: Garden City Publishing Co., 1900.

Braun, E. Lucy. *Deciduous Forests of Eastern North America*. 1950. Reprint, New York: Hafner Press, 1985.

Brown, Lauren. *Grasses: An Identification Guide*. New York: Houghton Mifflin, 1979.

Bruce, Hal. *How to Grow Wildflowers and Wild Shrubs and Trees in Your Own Garden*. New York: Alfred A. Knopf, 1976.

Buckman, Harry O., and Nyle C. Brady. *The Nature and Properties of Soil*. 7th ed. New York: Macmillan, 1969.

Campbell, Carlos C., William F. Hutson, and Aaron J. Sharp. *Great Smoky Mountains Wildflowers*. Knoxville: Univ. of Tennessee Press, 1977.

Capon, Brian. *Botany for Gardeners: An Introduction and Guide*. Portland, Ore.: Timber Press, 1990.

Carter, David. *Eyewitness Handbooks Butterflies and Moths*. New York: Dorling Kindersley, 1992.

Chester, Edward W., and William H. Ellis. "Plant Communities of Northwestern Middle Tennessee." *Journal of the Tennessee Academy of Science* 64 (3) (July 1989): 75–78.

———. *Wildflowers of the Land Between the Lakes Region, Kentucky and Tennessee.* Clarksville, Tenn.: Austin Peay State Univ., 1995.

Chester, Edward W., Richard J. Jensen, and Joe Schibig. "Forest Communities of Montgomery and Stewart Counties, Northwestern Middle Tennessee." *Journal of the Tennessee Academy of Science* 70 (3–4) (July–Oct. 1995): 82–91.

Chester, Edward W., B. Eugene Wofford, and Robert Kral. *Atlas of Tennessee Vascular Plants, Vol. 2.* Clarksville, Tenn.: Austin Peay State Univ., 1997.

Chester, Edward W., B. Eugene Wofford, Robert Kral, Hal R. DeSelm, and A. Murray Evans. *Atlas of Tennessee Vascular Plants, Vol. 1.* Clarksville, Tenn.: Austin Peay State Univ., 1993.

Clebsch, Edward E. C. "Vegetation of the Appalachian Mountains of Tennessee East of the Great Valley." *Journal of the Tennessee Academy of Science* 64 (3) (July 1989): 79–83.

Cobb, Boughton. *A Field Guide to Ferns and Their Related Families of Northeastern and Central North America.* New York: Houghton Mifflin, 1984.

Covell, Jr., Charles V. *A Field Guide to the Moths of Eastern North America.* Boston: Houghton Mifflin, 1984.

Cox, Jeff. *Landscaping with Nature.* Emmaus, Pa.: Rodale Press, 1991.

Cullina, William. *The New England Wildflower Society Guide to Growing and Propagating Wildflowers of the United States and Canada.* New York: Houghton Mifflin, 2000.

Dana, Mrs. William Starr. *How to Know the Wild Flowers.* New York: Charles Scribner's Sons, 1910.

DeSelm, H. R. "The Barrens of Tennessee." *Journal of the Tennessee Academy of Science* 64 (3) (July 1989): 89–95.

Diekelmann, John, and Robert Schuster. *Natural Landscaping: Designing with Native Plant Communities.* New York: McGraw-Hill, 1982.

Dirr, Michael A. *Manual of Woody Landscape Plants.* 4th ed. Champaign, Ill.: Stipes Publishing Co., 1975.

Duncan, Wilbur H., and Marion B. Duncan. *Wildflowers of the Eastern United States.* Athens: Univ. of Georgia Press, 1999.

Durham, Daryl, Edwin Bridges, Paul Hamel, Sam Pearsall, Larry Smith, and Paul Somers. *Conserving Natural Communities: Inventory and Classification.* Tennessee Dept. of Conservation, Ecological Services Division, 1985.

Eastman, John. *The Book of Forest and Thicket: Trees, Shrubs, and Wildflowers of Eastern North America.* Harrisburg, Pa.: Stackpole, 1992.

———. *The Book of Swamp and Bog: Trees, Shrubs, and Wildflowers of Eastern Freshwater Wetlands.* Mechanicsburg, Pa.: Stackpole, 1995.

Ellis, William H., and Edward W. Chester. "Upland Swamps of the Highland Rim of Tennessee." *Journal of the Tennessee Academy of Science* 64 (3) (July 1989): 97–101.

Ernst, Ruth Shaw. *The Naturalist's Garden.* Emmaus, Pa.: Rodale Press, 1987.

Ferreniea, Viki. *Wildflowers in Your Garden.* New York: Regina Ryan Publishing, 1993.

Fischer, Thomas. "How Do You Say That?" *Horticulture* 97 (1) (Jan./Feb. 2000): 41–44.

Foote, Leonard E., and Samuel B. Jones Jr. *Native Shrubs and Woody Vines of the Southeast.* Portland, Ore.: Timber Press, 1989.

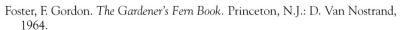

Foster, F. Gordon. *The Gardener's Fern Book*. Princeton, N.J.: D. Van Nostrand, 1964.

Fralish, James S., and Fred B. Crooks. "Forest Composition, Environment and Dynamics at Land Between the Lakes in Northwest Middle Tennessee." *Journal of the Tennessee Academy of Science* 64 (3)(July 1989): 107–11.

Gattinger, Augustin. *The Flora of Tennessee and a Philosophy of Botany*. Nashville, Tenn.: Gospel Advocate Publishing, 1901.

Gershuny, Grace, and Joe Smillie. *The Soul of Soil: A Soil-Building Guide for Master Gardeners and Farmers*. 4th ed. White River Junction, Vt.: Chelsea Green, 1999.

Gleason, Henry A., and Arthur Cronquist. *Manual of Vascular Plants of Northeastern United States and Adjacent Canada*. 2d ed. Bronx: New York Botanical Garden, 1991.

Gray, Asa, and Merritt Lyndon Fernald. *Gray's Manual of Botany*. 8th ed. New York: American Book Co., 1950.

Greenlee, John. *The Encyclopedia of Ornamental Grasses*. Emmaus, Pa.: Rodale Press, 1992.

Grimm, William Carey. *The Illustrated Book of Wildflowers and Shrubs*. Rev. ed. Harrisburg, Pa.: Stackpole, 1993.

Guthrie, Milo. "A Floristic and Vegetational Overview of Reelfoot Lake." *Journal of the Tennessee Academy of Science* 64 (3) (July 1989):113–16.

Hamel, Paul. *Tennessee Wildlife Viewing Guide*. Helena, Mont.: Falcon Press, 1993.

Harker, Donald, Sherri Evans, Marc Evans, and Kay Harker. *Landscape Restoration Handbook*. Boca Raton, Fla.: Lewis Publishers, 1993.

Heineke, Thomas E. "Plant Communities and Flora of West Tennessee Between the Loess Hills and the Tennessee River." *Journal of the Tennessee Academy of Science* 64 (3) (July 1989): 117–19.

Hemmerly, Thomas E. *Wildflowers of the Central South*. Nashville, Tenn.: Vanderbilt Univ. Press, 1990.

Hersey, Jean. *Wild Flowers to Know and Grow*. Princeton, N.J.: D. Van Nostrand, 1964.

Hightshoe, Gary L. *Native Trees, Shrubs, and Vines for Urban and Rural America*. New York: Van Nostrand Rheinhold, 1988.

Hinkle, C. Ross. "Forest Communities of the Cumberland Plateau of Tennessee." *Journal of the Tennessee Academy of Science* 64 (3) (July 1989): 123–29.

Holmes, Roger, ed. *Taylor's Guide to Natural Gardening*. Boston: Houghton Mifflin, 1993.

Hull, Helen S. *Wild Flowers for Your Garden*. New York: M. Barrows & Co., 1952.

Jacobs, Don L., and Rob L. Jacobs. *Trilliums in Woodland and Garden: American Treasures*. Decatur, Ga.: Eco-Gardens, 1997.

Jones, Ronald L. "A Floristic Study of Wetlands on the Cumberland Plateau of Tennessee." *Journal of the Tennessee Academy of Science* 64 (3) (July 1989): 131–34.

Jones, Jr., Samuel B., and Leonard E. Foote. *Gardening with Native Wild Flowers*. Portland, Ore.: Timber Press, 1990.

Kress, Stephen W. *The Bird Garden*. New York: Dorling Kindersley, 1995.

Kricher, John C. *A Field Guide to Ecology of Eastern Forests, North America.* New York: Houghton Mifflin, 1988.

Leopold, Donald J., William C. McComb, and Robert N. Muller. *Trees of the Central Hardwood Forests of North America.* Portland, Ore.: Timber Press, 1998.

Little, Elbert L. *The Audubon Society Field Guide to North American Trees, Eastern Region.* New York: Alfred A. Knopf, 1980.

Luther, Edward T. *Our Restless Earth: The Geologic Regions of Tennessee.* Knoxville: Univ. of Tennessee Press, 1977.

Martin, Deborah L., and Grace Gershuny, eds. *The Rodale Book of Composting.* Emmaus, Pa.: Rodale Press, 1992.

Martin, William H. "Forest Patterns in the Great Valley of Tennessee." *Journal of the Tennessee Academy of Science* 64 (3) (July 1989): 137–43.

McKinney, Landon E. "Vegetation of the Eastern Highland Rim of Tennessee." *Journal of the Tennessee Academy of Science* 64 (3) (July 1989): 145–47.

Midgley, Jan W. *Southeastern Wildflowers.* Birmingham, Ala.: Crane Hill Publishers, 1999.

Miles, Bebe. *Wildflower Perennials for Your Garden.* Mechanicsburg, Pa.: Stackpole, 1996.

Miller, Neil A., and John Neiswender. "A Plant Community Study of the Third Chickasaw Bluff, Shelby County, Tennessee." *Journal of the Tennessee Academy of Science* 64 (3) (July 1989): 149–54.

Miller, Robert A. *The Geologic History of Tennessee,* Bulletin 74. Tennessee Dept. of Environment and Conservation, Division of Geology, 1974.

Neal, Bill. *Gardener's Latin: A Lexicon.* Chapel Hill, N.C.: Algonquin, 1992.

Nicholson, Charles P. *Atlas of the Breeding Birds of Tennessee.* Knoxville: Univ. of Tennessee Press, 1997.

Niering, William A., and Nancy C. Olmstead. *The Audubon Society Field Guide to North American Wildflowers, Eastern Region.* New York: Alfred A. Knopf, 1979.

Odenwald, Neil, and James Turner. *Identification, Selection and Use of Southern Plants for Landscape Design.* 3d ed. Baton Rouge, La.: Claitor's Publishing Div., 1996.

Parmer, Henry E. *Birds of the Nashville Area.* 4th ed. Nashville Chapter, Tennessee Ornithological Society, 1985.

Peterson, Roger Tory. *A Field Guide to the Birds of Eastern and Central North America.* Boston: Houghton Mifflin, 1980.

Peterson, Roger Tory, and Margaret McKenny. *A Field Guide to Wildflowers of Northeastern and Northcentral North America.* New York: Houghton Mifflin, 1968.

Phillips, Harry R. *Growing and Propagating Wild Flowers.* Chapel Hill: Univ. of North Carolina Press, 1985.

Pyle, Robert Michael. *National Audubon Society Field Guide to North American Butterflies.* New York: Alfred A. Knopf, 1981.

Quarterman, Elsie. "Structure and Dynamics of the Limestone Cedar Glade Communities in Tennessee." *Journal of the Tennessee Academy of Science* 64 (3) (July 1989): 155–58.

Ramseur, George S. "Some Changes in the Vegetation of the Great Smoky Mountains." *Journal of the Tennessee Academy of Science* 64 (3) (July 1989): 159–60.

Reichard, Sarah H. "A Method for Evaluating Plant Invasiveness." *Public Garden* 14 (2) (Apr. 1999): 18–21.

Rickett, Harold William. *Wild Flowers of the United States, Vol. 2: The Southeastern States.* New York: McGraw-Hill, 1967.

Roberts, Edith A., and Elsa Rehmann. *American Plants for American Gardens.* 1929. Reprint, Athens: Univ. of Georgia Press, 1996.

Seidenberg, Charlotte. *The Wildlife Garden.* Jackson: Univ. Press of Mississippi, 1995.

Shaver, Jesse M. *Ferns of Tennessee.* Nashville, Tenn.: George Peabody College, 1954.

Sinclair, Ralph, Will Hon, and Robert B. Ferguson. *Amphibians and Reptiles of Tennessee.* Rev. ed. Tennessee Game and Fish Commission, 1965.

Smith, Arlo I. *A Guide to Wildflowers of the Mid-South.* Memphis, Tenn.: Memphis State Univ. Press, 1979.

Smyser, Carol A. *Nature's Design: A Practical Guide to Natural Landscaping.* Emmaus, Pa.: Rodale Press, 1982.

Sperka, Marie. *Growing Wildflowers: A Gardener's Guide.* New York: Harper & Row, 1973.

Springer, M. E., and J. A. Elder. *Soils of Tennessee,* Bulletin 596. University of Tennessee Agricultural Experiment Station, Knoxville, and United States Dept. of Agriculture Soil Conservation Service, 1980.

Stearn, William T. *Botanical Latin.* 4th ed. Devon, Eng.: David & Charles, 1992.

Steffek, Edwin F. *Wild Flowers and How to Grow Them.* New York: Crown, 1954.

Stein, Sara. *Noah's Garden.* New York: Houghton Mifflin, 1993
———. *Planting Noah's Garden.* New York: Houghton Mifflin, 1997.

Sternberg, Guy, and Jim Wilson. *Landscaping with Native Trees.* Shelburne, Vt.: Chapters Publishing Ltd., 1995.

Stevenson, Violet. *The Wild Garden: Making Natural Gardens Using Wild and Native Plants.* New York: Penguin Books, 1985.

Taylor, Kathryn S., and Stephen F. Hamblin. *Handbook of Wild Flower Cultivation.* New York: Macmillan, 1963.

Taylor, Norman. *Wild Flower Gardening.* Princeton, N.J.: D. Van Nostrand, 1955.

Tekulsky, Mathew. *The Butterfly Garden.* Boston: Harvard Common Press, 1985.

Tenenbaum, Frances. *Gardening with Wild Flowers.* New York: Charles Scribner's Sons, 1973.

Tennessee's Natural Resources, Vol. 2, Pub. # 331b. Tennessee Dept. of Finance and Administration, 1966.

Thomas, R. Dale. "The Vegetation of Chilhowee Mountain, Tennessee." *Journal of the Tennessee Academy of Science* 64, (3) (July 1989): 185–88.

Torrey, Bradford, and Francis H. Allen, eds. *The Journal of Henry D. Thoreau.* New York: Dover, 1962.

Tufts, Craig, and Peter Loewer. *National Wildlife Federation's Guide to Gardening for Wildlife.* Emmaus, Pa.: Rodale Press, 1995.

Warden, John C. "Changes in the Spruce-Fir Forest of Roan Mountain in Tennessee Over the Past Fifty Years as a Result of Logging." *Journal of the Tennessee Academy of Science* 64 (3) (July 1989): 193–95.

Wasowski, Sally, and Andy Wasowski. *Gardening with Native Plants of the South.* Dallas, Tex.: Taylor Publishing Co., 1994.

Webb, David H., and A. Leon Bates. "The Aquatic Vascular Flora and Plant Communities Along Rivers and Reservoirs of the Tennessee River System." *Journal of the Tennessee Academy of Science* 64 (3) (July 1989): 197–203.

Wernert, Susan J., ed. *North American Wildlife*. Pleasantville, N.Y.: Reader's Digest, 1982.

Wharton, Mary E., and Roger W. Barbour. *A Guide to the Wildflowers and Ferns of Kentucky*. Lexington: Univ. Press of Kentucky, 1971.

Wilson, Jim. *Landscaping with Wildflowers*. Boston: Houghton Mifflin, 1992.

Wofford, B. Eugene. "Floristic Elements of the Tennessee Blue Ridge." *Journal of the Tennessee Academy of Science* 64 (3) (July 1989): 205–7.

Wofford, B. Eugene, and Robert Kral. "Checklist of the Vascular Plants of Tennessee." *Sida, Botanical Miscellany, No. 10*. Fort Worth: Botanical Research Institute of Texas, 1993.

Wyman, Donald. *Wyman's Gardening Encyclopedia*. New York: Macmillan, 1986.

Young, James A., and Cheryl G. Young. *Collecting, Processing and Germinating Seeds of Wildland Plants*. Portland, Ore.: Timber Press, 1986.

Index

The Spirit of Place was designed and typeset on a Macintosh computer system using QuarkXPress. Body text is set in 10.5/14 Goudy with display type set in Techno and Gill Sans. This book was designed and typeset by Cheryl Carrington and manufactured by C & C Offset Printing.